LIVING THE KABBALAH

Living the Kabbalah

A Guide to the Sabbath and Festivals
in the Teachings of
Rabbi Rafael Moshe Luria

SIMCHA H. BENYOSEF

Continuum New York

1999

The Continuum Publishing Company
370 Lexington Avenue, New York, NY 10017

Copyright © 1999 by Simcha H. Benyosef

Printed in the United States of America

Library of Congress Cataloging-in-Publication Data

Benyosef, Simcha H.
    Living the Kabbalah : a guide to the Sabbath and festivals in the
teachings of Rabbi Rafael Moshe Luria / Simcha H. Benyosef.
        p.   cm.
    Includes bibliographical references.
    ISBN 0-8264-1149-5
    1. Mysticism—Judaism. 2. Cabala. 3. Fasts and feasts—Judaism.
4. Lurya, Mosheh.   I. Lurya, Mosheh.   II. Title.
BM723.B43   1999
296.4'3—dc21
                                            99-11840
                                            CIP

To Mikail,
With love and gratitude

———————————————

Lord of the Universe,
May it be Your will
to make a pure garment
for the soul of my father and teacher,
Joseph ben David,
and for the soul of my rabbi and teacher,
Rabbi Aryeh Kaplan ben Samuel,
and elevate their souls
high, high up in Eden.

Contents

PART THREE: SECOND TABLETS

PART FOUR: DEALING WITH CONCEALMENT

Rabbinic Festivals
Purim

Chanukah

Acknowledgments

To Rabbi Rafael Moshe Luria, for his trust and kindness.

To Rabbi Iztchak Abadi, for reading the manuscript and verifying the accuracy of its legal (*halachic*) contents, for patiently answering the innumerable questions that came up at the most inconvenient times.

To Rabbi Joseph Pacifici, for being a pillar of strength and encouragement throughout this work. To Rabbi Moshe Schatz, for his generous help, in particular for the chapters on Shabbat, the New Year, and Chanukah. To Rabbi Abraham Sutton, for his friendly, untiring help during the first stages of this project.

To the two distinguished kabbalists who clarified difficult concepts and offered the oral teaching behind the succinct written word.

To J. G. L. for coining a translation for the Hebrew term *yichud*/soul-union. To "Ephraim, my precious son," for being my U.S. correspondent. To G & S. L., for their blessing and support. To H. D. L. for his help with the technical aspects of word processing. To S. A. L. for believing in this project. To R. L. for reminding me to smile. To Rafael Benzaquen, for his generous help condensing this manuscript.

To E. van Handel, for an excellent editing job of the first version of this manuscript. To Rabbi Eliezer Shore, for his skillful editing of the final version, but most of all, for helping me constrict the light of the manuscript without dividing it.

A special thanks to Baruch Lazewnick for his selfless help.

To Rabbi David Ackerman, there are no words . . .

I feel very fortunate to have had Frank Oveis, from Continuum, as my editor.

I thank the Almighty with all my heart for helping me to present this offering. May He rebuild the Temple in our generation, thus remembering His promise to the Matriarch Rachel, "Restrain your voice from weeping and your eyes from tears, for you will be rewarded for your deeds. [Your children] shall return from the land of the enemy" (Jeremiah 31:15–16).

Letter from
Rabbi Chaim P. Sheinberg

RABBI CHAIM P. SHEINBERG
ROSH HAYESHIVA "TORAH-ORE"
MORAH HORA'AH OF KIRYAT MATTERSDORF

Lag baOmer, 5756/May 6, 1996

Our era has all the characteristics of the birth pangs of the Messiah—in particular, a search for meaning amidst the concealment of the Divine Presence. A book is needed that helps one to develop an intimate relationship with the Creator through the depth and grandeur of the Jewish year.

Thank G-d, *Living the Kabbalah* fills this need. With it, those who are far from their heritage and life source can find a key to true closeness to G-d. Torah-observant Jews will also find that it enhances their practice of our holy Shabbat and festivals.

The author, who has performed a great service for all those who wish to experience the beauty of our sacred heritage, is to be commended for a job well done.

May the Community of Israel find truth and tranquility in your important book. May you produce many more of this genre and increase the sanctification of G-d's Name, and may all of us together merit to greet *Mashiach*/the Messiah. May all your offspring be filled with knowledge of *Hashem.*

With blessings from Jerusalem,

חיים פנחס שיינברג

My soul yearns and even pines for the courtyards of *Hashem*;
my heart and flesh will sing joyously to the Living God.

–Psalms 84:3

Preface

IN JERUSALEM THERE IS A KABBALIST who dedicates his life to teaching others how to search for God where He can be found, namely, at the days on the Jewish calendar where a special Divine energy is available. This is Rabbi Rafael Moshe Luria, a descendant of the father of kabbalists, Rabbi Isaac Luria of sixteenth-century Sefad, who is known as the holy Ari.[1]

In many ways, Rabbi Rafael Moshe Luria's work is a running commentary on the ultimate song of love, the Song of Songs. This allegory describes God's relationship with His beloved people, Israel, as a fire that many waters cannot extinguish.[2] Rabbi Luria amplifies God's call to His people to relate to Him as the Community of Israel, His Companion of the soul (*Kneset Israel, bat zivugo*).

Because Rabbi Luria's works are addressed to an audience of Torah scholars like himself, he initially refused to allow me to translate his books for the modern public. I pointed out to him, however, that in our time there is a spreading desire to reach a heightened state of awareness as a way to come close to God. Yet, the only thing available in print is a staggering amount of misinformation and of literal translations of Kabbalah that have very little meaning and are even dangerous because they lack the teachings that only the insiders to the tradition can give.[3]

Rabbi Luria finally agreed that perhaps the time had come to reveal some of these mysteries and he blessed my enterprise. This book was culled from his seventeen volumes; selection has been one of my most challenging tasks.

Kabbalah is an ancient Jewish tradition in which only the essential concepts are written down. The initiate receives supplementary teachings in an oral form, directly from masters who are hidden from the public eye. Any translation made by one who has no direct access to this secret tradition is as valid as a book on how to fly an aircraft written by one who has never been on a plane.

An example of an abstract concept generally misunderstood is the kabbalistic "levels" of soul. In the teachings of Kabbalah, the soul is not merely a spiritual force enclosed within the body, infusing it with life. There are higher levels of the soul existing beyond the body. The soul of man is an entire spiritual structure, the highest point of which is attached to God Himself.

Each level of the soul corresponds to a different mental state, ranging from alert consciousness, where the mind's concerns are mainly physical, to the highest meditative state, where one consciously cleaves to the Creator with every aspect of the being.

These higher states occur mainly during prayer. To the kabbalist, prayer goes beyond the opportunity to present requests to the Father in Heaven, Provider of all needs. More importantly, prayer means immediate contact. The series of formalized prayers are a ladder of ascent leading to a meditative state, or "expanded consciousness," as Kabbalah calls it, in which one becomes attached to the Beloved in a soul-union, *a yichud*.

It is almost impossible to describe these states because the intensity of the Divine force with which one comes into contact depends upon the individual's level of preparation and of spiritual arousal. In these higher states, one can have a profound experience of the immensity of God's love.

In this condition, human senses become a conduit for spiritual worlds. The heavenly realms, ethereal as they may be, also contain delight of the senses—but without the physicality.

For example, when a person speaks on the telephone, he is aware that the mechanism is only a means for allowing communication with another person.[4] Similarly, when searching for Divine love, one strives for a feeling similar in kind to the one generated by human love—yet without any physicality.

Rabbi Aryeh Kaplan discusses the highest level of the soul:

> Normally these are things that you cannot be aware of: they are outside the realm of experience. In this dimension beyond logic, you can become one with the Divine yet still maintain your own identity; your *ani*/I becomes *ain*/nothingness. Here, one plus one equals one.
>
> In the highest level of your soul you are able to transcend human logic. At this point, all the souls of Israel are one. You then realize that in the true concept of *ani*/I, your inner and unique essence is really everybody. The full measure of this lofty state will only be available to us in the ultimate future, but the briefest of contacts suffices for love to engulf you: *ahavat Israel*/loving your fellow Jew suddenly becomes much easier.[5]

A soul-union with the Almighty involving this lofty level is what Kabbalah calls *binyan shalem*, which literally means "complete structure," evoking the total union with God of the collective spiritual structure of the people of Israel, as it was in the Giving of the Torah, and in the days of the Temple.

The expression *binyan shalem* is generally understood as a reference to the rebuilt Temple, for this was the purpose of the Temple: to make possible such a mystic union between God, the Source of holiness, and man, the dweller in the physical world.

Indeed, the initial task of the Redeemer—the Messiah—will be to arouse in the heart of the Jewish people a yearning for this soul-union with their Creator.

This book is addressed to anyone who would like to make such a relationship the purpose of his or her existence. It is an all-consuming experience, a love that goes beyond death, when it will continue to grow free of physical restraints.

If you are at the first rungs of your personal ladder of ascent, you will find in this work many new concepts. And even if you are familiar with most of the background information, you may find that you have never heard Judaism taught in this manner. Finally, you will close the book with precise instructions on how to reach these states of expanded consciousness.[6]

Due to the unique relationship between God and Israel, when celebrating a Jewish festival, we are not just commemorating a past event, we are renewing the original event in the present. The Hebrew term for weekdays is *chol*, which also means "sand." As the term suggests, on weekdays, Jews are separated from each other as grains of sand. However, on Shabbat and festivals, God shines a luminous energy upon us that unites us as a group.

Each one of these special times becomes an opportunity to reach an expanded state of consciousness where we feel a current of live energy vibrating within us. The lights illuminating each festival and imbuing it with its particular form of energy return every year, so that we have a further opportunity for growth and closeness to the Divine.[7] During Passover, we taste the spirit of freedom; on Shavuot (Pentecost) we are given the Torah anew; and on Sukkot (the Festival of Booths) we are imbued with joy. Yet the energy we draw in these three festivals is to last us not only during the time of each festival, but, rather, for the entire year.

Of course, God has no gender. Nevertheless, throughout the book I follow the practice of the Scripture and refer to the Almighty using the masculine pronoun. Similarly, this book is intended for both men and women. I address the reader in the masculine to avoid burdening the reader with the form he/she.

This book introduces the concept of being God's Companion of the soul and outlines the history of this facet of mankind's relationship with God, grounding this philosophy in the biblical texts familiar to most readers.

The book is divided into four sections. Part One covers Shabbat, the day on which God asked His Companion of the soul to free herself of any activity and devote her time to enjoy His closeness. Part Two focuses on the contents of the First Tablets God gave His people at Sinai, covering from Passover—the redemption from Egypt—until Shavuot, the time in which Israel received the Torah.

Part Three covers the Second Tablets Moses brought to Israel after the sin of the Golden Calf, with the festivals that allowed them to recapture the Sinai state of consciousness. Finally, Part Four evokes Israel's present situation: the concealment of the Divine Presence seen through the destruction of the Temples and the rabbinic festivals of Purim and Chanukah.

Although these four sections of the work contain a road map and detailed instructions on how to achieve the intimate relationship described in this book, the Epilogue may be seen as an aerial map to provide perspective. This final section contrasts the Creator's bond of Companion of the soul with the people of Israel, following this special closeness from its inception—before the Creation of the world—until the acquisition of the Promised Land.

The main object of the Epilogue is to alert the reader to the fact that the Divine energy described in the four sections of the book comes and goes: it is not stationary. The Conclusion provides specific directions to recover this energy when one loses it, thus shortening the interim periods of concealment.

The key to penetrate the heavenly realms, as Rabbi Luria teaches, is spiritual arousal. The chapters that follow are aimed to produce in the reader the searing emotion needed to enter the altered state of consciousness in which one relates to God as part of "the Community of Israel, His Companion of the soul."

A first reading of the book will acquaint the reader with the terms and antecedents of this new relationship. One who is moved by the words, and desires this relationship more than anything else in the world, will first strive to attain the quality of Shabbat described, following the instructions outlined throughout the book.

However, merely following the instructions in a cold and intellectual way will not produce the altered states we are alluding to, even for a reader with a background in Jewish thought. For above and beyond the steps one takes is the necessity for spiritual yearning, which produces the enhanced state of consciousness.

Thus, it is preferable that you read the book initially without expectations, and as you are doing so, absorb the different kabbalistic concepts gradually introduced throughout the chapters.

Long before the close of the book, you will know whether this is what you have been looking for and, most importantly, whether you are ready for the consequences of your choice. Making a firm commitment does not mean that you will not fall, but only that you will get up again and proceed in your ascent. When your decision is boosted by your determination, it will be rewarded by a beam of love that will guide your every step and will help you aim daily for the unforgettable space you leave behind at the end of each Shabbat.

When you attain a single Shabbat in which, throughout your prayers, you can feel an intimate state of communion with your Creator, you will then move on to the festivals. When approaching the upcoming festival, read the appropriate section as a means of preparation. Use the teachings that you internalize in the prayers of the festival; they will open your mind and heart, sharpen perceptions, and enable you to absorb and consciously experience the Divine luminous energy God is emitting *at this time*.

This is the secret of Kabbalah as Rabbi Luria teaches it: the key to arouse the searing emotion God asks of His beloved people. Learning about Kabbalah the way it is usually taught in translation (meditative states based on the Divine Names, the Sefirotic tree) before relating to God on a personal, emotional level is like learning the complex theory of musical harmony before ever having been touched by a piece of music.

And this has been my goal in translating Rabbi Luria's teachings: offering a guide to attain this ultimate experience of God's love despite one's involvement in the busy life of a twentieth-century person.

I asked Rabbi Luria whether it was fair to promise the reader that anyone who follows all the guidelines of the book is likely to have intimate personal signs of God's love that are supernatural in nature. Rabbi Luria said, "You cannot guarantee this because these signs are a gift from Heaven, but such quality of Divine service is generally rewarded with a personal bond in which you have a contact with Divine energy that is directed to you personally. When the signs do come, you cannot communicate them for they do not make sense to anyone else, but you are clearly aware of their existence beyond the shadow of a doubt."

Rabbi Luria paused for a moment and added, "There are some who finish praying and are unable to speak for a long time until the intensity of their personal signs begins to abate!"

Jewish prayer is not a way of asking God to satisfy your needs, as a person would give to another the object of a request.[8] Through prayer, we give substance to the way we relate to God, like the branches of a tree to its roots. The roots give life-energy to the branches, not in a giver/receiver relationship but automatically. The branches draw their sustenance through their connection with the roots.

Kabbalah offers a graphic representation of this relationship through an equation. As we will see, the soul has five levels: these are known as *nefesh, ruach,* and *neshamah,* which are within us, and two others, *chayah* and *yechidah,* in which our life force is not yet separated from God.[9] The global numerical value of these five Hebrew words composing the entire spiritual structure of the Jewish soul is identical to that of the combination of two other Hebrew words, *'anafim/* branches and *shorashim/*roots.

The human body parts draw life-energy from the brain and heart. Prayer has a similar function: man realizes that he has no independent existence, that he is only a branch bound to the Source of life, and asks the Root to infuse his branch with life-energy.

Prayer is thus known as the "service of the heart," but it is also a praise, for there is no greater praise than man's awareness of God as his Master, Creator, and beyond this, the Root of his very existence. Hence, prayer is the "service of the heart" in the sense that it essentially depends on the heart's contemplation of this bond.

The climax of Jewish prayer—the *Amidah/*standing prayer—allows us to soar way beyond the still point of inner harmony that meditation has to offer. The master of Jewish meditation, Rabbi Aryeh Kaplan, was once asked which technique was most effective. He answered,

The highest level is the closeness to and awareness of God. Many of our righteous people reached extremely high levels of consciousness and closeness to God without ever meditating. When you reach that level, in which you have a well-enough disciplined life, the entire concept of the Torah and commandments becomes a meditation.[10]

In fact, his widow observed that she never saw him meditate. In contrast, she often saw him stay a very long time immersed in his *Amidah* prayer.

A reconnection with the self as in meditation may be enough to bring about a soothing sense of inner peace, but it does not satisfy the deepest yearning of a Jewish soul: to become One with the Source of Energy that gave her existence.

It is to those who know how to make their prayer an ascent to a state of oneness with their Maker that the personal signs that Rabbi Luria mentions come about. And each of the chapters that follow will bring the reader one step closer to this goal.

Introduction: Fiery Coals

> Set me as a seal upon your heart, as a seal upon your arm, for love is strong as death, jealousy cruel as the grave. Love's sparks are fiery coals, a flame of the Divine. Many waters cannot extinguish love, nor can rivers drown it.
>
> —Song of Songs 8:6–7

A PASSIONATE YEARNING FOR GOD burns in the hearts of the children of Israel. This desire to attach themselves to God with all the levels of their souls is the very purpose of Creation. Every Jew is therefore asked "to love God your Lord, . . . and to attach yourself passionately to Him."[1]

Is it enough, however, to desire God's luminous energy in order to fulfill our physical or even spiritual needs? At the heart of our longing for a soul-union with God should be the wish that He delight in us—in Israel, His Companion of the soul. Indeed, from the very beginning of Creation, God wished to delight in us. This is the reason for our Creation.

Paradoxically, the source of our passion for God is rooted in worldly pleasures. God created a world that tantalizes us with its attractions so that we could then transmute this passion back to its Source. By restraining our desire for wordly pleasures, says the famed chasidic leader Rabbi Dov Baer, Maggid of Mezrich (1704–1772), we can elevate this desire to its source in holiness—a longing for the ecstasy of God-experience.

In the courtyard of the holy Temple stood an altar upon which early each morning the priest would place a fire. Afterward, the morning sacrifice was offered and a fire descended from Heaven and consumed the sacrifice. We may ask, if the fire had already been set by the priest, what did the heavenly fire add?

The answer may be found in the words of the Maggid quoted above. The Ari teaches that the fiery ecstasy of spiritual delight is concealed under a layer of physicality. This concealment is different for every individual; it may be food, drugs, sex. Whatever the nature of your physical desire—*that* is the main covering of your spark,

1

and it is by removing this particular veil that you can most awaken spiritually. This is particularly true if the object of your desire involves a Torah transgression. Yet, even when it consists of a permitted activity, when regarded as an end in itself rather than as a means of serving God, the physical desire will still dim the light of your spiritual fire.

For example, let us say that you are addicted to and obsessed with the source of your physical desire, to the extent that from the moment you wake up in the morning, and during all your activities throughout the day, that most powerful desire distracts you at every moment. You constantly look for the moment when you will be able to indulge in the particular lust that drives you. Kabbalah teaches that one should not despair, for the higher the intensity of your addiction, the greater is your soul's power of holiness that for reasons hidden beyond the reach of your conscious mind have fallen into the realm of evil.

Should you find the superhuman strength needed to break your addiction, as well as to find the necessary stamina to sustain the change, and aim to recover your powers of holiness that were hiding beneath, you will attain spiritual greatness. As the sages teach, "The greater the person, the keener his evil inclination."

It is written:

A man's soul is the lamp of God, which searches the chambers of one's innards.[2]

By focusing on the root of desire, you will identify its nature, and by restraining from indulgence *at the time it burns most fiercely* you will remove this physical cover and reveal the essence of your Divine longing. The feminine voice in the Song of Songs—which represents the Community of Israel—then finds its echo within you in its lament:

On my bed, at night, I sought the One my soul loves.
I sought Him but I did not find Him.
I must rise now and walk through the city,
in the market places and in the streets;
I will search for the One Whom my soul loves![3]

It is generally at night, after a busy day's work, that the physical fire begins to glow. But it is not by way of what is external to you, "through the city," that you will find "the One," but within: by checking this desire, you will in fact be drawing down upon yourself the heavenly flame.

Here lies the basic difference between the Temple fire that was lit by human hands, and the fire that descended from Heaven. The fire below is lit through the arousal of human passions. The same fire that rages within you, inciting you to indulge, will become your reward. Slowly you will be able to give yourself over to serving the Almighty with an identical fire, but this time with passionate attachment to God. This is the second fire, a flame undimmed by a physical cover that descends to meet the human spark from below. This will lead to an altered state of consciousness in which you will be permeated by the intimate experience of God's love. In the verse, "Is Ephraim My precious son, is he the child of My delight . . . ?"[4] God refers to Israel by the name *Ephr*aim, which begins with the same three letters as *epher*/ashes. "He who is searching for the fire of holiness should look for it in the ashes," says the Maggid. Though the pleasures of this world are ashes compared to the ecstasy of spiritual union, one who wants a fiery attachment to God should examine his baser instincts in order to uplift them.

By elevating the *epher*, Israel becomes the object of God's delight, and, by the act of restraint, Israel becomes a giver desiring to please the Beloved. Eventually, you will relate to God less as a Father in Heaven, Provider of all needs, and more as a Companion of the soul. You will realize that every time you restrain yourself from a mundane pleasure you move one step closer to Him.

This elevation is part of the continuous process of refinement and transmutation that must proceed until all Creation is reunited with its Creator. The impetus for this elevation originates in God's will to delight in Israel, which the kabbalists call the arousal from above. Yet it consummates solely as a result of the arousal from below—the observance of the *mitsvot*/commandments—the Divine service with which we were entrusted.

The purpose of this arousal from above is not for us to forget the mundane world and enter into a state of total oneness with God. On the contrary, we are meant to be the physical vehicle through which God reveals Himself in the world. The arousal from above—His will to delight in Israel—is likened to water, which flows downward and extinguishes fire. Israel's arousal from below is likened to fire that leaps upward. In our present dimension, water douses fire.

When the Divine will becomes overwhelming in its desire to descend and give to Israel, the result is that we begin to relate to God solely as Provider of our needs. The fire of passion that compels us to rise up to our Beloved and to give pleasure to Him is then doused by materiality. At this level, fire and water are contradictory and cannot exist together.

But at the highest level, these two aspects are complementary to the point of becoming one. The very pain of the estrangement from God arouses our fire once again, and we become even more inflamed by the desire to cling to Him. We now long to cause God delight by observing His commandments and weaving the consciousness of God into our way of life. This consummates in a soul-union at the level of our heavenly souls that arouses God's overwhelming desire to give. This water then puts out the new fire, unless. . . .

Unless Israel's arousal from below reaches the point at which "love's sparks become fiery coals." Water cannot extinguish such a fire, and the thirst for passionate attachment becomes permanent, so that "many waters cannot extinguish love, nor can rivers drown it."

We therefore end the daily *Amidah*/standing prayer with the words, "May He who makes peace in His heavens, make peace upon us and upon all Israel." The Hebrew word for Heaven, *shamayim*, is composed of the words *esh*/fire, and *mayim*/water. The word *shamayim* alludes to the higher level of soul-union, where the fire of desire is not extinguished by the waters of satiation.

As long as Israel's desire for God was fiery coals, the Temple in Jerusalem stood.

Having the Temple should have satiated our longing, yet we still thirsted. There were two permanent physical fires in the Temple, which corresponded to the two spiritual fires. Inside the sanctuary stood the Menorah, the seven-branch candelabrum with its permanently lit center branch; in the courtyard, a constant fire burned in the *mizbeach/* altar. The flame in the inner sanctuary reflected the ever-growing inner desire, whereas the outside flame reflected the human desire satiated by God's bounty. "As long as these two fires burn," said the Greek leader Antiochus, who wanted to destroy the Temple, "we are powerless to harm Israel."

Kabbalah teaches that every physical entity has a spiritual counterpart. And any weakening of a spiritual element is immediately revealed in its physical manifestation. When the fire of Israel's love of God diminished, its counterpart in the Temple slowly died out, until the Temple was destroyed.

Yet there is still hope. The Talmud promises: "If Israel were to keep two Sabbaths, they would immediately be redeemed." Israel's relationship to God can be restored through Shabbat—the highest level of soul-union, in which fire and water unite as they do in Heaven.

Shabbat is our chance to experience how love and restraint are really complementary. By refraining from certain physical activities on Shabbat, we can taste the outpouring of God's love.

Keeping Shabbat can bring us to our ultimate goal, which Kabbalah calls a "face-to-face" relationship with the Almighty. We give pleasure to God because our desire to attach ourselves to Him is ever increasing, and His wish to give to us is fulfilled as He responds to our thirst. That is the purpose of Creation, where each side gives unconditionally to the Beloved.

PART ONE

SHABBAT

1

The Infinite Light

S HABBAT IS THE DAY OF THE WEEK in which God invites us to share perfect intimacy with Him by helping us reach a higher state of consciousness in which our spirit merges with the Divine. On Shabbat, we can focus all our emotions on God with laser-beam intensity and feel attached to Him with all aspects of our soul.

Let us examine the verse where God gives us the commandment to keep Shabbat. It is in the Torah portion known as *Ki Tisa* (Exodus 31:13, 17):

> The Israelites shall thus keep the Shabbat, making it a day of rest for all generations, as an eternal covenant. It is a sign between Me and the Israelites that during the six weekdays God made heaven and earth, but on the seventh day [on Shabbat], He ceased working and withdrew to the spiritual.

There are seven different concepts alluded to in these verses—seven spiritual tools or "jewels" that can enrich our Shabbat observance and help us perceive higher dimensions. Each will be explained at length in a later chapter of this book, but are briefly presented here as follows:

1. "Making [Shabbat] a day of rest," making yourself a dwelling place for the Divine Presence (see chapter 4).
2. "As an eternal covenant. It is a sign between Me and the Israelites," referring to the union between the Almighty and the souls of the Community of Israel (see chapter 2).
3. "On the seventh day [on Shabbat], He ceased working and withdrew to the spiritual (*shavat vayinafash*)"—referring to the additional soul we receive on Shabbat (*nefesh* is the generic term for "soul"; see chapter 3).
4. "Making it a day of rest." We "make" the seventh day a Shabbat by preparing delicious meals to be served on that day. Savoring these meals helps us attain the spiritual delights (see chapter 4).

5. "On the seventh day." This is an allusion to God's Crown, or aspect of Kingship that is revealed to us on the seventh day (see chapter 5).

6. "I, God, am making you holy." The state of holiness allows us to discern the great difference between the closeness to God we experience on Shabbat as opposed to during the week (see chapters 4, 5, and 6).

7. Finally, on the above verses, the Talmud comments: God said to Moses, "I have a precious gift among My hidden treasures, and Shabbat is its name. Go and inform the Israelites." "Inform them" (*lehodi'am*) refers to *da'at*, the intimate knowledge of God that results from Shabbat observance (see chapter 2).

Becoming aware of these tools can initiate the process that leads us into the meditative realm of the Shabbat experience.

However, before explaining each one individually, there is a further point to be addressed. The commandment to keep Shabbat, as it appears in these two verses from Exodus 31, was given in relationship to the building of the *Mishkan*, the portable sanctuary that accompanied the Jews until they built the holy Temple in Jerusalem. The directions to build the *Mishkan* were given after the sin of the Golden Calf. Thus it is referred to as the "Sanctuary of Testimony," for it attested to the fact that God had already forgiven them for their backsliding into idolatry.

However, the commandment to keep Shabbat had already been given earlier, first in the Torah portion relating to the Manna, and again as one of the Ten Commandments.

> You must see that God has given you the Shabbat, that is why I gave you food for two days on Friday. (Exodus 16:28)

> For in six days God made the heaven, the earth, the sea and all that is in them, but He rested on Saturday. God therefore blessed the Shabbat and made it holy. (Exodus 20:11)

In these verses, Moses informed the Israelites of the commandment to keep Shabbat in most general terms. He made no mention of the seven tools of revelation that could produce a higher state of consciousness. The detailed instructions of these "jewels"— as the *Zohar* calls them—came only after the sin of the Golden Calf, in Exodus 31.

This is because at the revelation at Sinai, the entire Jewish nation reached such an intense level of holiness that they were almost as angels. Thus, on their own, they were able to absorb a greater proportion of the Shabbat consciousness. Yet, after the sin of the Golden Calf, they fell back to their mortal level. Of this the verse says, "I said, 'You are angelic, sons of the Most High are you all.' But just like men shall you perish" (Psalm 82:6-7). At that point, Shabbat had to be transmitted in a different way.

God is known as *En Sof*/Infinite Being. The Torah, as God's will, shares this quality of infinity. Yet, we cannot directly perceive this level of Torah. It is like a powerful light concentrated beneath a surface. Any light that appears above the surface is an extension of that which is concentrated beneath. Any beam of Infinite Light that appears above the surface stems from the gathering underneath, much like a branch connected to the roots of the tree.

In the same manner, the Torah has a revealed dimension and an esoteric tradition. The revealed side, the Written and Oral Torah, is transmitted in the form of letters. The letters are like vessels containing the light, condensing it to fit their size and quality. Yet, since the mysteries of the Torah are the very essence of the Infinite Light, the finite quality of the letters cannot represent this source of wisdom in all its complexity. The wisdom cannot be captured in words, but remains in the aspect of "sight and perception"—a seeing with the heart, which means a direct perception of the ideas.

This helps us to understand what the Ari taught. The Ari explained that the mysteries of the Torah are a *kabbalah*–"something that is received." It is not a knowledge that can be attained through the finite quality of the letters, but a perception that must be "received" from a master who himself received from one before him. The perception of the esoteric tradition is then a merging of spirits with the Divine which, by its very essence, cannot be condensed into letters.

The revelation of the secrets of Kabbalah was first entrusted in written form to Rabbi Shimon bar Yochay, known as Rashby, a second-century sage, who composed the *Zohar*. Although there were many sages before him who had gained a level of expertise in the esoteric teachings of the Torah, only Rashby was given permission to transmit the *Zohar* in the form of letters because he lived after the destruction of the Temple.

As long as the Temple stood, a Divine light permeated the world. The secrets of the Torah could remain in the form of "sight and perception," a form that went beyond the boundary of letters. However, after the destruction of the Temple, the light was dimmed. Yet, Rabbi Shimon received permission from Heaven to transmit a few of these secrets in writing, so that a choice body of students could receive the light through the conduit of letters.

As later generations decreased in holiness, the light was further dimmed. Once again, Heaven gave permission for a sage, the Ari, to commit a greater proportion of Torah secrets to writing. This was a condensation of the light, but was nevertheless permitted because the heart-vision of each generation was diminishing, necessitating the conduit of letters in order to transmit the Divine light.

A few generations after the Ari came the Baal Shem Tov, who fulfilled the same function. Yet, interestingly enough, neither the Ari nor the Baal Shem Tov was able to confine his overwhelming perception of the Infinite Light to writing. They transmitted their teachings orally; it was their students who wrote them down. Even Rabbi Shimon wrote only the first "Mishnah" of the *Zohar*, the main body of the *Zohar* being written down by his disciples some seventy years after his death.[1]

As the generations continued to decrease in wisdom and holiness, more and more Torah secrets had to be presented in written form, otherwise people would have been unable to perceive the light.

The same is true of the commandment to observe Shabbat, whose importance is equal to that of the entire Torah. Shabbat is also said to be infinite—in the words of the Bible, "an inheritance without limitation."

Before the giving of the Torah, Israel was on the level of "angelic beings," "sons of the Most High," and thus the light of Shabbat was given to them directly, not in the limited form of letters but as the unbounded light of *En Sof.* "You must *see* that God has given you Shabbat." Not as a revelation that can be contained in words, but in a way that can be seen only with the heart.

After that, on every succeeding Shabbat, Israel could soar to unprecedented heights, until the previous Shabbat would seem like a weekday in comparison. For on every Shabbat there shines a light that can make one feel that he has never observed a Shabbat before. Every Shabbat becomes like the first. Hence the Talmud teaches that if Israel had only kept the first Shabbat, they would immediately have been redeemed, meaning to say that every Shabbat is "a first Shabbat" from the viewpoint of the new light created for that individual Shabbat.

This is how it was supposed to be, before the sin of the Golden Calf, when the Israelites were on such a high spiritual level that they could, on their own, draw the higher consciousness of Shabbat from its very Source. Hence, the seven Shabbat jewels would only have clouded their Divine awareness and prevented their contact with the Infinite Light.

After the sin, however, when they could no longer relate to Shabbat from the viewpoint of "sight and perception," the seven jewels of Shabbat had to be spelled out to them. Their physical letters would become conduits through which the Israelites would absorb the light and benefit from it. Nevertheless, even after the sin of the Golden Calf, those righteous people who had achieved a degree of holiness were still able to experience Shabbat in all its original radiance.

"I have a precious gift among My hidden treasures, and Shabbat is its name. Go and inform the Israelites," said God to Moses after the Golden Calf. The Almighty was saying that although the sin had dimmed the people's ethereal lights and that from then on they would have to exert themselves considerably to regain the light, still the gift of Shabbat was that its light was not obstructed by their physicality like all the other lights. On Shabbat, they would be able to absorb the light of the Torah without the effort required during the week. On every Shabbat, the amount of light revealed to them would be in direct proportion to the intensity of their spiritual longing.

In the following chapters we will examine the "jewels" of the Shabbat experience available to us. We will learn how to focus our minds on God with increasing sharpness, until the myopia we have inherited from the perpetrators of the Golden Calf completely falls away.

2
Soul-Union of Shabbat

"Make it known to the Israelites"
> —Tractate *Shabbat* 10a

If you turn away your foot on the Shabbat
and refrain from your affairs on My holy day;
if you call the Shabbat a delight
and God's holy [day] honored;
if you honor it by not doing your business,
attending to your affairs,
or speaking of [weekday] matters,
then you will delight in God.
I will let you ride the heights of the earth
and enjoy the inheritance of your father Jacob,
for God's mouth has spoken.

> —Isaiah 58:13, 14

FROM THIS PASSAGE WE LEARN of the reward for observing Shabbat. To those who honor and delight in Shabbat to the best of their ability, God "will let you ride the heights of the earth and enjoy the inheritance of your father Jacob." According to Maimonides, this is the earthly reward one receives for keeping Shabbat. There is still another reward that awaits the Shabbat observer in the world to come.

> God said to Moses, "I have a precious gift among My hidden treasures, and Shabbat is its name. Go and make it known to the Israelites."
>
> —*Shabbat* 10a

This precious gift, hidden away, is not Shabbat itself, for the injunction to observe Shabbat was explicitly stated in the Ten Commandments. The gift, says the Talmud, is the reward for keeping Shabbat which one will receive in the future world. The reward in this world is revealed by Isaiah. The reward in the world to come is not

11

recorded in Scripture; it is the hidden treasure of which God told Moses to inform Israel.

The knowledge of the reward for keeping Shabbat is not merely auxiliary to the commandment, it is a necessary part of Shabbat observance. In almost no other mitsvah are we told the reward for keeping it. As the sages have said, "Be as careful with a light mitsvah as with a weighty one, for you do not know the reward given for the mitsvot" (*Ethics of the Fathers* 2:1). Yet, here we are informed twice. This knowledge itself helps us to achieve a higher state of consciousness which enhances our ability to feel and appreciate Shabbat.

> Beloved is man, for he was created in the image [of God]. Informing him that he was created in the image [of God], as it is written, "In the image of God He made man" (Genesis 9:6), indicates even greater love.
>
> Beloved are Israel, for they are called children of the Omnipresent. Informing them that they are called children of the Omnipresent, as it is written, "You are children to the Lord your God" (Deuteronomy 14:1), indicates even greater love.
> —*Ethics of the Fathers* 3:18

Sending an anonymous gift to a friend is surely an expression of love. Informing him of its source may cause the receiver to love his friend the giver in return. By informing us that we are His children, with the ability to acquire a higher state of awareness, God expresses His love and asks us to reciprocate. God yearns for Israel to reach a higher state of consciousness. Informing us of His love is meant to arouse the same powerful emotion in us.

We see this same dynamic at work in two different places in the daily prayer service. Before the recitation of the Shema prayer, we say a blessing over God's love for Israel that begins "With an eternal love You have loved us, Lord, our God," and concludes, "Blessed are You, Lord, who chooses His people Israel in love." Immediately afterward are the words of the Shema:

> Hear, O Israel, the Lord is your God, the Lord is One! You shall love the Lord your God with all your heart, with all your soul, and with all your might.

For the knowledge that God loves us infinitely impels us to love Him with heart and soul until we become one with Him.

In addition, the code of Jewish law states that during the repetition of the Amidah prayer, in the section known as *Kedushah*, we should lift our eyes to Heaven. The mystical work *Sefer Hechalot* describes God's response:

> Inform My children that when they sanctify Me with the words of the *Kedushah*, "Holy, holy, holy is the Lord of Hosts," they should lift their eyes to Heaven and be carried aloft at this time, for I have no greater pleasure in the world than the moment that they lift their eyes to Mine while My eyes are on theirs. At this time . . . I hasten their redemption.

The function of the *Kedushah* is to produce in us a higher state of consciousness in which we are more aware of our relationship with the Divine. According to the *Sefer Hechalot*, God informs us of His love for us in order to arouse us to respond in kind.

Soon after the recital of the *Kedushah* comes the blessing in which we pray for wisdom and understanding. This refers to a special type of soul-union that can occur only when the love between man and God is reciprocal.

EXCLUSIVE LOVE

There are various types of love that bond us with the Creator. One is reminiscent of the love of the Father for his child, as the verse says, "I loved Israel when he was still a youth" (Hosea 11:1). A father loves his child even if the child does not reciprocate his love. And if the love is mutual, it still need not be exclusive; a father's love for his favorite son does not diminish his affection for his other children.

There is a different level of love called *da'at*/knowledge. It is the higher state of consciousness in which one achieves a passionate attachment to God. In this higher form of awareness, each spirit merges with the other, so to speak, until they become one.

Da'at is the biblical term for the marital union, "And Adam *knew* Eve." It is the metaphor used in the Song of Songs to describe God's love for Israel. To reach the oneness and passionate attachment of the marital bond, both husband and wife must feel the love with equal intensity, and the love must be exclusive. To cleave to God on the level of *da'at*, the love must be mutual and exclusive; we must focus upon Him all our emotions. Anything short of this cannot be called binding to God with passionate attachment.

This is the soul-union of Shabbat, when we "delight in the Lord." Shabbat is a covenantal sign, a day of special unification between God and Israel. It is the only day of the week in which we can achieve complete intimacy with the Divine. For on Shabbat, God informs us of His love for us, revealing that our love is important to Him; that He wants us and enables us to love Him. "I have a precious gift among My hidden treasures, and Shabbat is its name. Go and inform the Israelites." The Hebrew *lehodi'am*/inform stems from the word *da'at*. During the six days of the week, our relationship with the Almighty is like the love of a father and child. Only on Shabbat do we attach ourselves to God through *da'at*, that special illumination of the relationship between the Creator and "the Community of Israel, His Companion of the soul."

All week we prepare ourselves to achieve the soul-union of *da'at* on Shabbat. Saying Shema and Kedushah daily reminds us of the powerful love bond that will take effect on Shabbat. And God has informed us of the reward to make us understand that Shabbat observance leads to a closeness to Him that cannot be achieved in any other way.[1]

THE BLACKSMITH AND THE BRIDE

In the Ten Commandments, we are given a "reason" for the Shabbat rest:

> Remember the Shabbat day to keep it holy. You can work during the six weekdays and do all your tasks. But Saturday is the Sabbath to God your Lord. Do not do anything

that constitutes work. . . . It was during the six weekdays that God made the heaven, the earth, the sea . . . , *but He rested on Saturday.* God therefore blessed the Sabbath day and made it holy.

—Exodus 20:8–11

The commandment to keep Shabbat is different from all the others in the Decalogue. The other commandments, against murder and idolatry, or to honor parents, were not given in order to teach us to emulate God. Yet on Shabbat we are commanded to rest because He did so. What does our human rest have to do with Divine rest?

In the *Kiddush* prayer recited Friday night over wine, we say the following verses:

God blessed the seventh day and sanctified it, for on it He ceased from all His work that God created [so that it would continue] to function.

—Genesis 2:3

From a casual reading it would seem that God finished the work of Creation on the sixth day, and therefore rested on the seventh because the work was finished. Our sages, however, say that with the oncoming of Shabbat, not all God's work of Creation was finished and certain parts of Creation remained incomplete. The Midrash compares this to a blacksmith who raises his hammer to strike the anvil, then sees that the day is waning and Shabbat is coming, so he sets down his hammer without striking, leaving his work unfinished.

This teaches us that God ceased working not because He had finished, but because Shabbat had come. Had God completed all His work on the sixth day, it would have appeared as if He had rested because there was nothing more to do. Of course, He could have completed all His work before the arrival of Shabbat. But He wanted to teach us that a person can never finish all his work, yet he must put it aside, just as God did, in order to experience Shabbat.

THE HIDDEN LIGHT

On the first day of Creation, when God said, "Let there be light," He created an Infinite Light that permeated all Creation. Yet God saw that one day wicked people would arise. Concerned that they might misuse this spiritual illumination, God concealed the light, allowing it to be perceived only at special times, such as Shabbat and festivals. At these times, God unites with the soul-root of all Israel to produce an intense Divine awareness.

But in order for this soul-union to be complete, both sides must be mutually committed. For Shabbat to be a day of revelation of the hidden Light and of passionate union with the Divine, there must be a complete cessation of work by both parties. God sanctified the Shabbat day by stopping all work in order to join Israel in perfect intimacy. And He asks His people Israel to cease their work on Shabbat as He did. Just as He left His creative task unfinished to join His partner, so Israel must do the same, putting aside any worldly preoccupation—in deed as well as in thought—in order to cleave to God in passionate attachment. Without total disengagement from all worldly concerns, no soul-union can take place.

Once we can completely uproot any thought of worldly needs and feel that our weekday goals are completed, we will be able to reach the level of *da'at,* where the only thing that matters is intimacy with the Creator.

THE MANNA

"The Lord blessed the seventh day and He sanctified it."

According to the Midrash, God blessed and sanctified Shabbat with Manna. During the week, enough Manna fell from Heaven to fulfill each person's daily needs. On the eve of Shabbat, two portions fell, one for Friday, and one for Shabbat. Sanctifying Shabbat with Manna means that on Shabbat the Manna did not fall at all. Unlike earthly produce, which grows by itself, the Manna had to be created anew each day. By withholding Manna on Shabbat, God showed that He set aside His work to dedicate that day to His attachment to Israel.

The Manna represents a person's livelihood, one's "daily bread." A person who wants to observe Shabbat can ask, "But if I don't work, how can I make a living?" Yet the *Zohar* says that precisely because of the cessation from work do we merit the sustenance of the week. God "blessed and sanctified Shabbat with Manna." Sanctification means pulling back from the physical to the inner state of union. When one enters into a soul-union with God, the Source of blessing, on Shabbat, then all one's efforts throughout the week will succeed. As the *Zohar* teaches, Shabbat is the wellspring of all blessing.

God ceased His work to make Shabbat a source of blessing. By our ceasing our worldly occupations, we connect to God on Shabbat, to receive His blessing and sustenance all week.

A SIGN FOREVER

The Children of Israel shall keep the Shabbat, making the Shabbat for their generations an eternal covenant. Between Me and the Children of Israel it is a sign forever that in six days God made the heavens and the earth, but on the seventh day He ceased working and withdrew to the spiritual.

—Exodus 31:16–17

The Rashba explains that the only way to achieve closeness to God is through the "sign" He gave us for that very purpose: the cessation of activity on Shabbat. As with any sign it is verifiable. When we have given ourselves totally to the Shabbat experience, we will find that our awareness of Divine Providence in our daily life is heightened.

Although in the initial stages of Shabbat observance we have no conscious perception of the occurring soul-union, we nevertheless become increasingly sensitized to the special closeness to God available on that day.

A non-Jew studying Judaism in preparation for conversion, who wants to experience Shabbat, is always told to perform deliberately at least one act of work each

Shabbat—one minor desecration—until he converts and receives Shabbat as a covenantal sign. The Talmud warns that a person who keeps Shabbat without having first received the covenant endangers his life, like one who interferes with a lion's intimate relations with his lioness. Only a person who is part of the covenant can aspire to the soul-union reserved for Shabbat observers.

THE QUEEN-BRIDE

> Come, my Beloved, to greet the Bride
> Let us welcome the Shabbat presence. . . .
> Come, O Bride, O Shabbat Queen!
> —Rabbi Shlomo HaLevy Alkabetz

This hymn, sung in the synagogue before sunset on the eve of Shabbat, is based on the Talmud's description of how the sages greeted the holy day:

> Rabbi Chanina would wrap himself in his cloak and say, "Come, let us go and greet the Shabbat Queen!"

> Rabbi Yannai would don his garment and say, "Come, O Bride! Come, O Bride!"
> —*Shabbat* 119a

The Shabbat Queen is Israel's bride. Each weekday has a partner: Sunday and Monday, Tuesday and Wednesday, Thursday and Friday. "Only I have no partner," Shabbat complained to God, according to the Midrash. "I will give you Israel as a partner," the Almighty replied. Thus we recite in Kiddush the verse "Remember the Shabbat day to sanctify it." In Hebrew, the word for "sanctify" also means "marry"—*lekadesh*.

Shabbat arrives at sunset on Friday. But we do not stop work at sunset. We must prepare to greet the Queen-Bride. We must bathe, dress in our finest clothes, and stop all work at least eighteen minutes before sunset. Finally, before greeting Shabbat, we must feel that all our work is done, so that we can totally give ourselves to the soul-union of Shabbat.

Returning to our blacksmith, we can well imagine that if, when he lifted his hammer, he had seen his beautiful bride coming toward him, resplendent in her wedding gown, how frustrated he would have felt for not having put down his hammer earlier, even before finishing his work.

God concealed the light of Creation to avoid its misuse, but He reveals it on Shabbat. This effulgent light hid the soul-union between God and the souls of Israel, His Companion of the soul, and it revealed its iridescence only because of the restraint God placed upon Himself by stopping the work of Creation upon the arrival of the Bride, Shabbat. By placing a similar restraint upon themselves, Israel would be able to receive the sign God was giving them that would enable them to experience totally this intimacy with the Beloved.[2]

3
The Additional Soul

On the Shabbat, [God] ceased working vayinafash/*and withdrew to the spiritual.*

T O UNDERSTAND THE CONCEPT of Shabbat additional soul we must first discuss the three dimensions of the soul.[1] These are the *neshamah* (from *neshimah*/breath), the *ruach* (literally, "wind"), and the *nefesh* (from *nafash*/rested).

The *neshamah* rests upon the brain; the *ruach* dwells in the heart; the *nefesh* is attached to the liver. The *nefesh* and the *ruach,* which are responsible for human emotions, are directly connected with the body. However, because of its lofty origin, the *neshamah* is not completely attached to the body; body and *neshamah* are two separate entities dwelling together.

At the moment of death, the *neshamah* leaves the body. The *nefesh* remains, and the *ruach* fluctuates back and forth, returning annually on the anniversary of the death to dwell in the body for that day.

The *nefesh* is bound to the body's material needs and tendencies. It is an animating force, the motivation behind our basic life forces such as eating and drinking. The *neshamah* deals exclusively with matters of the spirit. It is an intellectual soul longing to serve the Creator; its goal is to teach man how to make his life a constant fulfillment of the will of God.

The *ruach* is in constant movement between the *nefesh* and the *neshamah*. On weekdays, the *ruach* attaches itself to the *nefesh;* on Shabbat, in which the *ruach* is not involved in any mundane activity, it separates from the *nefesh* and attaches itself to the *neshamah*. In addition, for the duration of Shabbat, each Jew receives a *neshamah yeterah*, an additional soul. When Shabbat departs, the *ruach* returns to the *nefesh*, and the *neshamah yeterah* returns to Heaven.

Just as there are two "sides" to Shabbat observance—outwardly, it is a day of rest, but inwardly, it is a time of soul-union with our Maker—so does the additional soul have an inner and outer purpose. This outer purpose is, as Rashi explains, an expanded heart, or in other words a sharpening of our sense perceptions comparable

17

to the effect of mind-altering drugs which heighten the ability to see colors, taste food, appreciate sound, and the like. This outer purpose helps us fulfill the commandment of delighting in Shabbat.

The inner purpose of the additional soul is to help us focus our entire mind on the Almighty. As a result, our ability to feel His Presence is intensified, particularly at the moment of prayers. This special focusing power of the mind also results in a higher level of understanding, which greatly enhances the pleasure of learning Torah on Shabbat.

Shabbat provides a unique opportunity to study the Torah for the sake of giving pleasure to the Beloved, without thinking of the reward we will gain. At the time you are absorbed in his study, your body ceases to call attention to its material needs. As a consequence, you are able to soar to new heights, boosted by your increased understanding of God's Torah.

On Shabbat the gates of the light of the Torah are opened. The mysteries of the Torah that you begin to grasp increase your faith in the Divine Wisdom and intensify the delight that floods you at the time of prayer.

We see an allusion to the increased understanding of Shabbat in the account of the commandment of the Paschal lamb that the Israelites were to sacrifice on what is referred to as the "Great Shabbat," namely, the Shabbat preceding Passover. At the time of the Exodus, on the tenth of Nissan, they were commanded to take one sheep per family.

On this day, which at the time fell on Shabbat, the Egyptians saw the Israelites taking the object of their worship, sheep, to slaughter. The Egyptians could not raise a finger to prevent them because at this point, they were totally overwhelmed by the devastating plagues. It is due to this miracle that every Shabbat preceding Passover is referred to as the "Great Shabbat" even if it does not fall on the tenth of Nissan.

When Moses told the Israelites to take a young sheep and slaughter it in fulfillment of the commandment of the Paschal lamb, he revealed to them the underlying reason behind this instruction. Essentially, this commandment was to help them put a stop to their idolatrous practices, as the commentators derived from Moses' transmission of the Divine order. The literal translation of this verse is: "Withdraw and take sheep according to your families."[2] Due to the apparent repetition of the verb, "withdraw and take," some commentators understood the first expression as an injunction to put an end to idolatry, namely: "Withdraw [from idolatry] and get yourselves sheep for your families." It is not by chance that Moses chose to tell the Israelites the secret teaching of the Paschal lamb on a Shabbat. Beyond the inner peace of this day which is naturally conducive to a deeper level of understanding, it was the best time for them to learn that they had an additional soul which would help them to grasp the teachings of the Torah if they so desired.

According to this interpretation of the verse, if Moses had not explained to the Israelites the mystery of the Paschal lamb, they would not have put an end to their own acts of idolatry. Neither the ten plagues nor any of the miracles that God wrought on their behalf had stopped their involvement with idolatry.

Moses knew that they would only acquire the strength to stop when they fully understood how they were destroying their spiritual makeup through their activities. He therefore waited for Shabbat so that they would be able to focus their entire minds on what he was teaching them with the help of the additional soul. Hence, the Shabbat preceding Passover is referred to as the Great Shabbat, for it was on that day that God's Name was sanctified when they were able to abide by His will.

Whereas the *neshamah* that a person has during the week enables him to understand the outer aspects of the Torah, the *neshamah yeterah* enables him to understand its mysteries. "Let Him kiss me with the kisses of His mouth," says the first verse of the Song of Songs, which Rashi interprets as:

> Let Him be intimate with me again, and transmit to me the innermost secrets of His Torah directly, "mouth to mouth," as He did at Sinai when He revealed Himself to us "face-to-face."

Thus, it is traditional to read the Song of Songs at the onset of Shabbat to remind us that on this day our wish will be fulfilled through the presence of the additional soul.

Hence, the outer purpose of the additional soul—the sharpening of the senses—is to feel the Shabbat *oneg*/delight.

JOY VERSUS DELIGHT

The fine distinction between enjoying ourselves through the harmony and physical pleasures of Shabbat versus delighting in the spiritual joy we may attain this day calls for a redefinition of the terms "joy" and "delight."

As specific situations in man's life give rise to joy, the happiness that takes hold of him makes him momentarily forget everything that may be oppressing him. For instance, a person who discovers new levels of meaning in the Torah after hours of analytical study feels great joy stemming from the illumination of wisdom he has received. Although the other parts of his body are not experiencing his joy directly, they share in his joy despite the fact that their individual burden is not lighter.

In contrast with joy that is felt in the mind, *oneg*/delight is also expressed as an illumination of joy, but this time all the parts of the body share in it equally, as if one were rejoicing for many different reasons simultaneously. The vibrant delight known as *oneg* infuses each and every part of our body in equal measure, reaching beyond the body to our soul.

Reaching the *oneg*/delight of Shabbat allows man to devote all his being to the service of his Creator. This, in turn, serves to enhance the inner function of the additional soul, the sharpening of the mind of those who thirst for closeness to God, allowing them to grasp the inner message of the Torah.

The additional soul also gives us an expanded consciousness to eat and drink with a joyful heart. We no longer have to fear the power of the animating soul to pull us down as it does throughout the week. The *ruach* is now free to attach itself to our *neshamah*. This increased power of our intellectual soul, coupled with the awareness of the altered state within our reach, gives us an added measure of self-control to avoid the "down" of overeating.

Aware of the way in which one's spiritual consciousness is lowered while eating, Torah sages usually interrupt their meals at frequent intervals in order to break the strength of their desire. The time of these interruptions is usually spent discussing the Torah. The goal is to raise the consciousness so that the taste of the food is not an end in itself. The interruptions make it easier to enjoy the savory taste while consciously aware that the pleasure one is deriving is a reflection of the Divine in the food. When a meal is conducted in this manner, the pleasure of the food becomes a conduit to achieve the spiritual joy of passionate attachment to the Almighty.

Another traditional way of interrupting the Shabbat meal is with song. Music is one of the seven wisdoms given to us to find God through His concealment within nature,[3] and consequently, it has been used as a means of arousal to enter a prophetic trance since the beginning of times.

Aware that the sound of music induces a high state of consciousness sensitizing man to feel his additional soul, the Ari wrote poems for each of the three Shabbat meals. His songs, like the many others that are readily available in print, have a refrain that takes the role of a mantra which clears the mind of all thoughts until all that remains is the longing.

The sharpening of our sensory perceptions, the product of our additional soul, allows us to use all our physical senses as a means to lift the veil of concealment separating us from the Beloved.

THE TWO TABLETS

It is known that the Tablets of the Ten Commandments were given twice. The first set, before the sin of the Golden Calf, were shattered by Moses; the second were given after God forgave the people for their transgression. In both sets of Tablets, the commandment of Shabbat is mentioned. Yet the wording is slightly different.

1. Remember the Shabbat to keep it holy. You can work during the six weekdays and do all your tasks. But Saturday is the Shabbat to God your Lord. . . . It was during the six weekdays that God made the heaven, the earth, the sea and all that is in them, but He rested on Saturday. God therefore blessed the Shabbat and made it holy.[4]

2. Observe the Shabbat to keep it holy, as God your Lord has commanded you. You can work during the six weekdays, and do all your tasks, but Saturday is the Shabbat to God your Lord. . . . You must remember that you were slaves in Egypt, when God your Lord brought you out with a strong hand and an outstretched arm. It is for this reason that God your Lord has commanded you to keep the Shabbat.[5]

The rationale behind Shabbat serving as a reminder of God's own rest is clear. However, it is not clear why Shabbat is a reminder of the Exodus.

The reason is that without the light of Shabbat, derived from the additional soul, the Israelites would have been unable to cease the idolatrous practices they had learned in Egypt, and therefore, never have been able to escape slavery. It was the Shabbat experience that enabled them to leave.

This was stated in the second set of Tablets, after the sin of the Golden Calf, for the Israelites had once again fallen into idolatry. They had regressed to an Egyptian mentality. Now, they had the additional task rectifying their sin. Hence, just as the light of Shabbat had initially helped them put an end to idolatry, so would it now help them rectify the making of the Calf.

Throughout the Bible God repeatedly refers to "My Sabbaths,"[6] referring to the two aspects of Shabbat. The closeness to God experienced on Shabbat empowers man not to sin. Yet if he does fall into transgression, Shabbat will also light his way back to God as it once did, prior to leaving Egypt.*

---

* A fine human voice is the most powerful channel to reach passionate attachment to the Divine, and indeed it was the haunting beauty of the Levites' song in the Temple that moved repentants to tears before presenting the offering that would restore the intimate bond they had lost. I dedicate this chapter to my son James, in recognition of the *oneg* he gives us with his Shabbat songs, and in particular, "I will build a sanctuary in my heart."

4
Reaching the Shabbat Delight

HONOR AND DELIGHT

If you call the Shabbat a delight, and God's holy [day] honored; if you honor it by not doing your business, attending to your affairs, or speaking of [weekday] matters, then you will delight in God.[1]

FROM THESE VERSES THE TALMUD derives two commandments pertaining to Shabbat, to delight in it and to honor it. Together, these lead to the final promise, "then you will delight in God." Note that the verse does not say, "If you enjoy the Shabbat delights," but rather "if you call *the Shabbat* a delight"—if you realize that the day itself is the source of delight. For much higher than the physical pleasures we enjoy on this day is the *oneg* that we are able to achieve, a pleasure so intense that it has the power to connect man below with all the levels of his soul above, and hence to God Himself.

According to Maimonides, honoring Shabbat involves physical preparations such as cleaning and putting the house in order, planning gourmet meals and shopping for the finest ingredients, cooking with love and care, setting flowers on the dining table, arranging the Shabbat lights, showering and donning one's finest attire. All this is meant to honor Shabbat's arrival as one would honor the arrival of a king. One need not worry about straining one's budget, because, as the sages have promised, every penny spent on honoring Shabbat will find its way back into your purse.

Making Shabbat a source of spiritual delight means arousing yourself by savoring each morsel of the special meals you have prepared and drinking the fine wine you have bought for the occasion. Furthermore, on Shabbat we have a keener sense of sight that opens us to the beauty of the array of food against the background of a white tablecloth and fills our eyes with the glow of the Shabbat lights. On Shabbat, says the Talmud, food has a special taste. Meals characteristically last for hours and include many courses.

INNER AND OUTER

Let us examine how we achieve this merging of our physical body with our spiritual essence to serve the Creator.

We see that "honoring Shabbat" involves activities that are exterior to the body, such as cleaning the house and donning fine clothing. "Delighting in Shabbat" is related to internal pleasures such as eating and drinking. Furthermore, "honor" is something you do before Shabbat, in preparation for its arrival, while "delight" occurs on Shabbat itself.

There is a deeper dimension to these two commandments. "Honor" and "delight" correspond to two types of spiritual illumination, inner and outer. Kabbalistically, these are referred to as the Surrounding Light and the Inner Light. These two illuminations are present at every level of Creation and are reflected in many areas of Jewish thought.

The Inner Light is a Divine force intended to enter man's body and arouse him spiritually. A person who is close to God feels this force as it enters him and is painfully aware of the times when it is absent. The Surrounding Light is a luminous garment around man that sensitizes him to the spiritual energy available around him[2] and sharpens his intellect.

Torah study, for instance, purifies our Inner Light, since it helps refine our character traits and purifies our mind and heart. Fulfilling commandments, on the other hand, purifies the Surrounding Light, since most commandments pertain to the world around us. Thus our actions and the physical world around us become refined. When the two simultaneously act upon a person, from within and from without, a human being is transformed until he becomes a sanctuary for the Divine Presence.

JACOB'S LADDER

The concepts of Inner and Surrounding lights are closely connected to the commandments of the Torah. According to the sages, the number of human body parts equals the number of commandments, 613. By fulfilling God's will through His commandments, each organ becomes a vessel to contain within it and be surrounded by Divine light. When the entire body radiates with Divine energy, a person becomes a "dwelling place"—a Temple—for God's Presence.

This is the secret of Jacob's ladder. Upon awakening, after seeing the heavenly ladder, the Patriarch exclaimed:

> If God will be with me, if He will protect me on the journey that I am taking, if He gives me bread to eat and clothing to wear.[3]

The "bread" here refers to the Inner Light, while the "clothing to wear" alludes to the Surrounding Light. Jacob was praying that God would bless him with both inner and outer realization, until both these aspects became one.

It is taught that the heavenly ladder was the pictorial representation of God's desire to have a Temple on earth—and indeed, the place where Jacob slept would later be the site of Solomon's Temple. It was a place where man's Inner and Surrounding Lights could merge with the Divine essence. Jacob was concerned that he would be unable to meet the challenge of drawing down both aspects of God's light. He therefore asked the Almighty to grant him the luminous energy as a gift.

But according to the Talmud, God did not grant him this request. For these were the aspects of himself that Jacob had come to the world to perfect. Only through his own efforts could he rise up the ladder and bequeath his spiritual accomplishments to his children. Jacob's soul included the collective souls of all Israel. If God had granted him his wish, then his descendants, the Children of Israel, would not have had the opportunity to fulfill their Divine mission. Man is placed in this world in order to attain, through his personal struggle, the refined spiritual delight for which he was created.

Consequently, rather than regarding as cumbersome tasks the difficult and often lengthy preparations for Shabbat, we should remember that they are unique tools for perfecting our vessels to receive God's light. "A person who does not work on Friday won't eat on Shabbat," says the Talmud, meaning that without intense spiritual work to refine ourselves and the world around us, we will never come to the inner delight of God's Presence that we enjoy on Shabbat.

THE CONCEPT OF "DELIGHT" AND THE FUNCTION OF PRIESTHOOD

According to Isaiah, the ability to reach the *oneg*/delight of Shabbat is "the heritage of your forefather Jacob." Where do we see the connection of physical pleasure and spiritual delight in Jacob's life? More specifically, is there a biblical antecedent giving substance to the idea of using the pleasure of food as a means of attaining a higher state of consciousness?

In his early years, Jacob is described as "sitting in the tents" of Noach's sons, Shem and Eber, studying Torah. In contrast, his twin brother, Esau, is presented as a skilled hunter who knew how to attain physical pleasure, except that he stimulated his senses through the forbidden paths.

The kabbalists understand Jacob's description—"sitting"—as indicating that initially he lacked the ability to transfer the mind-expansion of worldly pleasures to the service of God.

What about his father Isaac? How did Isaac stimulate his senses in order to attain a state of communion with God? It is written: "Isaac enjoyed eating Esau's game and favored him."[4]

At first glance, it seems unlikely that a person with the spiritual stature of Isaac would regard the taste of food as a sufficient cause for favoring one son over the other. The patriarch's attitude to food was further stressed when, prior to blessing his first born, he requested a serving of venison.

From the zeal that Isaac's wife and sons applied to getting him the savory meal he had requested, we can see that they understood it was Isaac's way of becoming attuned to the spiritual dimension. The taste of venison was the prism he needed to switch to a higher state of awareness. Having attained mind-expansion in this manner, he was able to draw down the Divine luminous energy he needed to transfer his essence to the son who would carry on Isaac's function in the world.

After Jacob bought from Esau the rights of the first born, which included personal involvement in the Divine service, he also acquired Esau's ability to stimulate his senses. Jacob, however, used the stimulation of his senses to enhance his Divine service. As we will see, Isaac's blessing, compounded by the years Jacob spent with his evil uncle, Laban, would give Jacob the ability to use the concept of *oneg*/delight as a means of cleaving to God.

In fact, what happened after the blessing? The biblical scene shifts to Jacob as he received the vision of the heavenly ladder whose feet stood on earth and whose top reached Heaven. The Ari explains that the ladder illustrates the process of Jacob's growth. At the beginning he sat at home studying Torah, which represents the top of the ladder reaching up toward Heaven.

On his way to the home of the devious Laban, he was going not only to find a wife but also to practice the skill he had just acquired by becoming a ladder standing on the ground. He had to use the pleasures provided by "the ground" as a means of ascent. Although God intimated that He wanted Jacob to become a dwelling place for His Divine Presence through his own efforts, He nevertheless promised him help when He saw Jacob's fear that he would not be equal to the task: "I am with you. I will protect you wherever you go."[5]

Jacob did indeed need Divine protection to preserve his holiness, for he was going to an atmosphere where evil reigned. It was there that he had to learn how to use physical pleasures in holiness as a means to reach spiritual arousal so that he could teach it to his children. An intrinsic part of the Divine assistance he received was Rachel, Jacob's earthly soul mate whom he met directly after his vision. "Jacob loved Rachel so much that the seven years he worked for her seemed like no more than a few days."[6]

The union with his soul mate taught Jacob how to feel a love that totally fills the mind, where everything else is in the periphery of the consciousness. Jacob thus learned that relating to God as part of the Community of Israel, His Companion of the soul, entails the same directed consciousness.

After inheriting the Divine service of the first born, which gave him the skill to use physical delight as a means of reaching passionate attachment to God, Rachel was the earthly model Jacob received to complete his apprenticeship.

Initially, it was God's will that the Divine service of drawing down luminous energy that Jacob had inherited be fulfilled by all future firstborns. The physical delight these would experience in holiness would serve as a magnet to draw down the Divine energy. However, after the sin of the Golden Calf came the fear that the arousal of a high degree of sensual gratification would increase in equal measure man's vulnerability to evil.

The Divine service of the first born was therefore entrusted to those who had not been involved in the sin of the Golden Calf: the tribe of Levi and the priesthood. The priests' inborn ability to combine awe and love of God would enable them to experience sensual enjoyment when partaking of the Temple offerings while focusing their attention on the Divine source of their delight.

PLEASURE AND THE SHABBAT EXPERIENCE

On Shabbat God sends us His luminous energy: that is the Shabbat "gift." By anticipating and preparing for Shabbat throughout the week, we transform our body and our possessions into vessels that can hold the Divine Shabbat light. Clothes that are purchased specifically for use on Shabbat acquire a level of holiness similar to that of the priestly garments used in the Temple. This holiness subsequently influences and uplifts the wearer.

With the arrival of Shabbat, we move farther inward. Now we experience the delight of Shabbat. Maimonides explains that if you prepare a meal *with the intention* of honoring Shabbat, this meal acquires an intrinsic holiness which helps to refine our inner vessels to the point where they are flooded by the intense pleasure of the Divine.

This, then, is the meaning and implication of the delight of Shabbat, Jacob's legacy to us: the ability to use the Shabbat food and drink as a means of arousal from which you can attain the spiritual fire of the Shabbat delight.

Delighting in Shabbat by savoring the delicacies prepared raises our consciousness to the spiritual level of the Holy Temple. In the Temple, the priests consumed the highest offerings which infused them with holiness. On Shabbat, this concept of delight is revealed in its full force, influencing all our character traits. It is from this fountain that the blessings and holiness spring forth. Thus, the Talmud teaches: He who delights in Shabbat is granted his heart's desires, for it is written, "take delight in God and He will give you the desires of your heart."[7]

What is "the desires of your heart"? To be able to feel the attachment to the Almighty as the Companion of our soul. This is indeed a "high," but one whose essence is holy. Our forefather Jacob paved the way for us to reach this elusive experience by showing us how to arouse ourselves in holiness through the physical pleasures of Shabbat.

As we take leave of the Shabbat Queen, we will direct the energy filling us toward the Divine service of the six weekdays in the knowledge that the fruit of our labor will be an unprecedented "high" on the following Shabbat. Hence, every Shabbat experience builds on the previous one, to the extent that our Divine awareness of the preceding Shabbat is almost like a weekday consciousness compared to that of Shabbat that follows.

5

The Light of the Crown

WE HAVE SEEN HOW VARIOUS LEVELS of Shabbat observance lead to a communion with the Divine. These include putting aside one's work in anticipation of the Shabbat union, preparing for Shabbat to draw down the Surrounding Lights, using the senses to reach the delight of the spirit, and finally, the more ethereal pleasure that every Jew is meant to experience—the higher state of consciousness in which body and soul experience Shabbat together.

In this chapter we will learn how to make this joy a permanent reality in our lives, by directing our efforts to the spiritual pursuits of Shabbat. Prayer—the direct communication with the Beloved—is the most important of these.

A GLANCE BACK TO CREATION

God wanted to create the world in order to bestow His goodness upon His creatures. That goodness was the chance for the creatures to attach themselves to God's own Presence, the ultimate source of blessing. God furthermore desired that we attain this goodness through our own efforts. Each one of us would then be able to cleave to Him, as attached to Divinity as the soul is to the body.

God therefore created a world of free choice, of good and evil. Every move we make toward goodness refines us and makes us into purer vessels to hold the Divine light; every selfish act sullies us and obscures the Divine light.

In order to give man free will, God chose to conceal His Presence. He constricted His Infinite Light into four spiritual dimensions, known as heavenly worlds. Only in the last of these stages—our physical world—is the concealment great enough to allow us free choice and the opportunity to refine ourselves and become one with the Source of light.

Hence, when the individual perfects himself through the observance of God's will as revealed in the Torah, he fulfills the ultimate goal of Creation. He can become like an angel, a pure vessel for the Infinite Light to dwell in. He can then meet his Creator at a high level of consciousness, in those spiritual worlds involving a lesser degree of constriction.

This ideal state was achieved by each Israelite at the Giving of the Torah, after they had removed from themselves the impurity of the Egyptian bondage. However, when they were unable to maintain this level, and fell through the sin of the Golden Calf, they could no longer become one with their Maker. It was then necessary to make a "holy space" where the Divine Presence could dwell. In that space, the Sanctuary and Temple, the Israelites could regain their former holiness through repentance and sacrificial offerings. Then they could once again absorb the Divine energy within them.

During the entire First Temple period, the Jewish people absorbed the powerful Divine radiance generated by the Temple vessels such as the Ark of the Covenant and the holy *Menorah*/lamp. In the Second Temple, however, the Ark and the Tablets were no longer present. Only the luminous energy of the Menorah shed Inner Light to the Israelites. As a result, their awareness of God was much weaker.

To counteract this gradual concealment of the Divine Presence, the members of the Great Assembly composed the formalized prayer service recited three times daily. Their intention was that the external organ of the voice should draw the Surrounding Lights into a person's consciousness. Then the Inner Light—and with it the understanding of the heart—would be strengthened accordingly.

Furthermore, the sages foresaw a time when even the luminous energy of the Menorah would be missing. Then there would be almost no awareness of God's Presence, and only the words of our lips would save us from losing all contact with the Beloved.

During our morning prayers, the spiritual worlds that normally block our perception of God are lifted so that, at least in our consciousness, we can once more enter the Holy Temple, the "space of no evil," where we can attain intimate communion. The prayers are our "ladder of ascent" to return to the Source. As we saw, man's soul has many different levels, from the spirit infusing life into his body, up to his source on High—his soul-root. Rabbi Chayim Vital, the main disciple of the Ari, explains the soul's contact with the Creator:

> The root of the soul is very high in the World of Closeness and its branch is very long; it spreads through all the worlds until it is enclosed within man's body. And at each level, in each one of the heavenly worlds, the soul has a root. There is no soul that does not have an infinite number of roots, one above the other, and through its deeds, it merits to ascend from level to level. . . . When man is pure of any defilement he may aspire to cleave to the highest root of his soul.[1]

The expression "ladder of ascent" refers to man's ability to connect successively with all his soul-roots or points of contact with his Maker.

SERVICE OF THE HEART[2]

The legal parameters of prayer were instituted by the sages of the Great Assembly at the time of the Second Temple. Besides spontaneous prayer, which bursts naturally from an inspired heart, they composed the prayer book liturgy used today by Jews throughout the world. The sages of the Great Assembly were among the wisest and holiest in our history. Among them, as well, sat the last of the true prophets, thus guaranteeing that the prayers they composed truly reflected God's will and could bring a person to union with the Divine.

Prayers must be uttered with the lips, not just read silently. The sound of the voice has an arousing quality that aids one's concentration. However, although your voice carries your prayers, it is essential that the words reflect the feelings of your heart, for prayer is called "the service of the heart." Thus, there are two main requirements for the actual prayer: (1) to understand the meaning of the words you are saying,[3] (2) to be aware that you are standing before God.

Therefore, you must center yourself before beginning your prayers and release any extraneous thoughts you may have. You must first concentrate on the simple meaning of the words in order to switch from a monotonous reading of the prayer book to a communication with the One who is listening. Rabbi Alexander Ziskind, an eighteenth-century sage, advised that at every two or three words, you should pause to consider the meaning. In addition, he stressed the importance of clearly enunciating each Hebrew word and carefully distinguishing one word from the next.

The next goal is to address these words to the Divine Presence surrounding you. This goal is all-important, for a prayer said without an awareness of God's Presence before you cannot ascend. Ideally, the awareness of God should be sustained during the entire prayer.

STEPS OF THE LADDER

The daily prayers are composed of four sections: the Temple offerings, the psalms of praise, the Shema and its blessings, and the Amidah, the silent prayer. As we ascend through these steps, our normal consciousness can expand until we reach the heavenly realm of closeness to God, where the Divine Presence pervades all. It is in this space that we recite the Amidah.

As we begin the Amidah, we whisper the verse "God, open my lips, and my mouth will pronounce Your praise." We pray that God will sustain us during the last stage of our ascent. When we can hold our conscious intention of rising to meet the Beloved in this space, we are in an altered state: our lips become God's servants that He opens to pronounce His praise as we commune with Him.

In the final blessing of the Amidah, that of *sim shalom*/establish peace, God joins the collective soul of all Israel in a soul-union. The Hebrew word *shalom* carries a connotation of "perfection." Man's perfected state is realized while in this union with his Maker.

This heavenly bond occurs at the first point where the soul touches its Creator, and from which the Divine blessing and sustenance flow into the world. This point of meeting is known in Kabbalah as *ateret*, which means "crown." The Hebrew word *yesod* means "foundation." We will nevertheless render *Ateret haYesod* as "the Foundation Coronet," in order to distinguish this first spiritual point of meeting from that of "Crown."[4] This, as we will see, manifests itself on a higher level of closeness.

Although in our generation we have no conscious perception of the union in this dimension, we are nevertheless infused by the immediacy of an unknown Presence whose vibrant energy fills us with a total sense of fulfillment. The Amidah enables our soul to replenish its former luminous energy as it rises to the Source. The purpose of the prayers that follow the Amidah is then to bring this energy down with us to elevate our normal consciousness, helping to enhance our awareness of the Divine until the following Amidah prayer.

PRAYER ON SHABBAT[5]

Unlike the prayers of the festivals, in which the same Amidah is repeated morning, afternoon, and evening, the three Amidah prayers of Shabbat are each different. For each prayer attunes us to the special energy of that time of the day. Thus, on Shabbat eve, we say,

> You sanctified the seventh day to Your Name, the purpose of the work of heaven and earth. You blessed it above all days, and sanctified it about all times.

In the morning we say,

> Moses rejoiced in the gift of his portion, for You called Him a faithful servant. You gave him a crown of beauty when he stood before You on Mount Sinai, and two tablets of stone he carried down in his hands.

Finally, in the afternoon we say,

> You are One, and Your Name is One; and who is like Your people Israel, one nation on earth?

In addition, in both Shabbat evening and Shabbat morning prayers, we also add:

> They shall rejoice in Your kingship, those who observe the Shabbat and call it a delight.

On Shabbat we can lift the veil clouding our weekday consciousness to reach the intimate relationship we long for. Each one of the Shabbat prayers thus expresses the special nature of the time it is recited. The evening renews the sanctification of this relationship; the morning dawns with a new level of awareness given to us as a gift, and the afternoon is the time of intimacy.

YOU SANCTIFIED SHABBAT

> "You sanctified the Seventh Day and made it holy."

When the Jewish people first stood at Mount Sinai, they entered into the deepest possible relationship with their Creator. Their souls were "wed" to God, as it were. The

Midrash says that the Giving of the Torah was like a wedding ceremony; the Jewish people were the bride, the Torah was the wedding contract, and God held Mount Sinai over their heads like a canopy.

This union was supposed to be eternal, but when Israel sinned with the Golden Calf, the bond was broken. Nevertheless, they did retain the ability to renew this relationship, not as a gift from above, but through their own efforts at sanctifying the weekly Shabbat.

As we discussed previously, the commandment to observe Shabbat was given twice, in the first set of Tablets and in the second. In the First Tablets, it is called a day "on which God rested." In the Second Tablets, it is "a sign between Me and you for all generations,"[6] implying that, because of the Golden Calf, this "sign" would have to be renewed on each and every Shabbat.

Through the preparations we make during the week, we ready ourselves for this special time of intimacy. When we sanctify Shabbat and try to rise above our material nature, God, in turn, sanctifies us. As at Mount Sinai, He shines upon us the light of union. Thus we say, "You have sanctified. . . ." The word for "sanctify," *lekadesh*, is the same word as "to marry." You have brought us back to You in the bond of love we first left at Mount Sinai.

The Shabbat Morning Gift[7]

The Torah speaks of God in different ways, as our father, our brother, our companion, our king. It is through this last aspect, the gate of kingship, that He reveals Himself to the Jewish nation. The sages have said, "There is no king without a people." Simply put, this means that we must obey God's will and fulfill His commandments, much as we would obey the edicts of a human king. But, on a deeper level, it means that God's attribute of kingship is not manifest until we serve Him, for a king is not the same as a dictator.

The Jewish concept of king is not that of a sovereign monarch, but rather of a divinely selected ruler who has an intimate mental and emotional connection with his people. The nation willingly accepts the rule of such a king. At Mount Sinai, the Jewish people stood together, "like one person, with one heart," to accept God's kingship. At that point, we reached the level of faith referred to as "sight." Thus, the verse states:

> You are the ones who have been shown (lit., "made to *see*"), so that you will know that
> God is the Supreme Being, and there is none besides Him.[8]

According to the Ari, the people were "made to see" that there is none besides God. This means that the spiritual lights surrounding them suddenly entered their consciousness. The Talmud says that at the Giving of the Torah, the angels placed "crowns" on the heads of all the Israelites. These were the Surrounding and Inner Lights they had gained. However, with the sin of the Golden Calf, these lights were lost. Their spiritual vision was dimmed. Thus the verse says, "And the Children of Israel stripped themselves of their ornaments at Mount Chorev (Sinai)."[9] These "ornaments" were the lights of consciousness they had received.

Moses, however, did not lose his lights. In fact, he gained all the Surrounding Lights that the rest of the nation had lost. Thus the very next verse says, "And Moses took the tent," referring to the spiritual illumination that surrounds one like a dwelling, a tent.

All hope was not lost. The Jewish people could still regain their initial spiritual level. On Shabbat, Moses was able to give his people the lights they had lost. Thus it is written in the Shabbat morning Amidah, "Moses rejoiced in the gift of his portion." He rejoiced at the gift he gave his people—the fact that he could help them reach spiritual perfection—and he further rejoiced at seeing the preciousness of the Shabbat day. Only the Faithful Shepherd was worthy of this revelation during his lifetime; he was the one to transmit this revelation to all Israel after Sinai, as well as to future generations.

Moses' gift was that through his mediation the Crown would continue to shine on Shabbat. As Shabbat observers internalized their own "crown," made up of the light of the commandments they had observed throughout the week, the glow of their Surrounding Lights would be brightened by that of the Crown. At the moment we say the prayer, "Moses rejoiced . . . ." we actually draw upon ourselves the holiness of the day, available through the soul of Moses.

The *Zohar* explains that on Shabbat, the soul of the *Tsadik*/righteous rises to closer proximity with God. In the process of its own ascent, it elevates the collective consciousness of the people, until they reach the "Foundation Coronet," where the soul touches its Creator. The Tsadik then draws God's unconditional mercy down to the people of his time.

THE CROWN IN THE *MUSAPH*/ADDITIONAL AMIDAH[10]

The second Amidah prayer we offer on Shabbat is known as Mus*aph,* from the word *mosiph,* to add, alluding to the additional sacrifice offered each Shabbat in the Temple. However, according to the Ari, the word is also related to the name of Jos**eph,** which stems from the root *asaph*/gather. The Ari teaches that it is in this additional Amidah prayer that the people of Israel make use of the "Shabbat gift" they have just received, thus benefiting from Moses' continuing influence.

Equipped with the surplus of holiness of the first morning Amidah, we can now enter deeper into prayer. At this point, although we are not consciously aware of this, our souls can attach themselves to those of the truly righteous of past and present, those who, like Joseph, have risen in their lifetime to the Foundation Coronet. From that place, they can transfer spiritual elevation to those who are unable to attain it on their own.

The *Musaph* Amidah is the time when God brings to fruition His initial intention for Creation. It is in the *Musaph* prayer that the collective soul of His earthly companions rises to meet with Him at the height of their spiritual structure, for only at this point can God reveal Himself.

Let us draw upon the comparison of an earthly king. When a human king reveals himself to his subjects, he must also show them his crown. We are reminded of Rabbi Vital's teaching that an individual who is pure of any defilement may aspire to cleave to the highest root of his soul. Spiritually then, the soul-union at this level entails a Divine revelation reaching past the first point of contact, all the way up to the Crown.

As we saw, it was at the Giving of the Torah that the people of Israel united with the Creator at that point of their consciousness. Despite their sin, Israel recovered this lofty state through Moses' gift, but only for the duration of Shabbat. Although Shabbat leaves its mark on us, we lose a significant part of our Shabbat consciousness during the week.

Hence on the weekdays, the collective soul of God's earthly companions is unable to rise to Him. Thus, the King of the world hides His Crown so as to lower Himself and become One with His people despite their present deficiency. In other words, during the week, our union with the Creator takes place in the initial points of contact of our soul-roots.

On Shabbat, the Divine energy radiates with renewed power and the spiritual worlds return to their source: God removes our mental obstructions, not just for the duration of the morning prayers as He does during the week, but for the entire day.

We can now ascend to the "Crown," and, if it can be said, we give God back His Crown in the *Musaph* Amidah of Shabbat. We fully accept His kingship over us and cleave to Him at this level of closeness.

We have seen that in the repetition of the Amidah, we should lift our eyes to Heaven in the *Kedushah* and elicit the Divine response described by the *Sefer Hechalot*:

> For I have no greater pleasure in the world than the moment that they lift their eyes to Mine while My eyes are on theirs.

The hidden meaning of "lifting the eyes" is Israel's ascent to the Crown, as it were, high enough for "eye contact."

When two people in love with each other look into each other's eyes, there is no need for words. Each one of them has an experiential perception of the deepest recesses of the beloved's being; each one of them knows what the beloved desires without needing to be told.

"Ascending to the Crown" brings us back to Sinai, when we were close enough for the "sight and perception" of the Torah that is beyond the finitude of letters; we were close enough to know what our Beloved wanted and expected of us, beyond what was spelled out in the Torah, and we wanted more than anything else to forget our "selves" and rise to His expectations.

We now understand this wording of the *Musaph* prayer:

> A Crown will they give You, O *Hashem*, our God—the angels of the multitude above, together with Your people Israel who are assembled below.[11]

In the soul-union of the *Musaph* Amidah, then, the King is wearing His Crown, while Israel, His earthly companions, wear their own crowns of the Surrounding Lights they have gratuitously received. For the duration of the *Musaph* Amidah we are trans-ported back in time, to the Giving of the Torah, when both the Almighty and His soul-companion spoke "face-to-face." In the *Musaph* Amidah, God elevates the spiri-tual structure of our collective soul so that we can become One with Him, in a union of the higher levels of our soul.

ONE WITH GOD: AFTERNOON PRAYERS[12]

"You are One, and Your Name is One"

The commentators equate Israel's ability to reach their complete spiritual structure (*binyan shalem*) with the building of the Third Temple. For it is only when the Temple is standing—the space where no evil is allowed to dwell—that Israel will be able to make this spiritual ascent consciously. Nevertheless, the kabbalists explain that, in point of fact, this union is realized through the Shabbat afternoon prayers.

The essential difference between the *Musaph* and afternoon Amidah prayers is that, as we saw, during *Musaph* we rise through attachment to the Tsadik. However, in the afternoon Amidah, we may only elevate our consciousness on our own merits. Hence, it very often happens that one reaches a deeper sense of union during the *Musaph* prayer, even though the potential of the afternoon prayer is higher.

The wording of the afternoon prayer alludes to the soul-union of this time, in which the people Israel ascend even beyond the Crown, to what we may call the "Light of the Crown" and retain the impression of that illumination within themselves here below, "on earth."

You are One, and Your Name is One; and who is like Your people Israel, one nation on earth?

In the Amidah of the Shabbat afternoon prayers, it is possible to experience a total soul-union where we become part of God's essence. This union is associated with the building of the Temple because the bond also occurs "on earth," within each individ-ual who attains the degree of righteousness where his entire being becomes a vessel of Divine light.

To become "one with God" while "on earth" means previously fulfilling each of the Divine commandments out of a deep longing for *devekut*—a passionate attachment to God. Furthermore, the ability to reach "Heaven on earth" while remaining grounded in this world demands more than mere observance of Shabbat. It requires intensive preparation throughout the week, and most of all during the twenty-four hours preceding Shabbat.[13]

In the Shabbat afternoon Amidah, we can draw upon the light we absorbed throughout the *Musaph* prayer and soar to the crown of our spiritual perfection, join-ing the Creator in an intimate soul-union that may be felt in the deepest recesses of our being. Far from being sated, our longing for *devekut* will grow in intensity until the conclusion of Shabbat.

Thus, in the afternoon Amidah, we do not recite the prayer "They shall rejoice in Your kingship—those who observe the Shabbat and call it a delight," as we do in the previous evening and morning services, for at those times the soul-union is not yet complete. "They *shall* rejoice": the verb appears in the future tense. Still, we express our understanding that we are God's people, the vehicle of His kingship, yet we nonetheless wait in anticipation for the afternoon prayer, when we are actually admitted into the palace.

Hence, there is no mention of rejoicing in the afternoon Amidah; the joy we feel is contained because of its very intensity. We savor the intimate closeness in silence, for there are no words that could express it. At this point, our relationship to God is not like the thunderous Giving of the Torah; rather, it is like Elijah's "still, small voice."[14]

Consequently, the early sages, those who knew how to reach this space, suggest that from the early afternoon prayers until the close of Shabbat we sit for some time in seclusion to savor the ecstatic closeness to God and to study Torah while in this state of awareness.

Although the Surrounding Light helps us analyze the intricacies of the revealed Torah by drawing on our intellect, only the Inner Light of the soul can help us perceive the secret teachings of the Torah. These secrets cannot be grasped by the analytical study because they stem from a Source above the realm of human logic. It is by immersing ourselves in these studies in the afternoon of Shabbat that we may attain an experiential perception of the teaching, "God, the Torah, and Israel are One."

6
Sickness of the Soul

L ET US PAY CLOSER ATTENTION to the wording of the Shabbat afternoon Amidah prayer:

> You are One and Your Name is One; and who is like Your People Israel, one nation on earth? The splendor of greatness and the crown of salvation . . . .

The kabbalists understand the expression "splendor of greatness" as alluding to the soul-union. It is similar to the verse of Isaiah, "like the splendor of a man to dwell in the house."[1] That is, in intimate union with his wife. By the same token, "the crown of salvation" is associated with the verse, "A woman of valor is the crown of her husband."[2]

The additional Shabbat soul allows us to rise above our physicality, to merge with the "Companion of the Soul." Shabbat afternoon is the time we dwell in silent delight in what Isaiah calls the intimacy of "the house."

At this time, Israel is also likened to a "woman of valor" who is her husband's pride. She knows that they are one, and aims to give him joy with every fiber of her being. Thus, if during a time of togetherness she happens to be struggling with some inner turmoil, she holds back her tears rather than mar the joy her husband wants to share with her.

But were her husband to understand what she was silently going through for his sake, his love for her would increase a thousandfold. Were he able to remove the sadness from her heart, he would undoubtedly do so.

Such is Israel's devotion to their Beloved. Even when they are in the depths of sorrow, they marshal their inner strength to rejoice with God in times of their closeness, whether on Shabbat or festivals, or during prayer and observation of His commandments.

But God knows. When His Companion of the soul is torn with such inner strug-

36

gle, His love for her reaches the incandescence of fiery coals, until eventually He will remove the bitterness from her soul.

Kabbalah calls Israel "the righteous woman who acts in accordance with her husband's will" (paraphrasing the Talmud). When the People of Israel forget their sorrow so as to experience the Shabbat delight, they draw down God's unbounded love and receive in return the "endless inheritance" promised to Shabbat observers.*

This "endless inheritance," the spiritual as well as physical experience of God's love, is "sweeter than the drippings of the honeycomb or any taste," as we declare in "*Yedid Nefesh*"/"Beloved of the soul," the song sung at the onset of Shabbat, and once again during the third meal after the Shabbat afternoon prayers.

The song continues:

Majestic, Beautiful, Radiance of the universe, my soul is sick for Your love! Please, God, heal her, by showing her the pleasantness of Your radiance.

This echoes Israel's in the Song of Songs:

I conjure you, Daughters of Jerusalem, if you find my Beloved, tell Him that I am lovesick![3]

There are two types of lovesickness. One is of a person who is physically distant, but yearns to draw close to the beloved. The other is one who is so close, so much in love, that he is actually sick; his love is too intense for him to bear.

When Shabbat begins, we are on the first level. Then, Israel is referred to as a "bride." The word *kalah* in Hebrew means both "bride," as a noun, and "consumed with longing," in the form of a verb.

We come to Shabbat after a busy week, far removed from the Divine light. Then, at the beginning stages, we relate to our Divine Companion as a bride yearning for her beloved.

Like a perfumer whose senses have been dulled to the delicate fragrance of a rose because of his overexposure to coarser and artificial fragrances, so too we enter Shabbat dulled to its beauty. Continuous indulgence in physical pleasure has numbed our spiritual sensitivity. With the entrance of Shabbat, we are torn between our desire to cleave to the fiery coals of Divine love and our inability to do so. But our cry rises to Heaven, to penetrate ever so slightly the walls of separation. Then the King Himself opens the gate to reveal the reception hall.

As Shabbat progresses, we penetrate more deeply into the realm of the spirit. Our insensitivity is gradually transformed, and the yearning to draw near to God grows in strength to the point of lovesickness.

Maimonides discusses the intensity of this emotion:

A person should love God with a very great love until his soul is bound up in the love of God. Thus, he will always be obsessed with this love, as if he were lovesick.

* This chapter is dedicated to the memory of Eliahu ben Nissim, a very dear and unique human being, who passed on while I was at this specific point in the chapter, during the festival of Sukkot in 1996. May the Almighty cause his light to shine, binding him to the Source of Life.

[A lovesick person's] thoughts are never diverted from the love of that woman. He is always obsessed with her, when he sits down, when he gets up, when he eats and drinks. With an even greater [love] should the love of God be [implanted] in the hearts of those who love Him and are obsessed with Him at all times, as we are commanded, "with all your heart and with all your soul" (Deuteronomy 6:5).

This concept was implied by Solomon when he said metaphorically: "I am lovesick." [Indeed,] the totality of the Song of Songs is a parable describing [this love].[4]

Maimonides is referring here to one who has already reached the highest level of love and is unable to bear its intensity.

On Shabbat morning Israel receives a gift—Moses' portion. After experiencing the vibrant delight of the morning prayers, we await in anticipation for the afternoon Amidah, when we will come in direct contact with God's love for us. Readying ourselves for the surge of love we know will come, our state of longing is heightened, until by the early afternoon we feel consumed by the lovesickness Maimonides evokes.

We are ready to immerse ourselves in the Amidah prayer, totally oblivious to the physical. To those able to reach this level of arousal, God reveals His love as fiery coals. The person is left throbbing with emotion, sick with longing. At this point tears occasionally flow, unnoticed.

Such intensity of feeling is not restricted to Shabbat, however. Even in a weekday Amidah prayer a person can experience such moments of intimate communion. However, this level of closeness is most accessible during the Shabbat afternoon prayers, when the Light of the Crown reveals its glow, leaving us ablaze with an ever growing desire to become one with God. In the union of the Amidah at this time, we reach the essence of spiritual perfection, what the Kabbalah calls "Desire of desires."

Our soul-roots will remain in the intoxicating closeness of the afternoon prayers until the close of Shabbat.[5] As we tear ourselves away from the afternoon Amidah, our love of God has intensified to a searing emotion without ulterior motives. We no longer care: not about the benefits of this world, nor those of the world to come, nor even about the coming redemption. His love now fills the screen of our consciousness, not leaving room for anything else.

SHABBAT MEALS

The difference between the evening and morning prayers and that of Shabbat afternoon is reflected in the difference between the evening and day meals as opposed to the third meal of Shabbat. Although our senses delight in the evening meal, there is a note of melancholy. Our feelings still lack a degree of intensity. In the second meal our sense of delight reaches a peak as a result of the increased awareness of God that we have experienced in the morning prayers. By the third meal, however, the Shabbat delight has risen beyond our ability to bear: the person feels that his soul is aflame with love—about to depart from him.

We are reminded that in the afternoon Amidah we do not say that we will "rejoice in [God's] kingship" for joy is now inadequate to express our feelings. Similarly, in the meal that follows, we are beyond the need for stimulation through meat and wine. The love we feel at this time, intensified by the impending separation and descent into the weekdays, is comparable to that of the Israelites at the Giving of the Torah, the time in which "They had a vision of the Divine, and they ate and drank."[6]

Somehow, in this third meal, we can relate to this verse without the remoteness of weekday consciousness. Still under the effect of the afternoon Amidah, we *know;* we understand. And we sing of our pining for an ever greater closeness, like the one we felt in the desert, that God asks us to keep forever present in our minds:

> Go and call out to Jerusalem: "God says: I remember how you were faithful in your youth, your love as a bride, how you followed Me in the wilderness, a land not sown."[7]

We sing this moving message of our Beloved over and over again, until we are sick with the desire for His closeness and continue to be so until the Shabbat lights fade in the horizon.

In the Amidah that we recite at the close of Shabbat, our souls must part from their Source, and we must come back down to this world and our physical needs. As we saw, the soul-union arouses God's overwhelming desire to give, which is likened to water that will put out our fire unless . . . unless Israel's arousal from below reaches the point at which "love's sparks become fiery coals." Water cannot extinguish such a fire, and the thirst for passionate attachment becomes permanent, so that "many waters cannot extinguish love, nor can rivers drown it.[8] We therefore pray in the closing service to be able to draw the fire of His love during the weekday prayers so that we can use it as a torch to see through the weekday concealment.

As we have seen, we attain the peak of the *oneg* Shabbat in the Shabbat afternoon prayers, and by the same token it is written that our redemption is destined to begin at the time of Shabbat afternoon prayers.[9] The love of fiery coals inflaming the souls of His people as Shabbat departs reminds God of His desire for a Creation and to have a dwelling space within Israel below.

7

Hearing the Angel's Song

A T THIS POINT, I ORIGINALLY intended to conclude the Shabbat chapters. Nevertheless, I was plagued by a recurring thought: it was never my intention to write a book about the spiritual accomplishments of Jewish mystics, but about the ecstatic closeness that God expects every Jew to reach. In complete honesty to the reader, I had to face a few questions:

This "searing emotion" of Shabbat afternoon that Rabbi Luria writes about may exist in potential, but how many know how to reach it?

How many are consciously aware of the special ability to concentrate on God that their additional Shabbat soul bestows, particularly among those who do not dedicate their entire lives to study the inner teachings of the Torah?

Is it truly possible to experience the joy of *oneg*/delight on Shabbat and feel transported during prayer by the immediacy of God's Presence?

How many have crossed the bridge from love to passion, as Maimonides defines it?

The sad fact is that most of us do not attain the level of spiritual fulfillment and ecstasy reached by men and women of previous generations. "The bush was on fire, but was not being consumed."[1] We are insensitive to the fire of God's love that surrounds us, and as a result, we are unable to respond in kind.

And so I called Rabbi Luria and asked him: "You describe the delight of Shabbat as a Divine joy that reverberates in every part of the being. You constantly refer to the ecstatic delight, the still space of total fulfillment, the sickness of love. Yet, most people don't feel anything on Shabbat other than the physical rest and the pleasure to the palate. Are you trying to redefine Judaism?"

Rabbi Luria's answer was quick and to the point: "Hardly! They don't feel Shabbat because they don't prepare. You have to long for it! You have to consciously prepare yourself for Shabbat all week long if you want to feel it!"

Rabbi Luria highlighted the fact that in order to feel the additional soul on Shabbat we must first transform our body into a sanctuary for the Divine Presence. This is done by observing the commandments throughout the weekdays. Furthermore, to achieve the higher state of consciousness, we must prepare ourselves intensively during the twenty-four-hour period preceding the onset of Shabbat.

At this point I realized that in order to accomplish my original intention in this book, I had to include Rabbi Luria's specific instructions for the sixth day of the week, namely, Thursday night and Friday.

Initially I had not wanted to include this section. I felt that for modern readers— working people whose busy lives did not allow time for intense mystical pursuits—such an approach would be too demanding. Yet, I now had to admit that omitting the preparatory stage would make this book just one more description of mystical states unattainable to the reader, as impersonal as any textbook. Without the key to penetrate, the gate would remain shut.

THOUGHT, SPEECH, AND ACTION

Essentially, the main element of the preparation for the Shabbat experience is the yearning that we build up for it all week. And this depends upon the intensity of the daily morning prayers, which reach a climax in the prayer of Friday morning. Our Shabbat delight will be in proportion to the longing we have awakened within ourselves during those prayers.

We can all agree that it is easier to involve oneself in the physical preparations of Shabbat or even to be carried away by a passing fervor than to arouse a quality of love that grows in intensity without faltering. However, King David, the sweet singer of Israel, reminds us,

> The fear of God is pure, endures forever.[2]

Emotions waver. Love has its ups and downs, but a fear of God, based on the awe of His greatness, "endures forever." Furthermore, as we will see,[3] the true love of God, which burns like fiery coals, is a love imbued with the awe of God.[4]

When we read the prayers while contemplating their meaning, the different sections of the service become a ladder of ascent. In the introductory readings of the morning prayers, we relate to God as King and Judge. This gives us the distance and perspective to feel awe of Him. The psalms and prayers leading to the Shema enable us to penetrate the layers of concealment until we reach the intimate communion of the Amidah prayer, which leaves the imprint of love sealed within us.

In order to retain the Shabbat experience throughout the week, toward the end of the daily morning prayers, we recite the daily psalm that the Levites sang in the Temple. We make a point to relate each day to Shabbat. For instance, on Sunday, before reading the psalm we say: "Today is the first day of Shabbat (that is, the first day of the week leading to Shabbat), on which the Levites would recite . . . ." And on Monday, "Today is the second day of Shabbat," and so forth.

By counting the days in this manner, we are not only remembering Shabbat but also emphasizing that each weekday derives its blessing and sustenance from your Shabbat observance.

Since the introductory readings of the morning prayers have helped arouse our awe of God, the closeness we reach in the Amidah "endures." Consequently, in the afternoon prayers we no longer need a long introduction before the Amidah. We can reach the space where we were in the morning Amidah without difficulty.

Let us now examine what the main part of the Shabbat preparation is during the twenty-four hour period preceding its onset.

Shabbat has an inherent holiness that the kabbalists associate with the state of Shabbat *oneg*, or current of intense delight, which enables us to cleave to the Divine Presence.[5] We draw this holiness within ourselves and store it in order to experience it on the coming Shabbat—through the different elements of the preparation for Shabbat.

When body and soul *together* experience the Shabbat delight and one begins to taste the bliss of the additional Shabbat soul throbbing within, it is no longer possible to speak of Divine hiddenness because it becomes clear that the intensity of the feelings perceived is in exact proportion to the quality of one's preparation.

According to the Ari, the preparation covers three grounds: thought, speech, and action. The preparation in thought is done on the sixth night—Thursday night—and it concerns spiritual matters. The speech refers to the reading of the Torah portion of the week, as we will discuss, whereas the action constitutes the physical preparations for Shabbat.

The Ari revealed that the precious gift that God wants to give Israel on Shabbat is none other than the Infinite Light of Creation that God concealed, to be perceived only at special times, particularly on Shabbat.[6]

However, even on Shabbat, this light does not shine here below, as it did during the six days of Creation, nor will it do so until the ultimate future. Rather, it is Israel who can rise to this space of light by reaching an altered state of consciousness on Shabbat. There they are illuminated by the radiance of this light.

If we reexamine God's message to Moses for Israel, "I have a precious gift among My hidden treasures, and Shabbat is its name; go and inform the Israelites," we can detect a hint of this idea: whoever wants the gift has to prepare himself in order to be able to receive it, because God's house of treasures, where we have to go to collect the gift, is located in this "space of no evil." As long as our evil impulse has some hold over us, we cannot gain access into the holy space where His glory shines unrestrained.[7]

An essential part of this preparation is our effort to distance ourselves from the influence of the evil inclination. The latter does not just become inactive on Shabbat; rather, we receive a special help to distance ourselves from its grip.

We have to activate this help with our conscious intention. The problem is that the help becomes available around mid-Friday, a time in which we are most involved in our Shabbat preparations. The last of our concerns at this time is our negative inclination! And yet this is precisely the time when God intervenes on behalf of those who think of drawing His help to themselves and actively pray for it at this time.

The ultimate weapon—the only one that will make us remember to seek this special help—is a burning desire to cleave to God. According to Rabbi Luria, it is on Thursday night, all night, that God directs upon us the magnetic current of His desire. All we need is conscious intention to absorb it.

The goal, then, is to spend Thursday night involved in the study of the Torah's inner teachings, at whatever level you can grasp them.

In traditional *yeshivot*/study halls, Thursday night is a time for *mishmar*/vigil, in which students stay up all night studying. Ideally, the best time to study is in the second half of the night. Try and wake up a half-hour before dawn. Slowly push back this time until you can go to sleep in the early evening and wake up before midnight. Midnight does not mean 12 A.M., but rather half the night. According to Rabbi Nachman of Breslov, "the time for [the midnight prayer] starts six hours after nightfall, both in the summer and in the winter, and continues for two hours."[8] At this time, you can express your yearning for redemption by reading the midnight prayer service. This service concludes with a beautiful poem written by Rabbi Chayim HaKohen, in the form of a dialogue between the Holy One and Israel. Israel cries out:

> Pure One! You are not a God who desires evil.
> Until when will You refrain from being the Righteous One, the Redeemer?
> Return and clothe me in the garments of redemption
> A robe of charity with a multitude of pearls.

God replies:

> Companion of My soul, why do you complain?
> Your righteousness and love are not concealed from Me.
> Indeed, from the day of your exile, I too became a wanderer.
> Like a wandering bird I left My home. . . .
> I have not entered My House from the day you were exiled,
> So as not to be confronted with My overwhelming anguish. (Ibid., p. 48)

The soul-stirring prayers will remain with you throughout the night, inspiring you as you remain immersed in your Torah studies until the time comes to pray at dawn. Some people who are unable to remain awake the entire night will wake up before midnight to pray at this auspicious moment and then return to sleep, waking up in time for prayer at dawn, to bind the night to the day as Kabbalah teaches. Still others find it easier to stay up long enough to say the midnight prayer before going to sleep rather than waking up at this time.

If you are able to join a group of people with a similar goal, or even to organize one, the goal of waking will become much easier for you. Above all, you must give your body time to accustom itself to this night-study, for if you rush into it too fast, you may end up with a splitting headache that would hardly enhance your Shabbat delight!

A main part of the preparation your body needs in order to adjust to this different schedule is not to eat more than a very light dinner. If you have what is considered a normal meal in the evening you will not be able to wake up a few hours later, regardless of the extent of your willpower or desire to do so.

The night-study is a challenge if you have to work on the following day, but you will find that the body benefits greatly from short naps taken *whenever* sleep threatens to overcome you rather than at the time that it is convenient to nap. Attempting to sleep at any other time amounts to writing with an unsharpened pencil or waiting for the bus after its scheduled time. An additional benefit derived from these naps is that the total amount of time you need for your night's sleep will be reduced.

Napping at will may seem to be a luxury beyond the reach of most, but it is not the case. One may nap *anywhere* by reclining on a chair and closing one's eyes. Even a nap taken for a few minutes, your head resting on your arms folded over your desk, will prove to be refreshing—if not the last cry in comfort! If sleep comes when you are driving on a highway—as it often does to those who practice the night-study—pull over and lie back with your eyes closed for a few minutes.

It is God's deep desire that the Jewish people involve themselves in this study, particularly on Thursday night, for it enables them to draw down His love. The *Zohar* teaches that in response to the night-study, God assures: "I will walk with them in Eden, and they will not fear Me."

It is often at midnight that the righteous immerse themselves in their personal study of the Oral Torah, with the knowledge that the light available at this time will help them grasp difficult Torah insights. There is a tradition that even Moses, during his forty days on Mount Sinai, studied the Oral Torah by night, and the Written Torah by day.[9]

An entire night immersed in Torah studies will enable you to fan the burning desire for God's closeness which you seal within yourself in the Friday morning prayers. The love of God that we feel at dawn in prayer draws its strength from your night-study. You can then sail through the challenges of the sixth day without anger or impatience. You may be physically tired on Friday morning, but buoyant with a store of Divine energy you will need to draw on to complete successfully your Friday preparations.

All this is the preparation in thought. Preparation in speech involves reading each verse of the Torah portion of the week twice in Hebrew, and once in its accompanying Aramaic translation.[10] The symbolic meaning of this practice is that, all week, your Divine service is in the aspect of "translation," namely, the outside forces of evil that you must contend with do not allow you to relate to your Creator directly. On Shabbat, however, your service adopts the form of the holy Scriptures read in synagogue. When you hear the weekly portion read from a Torah scroll, you are returning to a "face-to-face" relationship with the Creator.

Ideally, advises the Ari, this reading should be done at midday on Friday, for then the forces of defilement rage most fiercely before they start to dissipate.[11] It is at that time that God sends His help.

Practically speaking, reading the Torah at this time is only possible for a Torah scholar. Most other people do not have the time or the Hebrew skills to complete the reading as well as prepare for Shabbat. However, you can start as early as Sunday, reading one portion each day, and save as little as a few verses for Friday noon.

The Ari teaches that the light of Shabbat begins to shine on the fifth hour on the sixth day—around mid-Friday—but yet in concealment. The implication is that, initially, the light reaches us in the form of strict justice. This means that on Friday afternoon things have a way of going wrong: dropping the chicken in sauce on the freshly cleaned floor, remaining "stuck" in traffic for over an hour, realizing that your spouse or children have suddenly turned into monsters. The frustration rises, and there goes your delight of that Shabbat!

But by expecting "trouble" you can distance yourself from the difficult situation and not let it affect you emotionally. Whereas during the week you might try to control your reaction in an effort to perfect yourself spiritually, on Friday your restraint is part of your inner cleansing, making space for the luminous energy of Shabbat.

Since the essence of Shabbat is "to delight in God," we may define the light of Shabbat as the desire for an intimate closeness. However, because our yearning for spiritual delight is often mistaken for physical lusts, around mid-Friday, we may feel a subtle desire for pleasure. It is no wonder, then, that the Serpent was able to cause Adam to sin precisely at this time. As he felt the first stirrings of desire for the spiritual delight of being close to God, he gave in to the temptation of the forbidden fruit.

Although on mid-Friday there is concealment of the Divine, we are subconsciously absorbing the energy of delight. Now is the time to distance ourselves from physical pleasures, to avoid their dimming effect on the spiritual delight we will experience on Shabbat.

Part of this separation lies in a critical examination of the past week, so as to remove the barrier that our transgressions have erected. Just as Abraham separated himself from his evil nephew Lot, just as Jacob took leave of the devious Laban, we too must leave behind all our misdeeds, willed or accidental, so that they do not obstruct the vibrant energy God emits on Shabbat. As Rabbi de Vidas points out in *The Beginning of Wisdom,* since our soul-roots are impressed above, every transgression ever committed and not rectified remains engraved in the heavenly counterpart of the soul and will prevent the soul-root from being included in the union with the Holy One at the time of prayer.[12]

After this moment of introspection, men may immerse themselves in a *mikveh*/ritual bath to express this separation and, by conscious intent, draw upon themselves the Shabbat holiness. This immersion is not required by the Jewish law and is mostly practiced by men, for women enter the realm of holiness through deed—their added responsibility to prepare for Shabbat.

The two essential functions of a mikveh are: (a) to remove the impurity of the menses, enabling a woman to reinstate intimacy with her husband, and (b) the last stage of the long process of conversion, so as to gain acceptance into the *Brit*/Covenant uniting God to the people of Israel.

The Talmud states that before the Children of Israel received the Torah, all the people immersed themselves in a *mikveh*. We have seen that the relationship with the

Almighty, as established at the Giving of the Torah, is renewed on every Shabbat. In this sense, a man who immerses himself in a *mikveh* before Shabbat renews the bond of the Covenant, while the women make the Shabbat intimacy possible through their preparations.

Those for whom Shabbat observance has become routine, who omit the intense involvement of the spiritual preparations we have outlined, may benefit from the blessings of physical prosperity in this world. Spiritual ecstasy in the world to come may still be their lot as well, according to the effort they have expended. Yet, as the Talmud says, Shabbat is a foretaste of the world to come. By spending Shabbat as a day of rest, good food, and company, we can enjoy a sample of this supreme delight without diminishing our future reward.

This is the key to arouse the searing emotion God asks of His beloved people. Studying the mysteries of the Torah allows us to know God and to cleave to Him with a love strong as death, passionate as fiery coals, a flame of the Divine, and to understand that without this passion, our lives are unfulfilled.

Too difficult? Stakes too high? Yet, think of what lies behind the veil of concealment! The delight of the world to come is so intense that we could not bear it while in our human form. The soul would just break from its bonds and rise to the Source, as we can see from the following incident, in the lifetime of the prophet Isaiah.[13]

Under King Hezekiah, Israel was at war. The Assyrians, led by King Sennacharib, were gaining ground under the eyes of powerless Israel. With Jerusalem in dire threat, King Hezekiah cried out in despair for the Creator's help. Overnight, God sent an angel who struck the enemy, and on the following day, the entire army of King Sennacharib was found dead.[14]

The verse says that the angel used his sword, but the commentators explain that this angel's weapon was his song. As the angel revealed himself to the enemy and sang, the exquisite delight that permeated the soldiers rose to such pitch that their souls were compelled to return to their Maker.[15]

Even though, on Shabbat, we are tasting a diluted version of the delight known as *oneg*, if one but once experiences a measure of this delight, one will find it difficult to return to physical indulgence. This is like a child who goes to an amusement park and starts with the roller coaster. Afterward, he might as well leave, for he will not be able to enjoy rides where the thrill is less intense!

If you strive for this space of supreme delight and, by Divine grace, attain it but once, your love will become permeated by a profound fear of estrangement. At this point the punishment you will most dread is the concealment of His love.

You will fear an explosion of anger, an act of self-indulgence of any kind, even if they are not transgressions. You will dread violating even a minor law, whether mentioned in the Bible or enacted by the sages, for any of these will rise against you on the following Shabbat, preventing you from experiencing the overwhelming lovesickness that invaded you at the close of the previous Shabbat. Thus the verse says:

> Hearken—for great pain is in my heart, like a blazing fire within my innards. No soul is left within me, and my strength is very weakened. . . .

> Wipe my sin away like a cloud, He Who sits in abiding concealment. Then I shall see and comprehend, the source of sapphire and of jade.[16]

One does not experience this quality of Shabbat without continued effort. Yet, as you approach it, you will find your morning weekly prayers growing stronger. No longer will they be a challenge in which you must use all your mental power to avoid foreign thoughts, while secretly looking forward to finishing so that you can start your day. The challenge remains, but it becomes charged with the positive energy of your longing to find your way back to the expanded consciousness of Shabbat.

As your experience of Shabbat and festivals intensifies, so will your ability to draw this enhanced consciousness to the weekly prayers. Whether the Hebrew of your prayers is new, or whether you have always spoken it, your Amidah will become longer and longer, even longer than when you were struggling with the unfamiliar words. In that space, you will know that this state of intimate communion with God is where you want to be.

Three steps backward: the Amidah is finished. Yet, you have brought down with you enough to keep your inner flame burning through the coming hours of the day.

You have entered the dimension of *da'at*/the intimate knowledge of God. In this dimension the bond is so closely knit that there is no space for anything else, nor anyone else, from above, or from below. This is the bond stronger than death that God evokes in His message to the Children of Israel, "Only you have I loved,"[17] where the Hebrew word for loved is *yada'ti*/(I knew), a form of *da'at*.

To enter this space, your iron will needs to be crowned by a Divine grace, but this heavenly favor comes readily when the bond you yearn for is based on your *cheshek*/desire rather than a paralyzing sense of awe. When you achieve this bond, nothing can break your passionate attachment to the Source of life.

8

From Shabbat
to the Festivals

THE FESTIVALS ARE DAYS OF JOY. Each commemorates a miracle that was performed for the people of Israel some time in their past. Recalling this miracle arouses our love for God, and as a result, God's love for us awakens in return. Furthermore, each year, at the same time, God joins the souls of His people to draw down the identical quality of Divine energy that was originally manifest.

Whether we "rejoice with trembling," as on Rosh Hashanah, radiate with love during Passover, or cleave to God on Shavuot with passionate attachment as in the Giving of the Torah, the experience becomes part of us. By preparing for the festival spiritually, we can actually experience these sensations and draw on them during the rest of the year, rather than merely observing the occasion intellectually.

In this, the festivals differ from Shabbat. Shabbat comes weekly. Its light is powerful, but established. The Song of Songs compares the Shabbat relationship to an intimate repast with an inseparable friend: "Eat, companions!"[1] However, the soul-union of the festivals is compared to an intoxication, for they are sporadic, and are the result of a spiritual influx from God. As the verse continues:

Drink and become intoxicated [with the love of God], beloved ones!

A similar metaphor can be found in Psalms:

Bread sustains the heart of man; . . . and wine to cheer the heart of man.[2]

We are sustained by bread. It evokes the delight and intimate closeness shared by those in an enduring relationship. The delight of Shabbat infuses our being and sustains us.

A soul-union that occurs only occasionally, as perhaps at the festivals, arouses joy, much like the sudden stimulation of wine. "Drink and become intoxicated"—become permeated with God's spirit.

The concepts of unique companionship versus intoxicating love find expression in the blessings pronounced under the marriage canopy. The sixth blessing reads as follows:

> Blessed are You, God, our Lord, King of the Universe, Who created *sasson, simchah, chatan, kalah, gilah, rinah, ditsah, chedvah, ahava, achvah, shalom, re'ut*—joy, gladness, groom and bride, mirth, glad song, pleasure, delight, love, brotherhood, peace and companionship.[3]

The combination of the terms "joy, gladness, mirth, glad song, pleasure, delight," which are expressions of joy, together with "love, brotherhood, peace and companionship," which are expressions of closeness, calls for an explanation. Furthermore, the four expressions of closeness seem to decrease in intensity, for love is stronger than brotherhood, and peace stronger than companionship. Finally, we need to understand why the words "groom and bride" are inserted in the midst of the expressions of joy.

The *Zohar* explains that at the beginning of their relationship, the bride and groom are in the stage of "drink and become intoxicated, beloved ones!" The novel quality of their coming relationship gives rise to a joy that, when stripped of physicality, could be compared to that of the festivals. As the marriage matures and the couple make God the third partner in their relationship by submitting to His will, they begin to experience the state of closeness mentioned in the second half of the blessing.

Furthermore, in these expressions, Kabbalah sees an allusion to the joy of festivals as opposed to the delight of Shabbat. On the festivals we experience the joy of loved ones coming together; on Shabbat we feel companionship and delight.

SIX EXPRESSIONS OF JOY

Sasson/joy alludes to the first day of Passover, as the verse says, "He led out His nation with joy."[4] *Simchah*/gladness alludes to the seventh day of Passover, on which we reexperience the exhilaration of the Israelites, who passed through the Red Sea and burst into inspired song.

On the festival of Shavuot we recapture the revelation at Sinai, when the entire Jewish nation united with the Creator. Their spontaneous declaration, "We will do [anything in order] to hear You," evokes—if it can be said—the selfless vows of a bride to her groom under the marriage canopy. The terms *chatan, kalah,* "groom and bride," placed after the "joy and gladness" of Passover, therefore reflect the Festival of Shavuot, which chronologically comes after Passover.

Gilah/mirth reminds us of Rosh Hashanah, the New Year, in which we "rejoice, *gilu,* with trembling."[5] Our fear of the impending judgment is nevertheless mingled with joy at the thought of the new potential for relationship with God that the upcoming year may hold.

Rinah/glad song reflects our feelings on Yom Kippur, after all our sins are forgiven. *Ditsah*/pleasure permeates us in the Festival of Sukkot, when we hide our love under the shadow of His faith, and *chedvah* is the delight of Shemini Atseret, when we experience God's private invitation, "Let us rejoice, I and you, together," through the gift that He gave us for that purpose, the Torah.

FOUR EXPRESSIONS OF CLOSENESS

The four expressions of closeness—*ahavah, achvah, shalom,* and *re'ut;* love, brother-hood, peace, and companionship—reflect different moments of the Shabbat experi-ence. Leaving behind a chaotic week on Shabbat eve, we begin to feel God's love. As the evening progresses, love turns into brotherhood as we are touched by the soul-union of the Friday evening prayers. On Shabbat morning comes peace, for through-out the entire *musaph* prayer, God joins our collective souls in a union involving the higher levels of the soul. Even if we lack the conscious perception of this, our prayers somehow reach an unusual depth, and we find ourselves not wanting to end, or let go of, the sense of fulfillment that permeates us.

Finally, by the third meal, the awe of God's greatness we felt at the onset of Shabbat turns into an intimate companionship. We continue to ascend, reaching the peak of our spiritual structure. But the connection far from decreases in intensity. At this point, we climb to the peak of our spiritual structure in a union known as *Jerusalem Above.* We then draw this Divine energy down to our souls within us, in a union known as *Jerusalem Below*, giving rise to what Kabbalah calls "the desire of desires."[6]

JERUSALEM ABOVE AND BELOW

When you reach a certain level of submission to God's will, your observance becomes a "relationship" in the true sense of the word, in that you can actually feel vibrating within you the Divine energy that God makes available on these days. This is not a soul-union, however; consequently, your Divine service, as well as your character traits, does not require the degree of perfection one must have to experience a soul-union. God responds to your love by sensitizing you to His Presence. You can enter into an altered state of consciousness in which you experience the luminous energy being directed toward you at the time.

In other words, in the state of mind called *Jerusalem Below,* Divine forces converge on a person, so that he, in turn, may illuminate the world around with God's light. In addition, this union reinforces the passionate attachment of his soul to the Creator.

In contrast, when one is wholeheartedly engaged in the observation of the com-mandments and the refinement of his character traits, even though he has not yet reached the perfection required for a Divine union, God helps his endeavors by allow-ing him to feel the Divine energy directed at Israel at the special times of holiness throughout the year.

When your Shabbat observance attains the quality described in the preceding chapters, and you begin to taste the bliss of your additional soul of Shabbat throbbing within, you then experience the *oneg* of the Divine luminous energy.[7] At this point, you can no longer speak of Divine hiddenness because you soon realize that the intensity of your feeling is in exact proportion to the quality of your observance of the com-mandments and to the refinement of your character traits.

PART TWO

THE FIRST TABLETS

9
Affliction

O N THE FIRST NIGHT OF PESACH, we commemorate the anniversary of our freedom from Eyptian bondage with a Seder.[1] We also commemorate our suffering in Egypt by eating *Matzah*/unleavened bread, "the bread of affliction," and bitter herbs. There are other holidays on which we celebrate deliverance; Pesach is the only holiday on which we also commemorate the affliction from which we were delivered.

This affliction increased when Moses first approached Pharaoh and asked him, in the Name of God, to release the Israelites. Pharaoh reacted to Moses' request by increasing their labor. Moses then complained to God:

> O Lord, why have You mistreated this people? Why did you send me? Since I came to Pharaoh to speak in Your Name, he has made things worse for this people, and You have not saved Your people.
>
> —Exodus 5:22–23

Then God told Moses:

> I am YHVH. I appeared to Abraham, Isaac and Jacob as *El Shaddai*, but I did not make Myself known to them by My Name YHVH.
>
> —Exodus 6:2–3

Let us analyze this brief but meaningful exchange. Moses was not questioning the reason for Israel's bondage in Egypt. He knew that it was necessary to purify Israel through suffering so that they would be capable of receiving the Torah. In fact, Moses had at first refused to go to Pharaoh because he felt that the Israelites needed more years of bondage to complete the purification. His claim now was that God's sending him to Pharaoh was a sign that the time of slavery was completed. He therefore asked why the bondage now became worse than ever: "Since I came to Pharaoh to speak in Your Name, he has made things worse for this people, and You have not saved Your people."

There is yet another element in Moses' complaint. He was also saying, "How is it possible that precisely now, when I spoke to Pharaoh in Your holy Name, the Tetragrammaton (YHVH), the Name denoting Divine compassion, the bondage became harder?"

MOSES' COMPLAINT

God replied:

> I am YHVH. I appeared to Abraham, Isaac and Jacob as *El Shaddai*, but I did not make Myself known to them by My Name YHVH.

The name Shaddai indicates a conduct of "measure-for-measure." When God relates to a person in this way, the person can absorb Inner Light within his inside organs only according to his degree of worthiness. Since God related to the Patriarchs as Shaddai, they received only as much as they deserved; and if they were given very intense light, it is because they worked on themselves to an inordinate degree to become worthy of it.

The Tetragrammaton, on the other hand, operates on the basis of pure love and kindness, bestowing Inner Light irrespective of the recipient's worthiness. To enable the recipient to absorb the light in his brain, heart, and liver, thus sharpening his intellect, emotions, and instincts, he is sent chastenings of love to refine him and ready him to receive the light.

God told Moses, "I did not make Myself known to [the Patriarchs] by My Name YHVH." The Patriarchs did not need chastenings of love; they had their own merit. The people of Israel, on the other hand, were not ready to receive the great light that God wanted to give them; and so they did need chastenings of love. Consequently, the years of slavery until Moses appeared on the scene served to rectify the errors they had committed until then.[2] From the moment that Moses went to Pharaoh in the Name of YHVH, however, the hardship of slavery intensified so as to refine them and allow the Inner Light to spread within them.

Israel's spiritual refinement can be compared to the refinement of gold. Just as gold must be purified by fire and then molded, so Israel had to be cleansed by suffering and then purified so as to be filled with Inner Light. The Torah commands us to remember the slavery and afflictions in Egypt in order to stimulate our awareness of God's lovingkindness in helping us purify our souls through this bondage.

As Rabbi Chayim Vital explains, the bondage that Israel suffered in Egypt prepared them to receive the Torah and the revelation of the great Name, the Tetragrammaton, which was hitherto hidden. The Torah can only be acquired fully through humility. On the rungs of spiritual elevation enumerated in the classic Mussar work *Messilat Yesharim*, the eighth level is humility, followed by fear of sin (pain of separation from God), which leads to the top of the ladder—Divine Inspiration. The Torah could be given only through Moses, who was "exceedingly humble, more than all the men on the face of the earth,"[3] on Mount Sinai, the lowest of mountains. Only by suffering bondage and poverty could Israel acquire the humility necessary for receiving the Torah.

Hence, on Pesach, we commemorate not only the redemption, but also the bondage because we recognize that the suffering God gave us enabled us to receive the Torah and to absorb the Inner Light. We eat bitter herbs to remember God's great kindness to Israel for sending them the bitter bondage that purified them and freed them from the forces of evil clinging to them.[4] Similarly, the Pesach offering was a gesture of thanksgiving to the Almighty for sending afflictions to Israel, as a gift of love designed to bring them closer to Him.

10

The Exodus:
Passionate Courtship

I N DISCUSSING THE FESTIVAL OF PESACH, the Torah says, "You shall eat *matsah*/unleavened bread because you left Egypt in haste."[1] What is the significance of this haste, which we are to commemorate for all time?

THE FOUR HUNDRED YEARS

Even before the birth of Abraham's son Isaac, God told Abraham that his descendants would be enslaved in a strange land for four hundred years.[2] Through this period of suffering, they would acquire the trait of humility that would allow them to receive the Torah and become a holy nation.

The prophecy of the four hundred years was passed down through the generations. The Israelites in Egypt knew it, and so they did not pray to God to redeem them before the appointed time. God, too, said to Israel: "Turn your eyes away from Me, for they overwhelm Me!"[3] As long as the time of redemption has not arrived, do not lift your eyes to Me in prayer, lest My control snap and I redeem you before the time.

Thus for one hundred and ninety years they silently endured forced labor. They witnessed their children being used as bricks in the very walls they were constructing. They saw Pharaoh bathing in their children's blood as a cure for his skin disease.

Finally:

> The Children of Israel sighed from their bondage and they cried out, and their cry rose up before God from the bondage.
>
> —Exodus 2:23

Targum Yonatan writes that these were not cries of self-pity. The Children of Israel were not bewailing their travail, for they were well aware that the painful exile had been decreed by God. Their groans were directed at the source of their bitterness, their estrangement from God. This cry God did not leave unanswered.

> God heard their groaning. . . . God saw the Children of Israel and God knew.
> —Exodus 2:24–25

We have seen that the verb "know" in the Bible often refers to intimacy. By lifting yearning eyes to the Omnipresent, the Israelites aroused His longing for them and His desire to redeem them. God then sent Moses to take them out of Egypt before the appointed time.

RESISTANCE TO MOSES

When Moses came to redeem Israel, he encountered resistance on two fronts: the Israelites at first objected to leaving because they believed that the appointed time had not yet come, and Pharaoh refused to let them go despite the plagues that afflicted him.

The Midrash relates that when Moses came to tell the Israelites that God wished to redeem them, they raised two objections: first, if they left before the appointed time, they would still be flawed, for the purification through suffering would not be complete. Second, in the environment of Egypt, the peak of impurity, they themselves had worshiped idols and had sunk to the forty-ninth level of impurity, one before the very end.

Moses replied, "Since God desires you, He will disregard both your accounting and your idolatrous practices!" God, as it were, desired to be attached to them; He therefore disregarded all considerations.

Pharaoh obstinately refused to let the people go because he knew that a time had been appointed for Israel's redemption, and he did not believe that an arousal of the heart could break the boundaries of reason. Therefore, God had to take Israel out "with great power and a show of force."[4]

The command to eat *matzah* "because you left Egypt in haste" commemorates God's haste to redeem Israel before the appointed time. God rushed to free them before they could fall into the fiftieth level of impurity; but He also rushed out of desire for them. As Israel's voice in the Song of Songs puts it:

> The voice of my Beloved! Behold it came suddenly [to redeem me], as if leaping over mountains, skipping over hills! (2:8)

The haste was Israel's as well, for God's love for Israel aroused Israel's love for God, according to the principle that love evokes love: "As water reflects a face back to a face, so one's heart is reflected back to him by another."[5]

11

I, and Not an Angel

THE EXTENT OF GOD'S LOVE FOR ISRAEL, listening to their cries despite the fact that, not having completed the prescribed time of their exile, they were steeped in impurity, comes through with particular intensity on Passover eve, as we read in the *Haggadah*: "I will pass through the land of Egypt, I, and not an angel. I will smite all the firstborn in the land of Egypt, I, not a seraph, I will execute judgment against all the gods of Egypt, I, not a messenger. I, the Lord, it is I and no other."

In contrast to the Exodus from Egypt, which was done through the intermediary of Moses, the plague of the firstborn was brought about by God Himself. Yet, this last plague was no different than all the others that were executed through Moses! Why would it require the direct involvement of the Divine Presence more than any of the others?

"I will pass through the land of Egypt on that night" does not mean that the purpose of the descent was to carry out the plague of the firstborn so that Pharaoh would finally agree to send them out of Egypt. Had the Divine purpose been exclusively to bring about the final plague, there was no need for God to come down Himself; He merely had to prevent His life-force from reaching them and they would have immediately become corpses! The main purpose of God's coming down was really to redeem them Himself, like a man whose son falls into a pit and who personally goes down to retrieve him.

Due to the direct Divine intervention, the revelation of God's luminous energy was so intense on Passover eve that the light in that night was as strong as daylight: the powers of evil in the Egyptian firstborn could not withstand it and died. Only the firstborn died because the root of impurity of each Egyptian household was concentrated in the firstborn. The revelation ended with the daylight, at the time the actual Exodus began.

The passionate courtship between God and Israel, as it was begun in Egypt, is described in Ezekiel, where God speaks of His beloved in moving terms (16:7):

> Your breasts became firm
> and your hair sprouted.
> You were [still] naked and bare
> when I passed by you and saw you.
> Then your time for love had come.
> I spread My cloak over you
> and covered your nakedness.
> I gave you My oath
> and entered a covenant with you,
> says the Lord God,
> and you were Mine.

"Your breasts became firm and your hair sprouted": to God's "eyes," from the point of view of time, the Israelites were ready to be redeemed. "You were [still] naked and bare": they still had to become physically involved in the actual observance of God's commandments with love and awe. This would purify their body and enclose them in ethereal garments of light.

We can read the Divine feelings, as it were, in between the lines. Despite this initial love and tenderness that would turn into a fiery passion, God is stressing His awareness that Israel was naked of the garments that they needed in order to relate to His Divinity.

The commandments are like ornaments that arouse the will of the King to the soul-union, even when the bodily parts have not yet become totally purified vessels ready to contain His Presence.

The purpose of the descent of soul to this world is to acquire the adornments of the Torah and commandments in order to be worthy of being consciously aware of this soul-union while in this world, and to a greater extent, after death when we fully become part of God's essence. Hence, this world is, in a sense, the corridor where we prepare ourselves for the soul-union that will take place in the next world.

According to the order of Creation, all Divine energy comes to the world through the intermediary of an angel or a seraph. These heavenly beings are only allowed to deliver the life force that they were entrusted with if the receiver is enwrapped by the garments of light of Torah observance and good deeds that the angel can readily identify.

While in the Egyptian bondage, the Children of Israel were devoid of garments, and consequently an angel, who can act only according to the order God built into Creation, could not have redeemed them. Hence the *Haggadah* reads, "I and not an angel; I, not a seraph; I, and no other." Only God Himself could break this order of Creation and so He did, making them a part of His essence.

The redemption came while the Community of Israel was still "naked and bare." God gave in to His desire for them—if one can speak this way—and helped them elevate themselves to Him by starting for them the task of purification they had to undertake: "I spread My cloak over you." God's message to His beloved is clear: "I gave you My oath, and entered a covenant with you."

From the time it was conceived in God's Thoughts, the special closeness of God and Israel was not to be a tempestuous relationship free of any responsibility other that their feelings toward each other. The passionate attachment of this union was not to be separated from the covenant, entailing terms to be kept on both sides. One is immediately adjacent to the other. It is only after "I entered a covenant with you," that we have "and you were Mine."

THE CONSEQUENCES OF HASTE

God was fully aware of the consequences of the arousal that resulted in the early redemption of His people. He knew that Israel would respond with passionate attachment to God's feelings when these were revealed to them. Overwhelmed by intense love, they would accept His Torah unconditionally, even before they heard what laws it would bind them to obey, by saying, "*Na'aseh VeNishma/*We will do and we will hear" (Exodus 24:7). He knew that they would follow Him into the desert without knowing how they would get food and drink. "I remember how you were faithful in your youth, your love as a bride, how you followed Me in the wilderness, a land not sown."[1] On the other hand, God was equally aware that they would make the Golden Calf and say, "This, Israel, is your god,"[2] because their purification had not been completed.

When the Israelites made the Golden Calf, God told Moses He wished to destroy them. "Moses began to plead before God his Lord. He said, O God, why unleash Your wrath against Your people, whom You brought out of Egypt with great power and a show of force?"[3] Moses' argument bore fruit. "God refrained from doing the evil that He had planned for His people."[4]

Moses' argument is puzzling. If Israel was guilty of idolatry, why should God's bringing them out of Egypt "with great power and a show of force" prevent Him from unleashing His wrath against them?

The expression "with great power and a show of force" hints of the prematurity of the redemption; had Israel completed its allotted time of bondage, the "great power and a show of force" against Egypt would not have been necessary. Moses' argument to God, then, was as follows:

The Israelites told You that they wanted to remain in Egypt until they were perfectly purified. Had they remained, they might have achieved the level of humility necessary for receiving the Torah fully. Then, after leaving the influence of the idolatrous Egyptians and experiencing the revelation of the Divine Presence at Sinai, they would never have committed the sin of the Golden Calf. If, in Your immense love, You took them out before their time, do not blame them for lapsing into idolatry.

COURTSHIP

The courtship of God and Israel, hasty as it was, went in stages. In a sense, God saw us. This led to loving us, wishing to attach His Presence to us.

Egypt was the beginning of the relationship, the initial seeing. "God saw the Israelites and God knew." It represented the initial move toward Israel. Next, it was

Israel's turn. They had to awaken to follow the Beloved. "I remember how you were faithful in your youth, your love as a bride, how you followed Me in the wilderness." It was only when we responded to God's overtures by following Him in the desert that He attached Himself to us forever by giving us the Torah.

This was the intention behind God's words to Moses, "Proof that I have sent you will come when you get the people out of Egypt. All of you will then become God's servants on this mountain."[5] Moses feared that if God redeemed Israel out of longing, love and the desire for eternal attachment would not necessarily follow. God therefore reassured him: If you follow Me out of Egypt, even now, before the time, I will bring you to Me forever. As a proof, I will give you My Torah, which is the highest expression of My will.

Indeed, in the first of the Ten Commandments, God proclaimed, "I am the Lord Your God who brought you out of Egypt."[6] I brought you out because of My desire for you. Now let My attachment to Israel become permanent. With the Giving of the Torah, the intoxicating love relationship of the Exodus left its temporary status and turned into an everlasting union between God and His chosen people.

12

The Song at the Sea

O N THE SEVENTH DAY OF THE EXODUS from Egypt, which we commemorate as the seventh day of Passover, the newborn Israelite nation found itself trapped. Behind it were the mighty horses, carriages, and soldiers of Egypt in hot pursuit; before it was the Sea of Reeds.

They jumped into the sea, thus proving the extent of their trust in the Divine Providence. Miraculously, the sea was split before them, and the Jews crossed safely. But the danger was not yet past, for the Egyptians, too, entered the sea-road.

At last the sea closed over the pursuers. Then, "the people were in awe of God. They believed in God and in His servant Moses. Then Moses and the Children of Israel sang this song to God" (Exodus 14:31; 15:1).

The *Zohar* notes that God illuminated them with His Supernal Wisdom, to the point that they were able to sing the Song at the Sea in perfect unison. And they sang: "I will sing to God, for He is lofty above all that is lofty";

> Horse and rider He threw into the sea....
> My strength and song is God; He has become my salvation.
> This is my God and I will enshrine Him....
> —Exodus 15:1, 2

Our sages note that the word "this" is used in the Torah when one points to something. On the shores of the sea, the Israelites beheld a vision of the Divine Presence so clear that they could "point" to God and say, "This is my God." At that moment, the simplest maidservant was able to see more of the Divine than the great prophet Ezekiel saw years later.

Unlike any other song, the Song at the Sea is written in the Torah scroll like a structure of staggered bricks. This design of space over print and print over space indicates that the Israelites were able to grasp the deepest secrets of the Torah contained in the white spaces between the black letters of the Torah scroll.[1]

We would have expected this elevated song to begin with a general statement of praise, such as: "My strength and song is God; He has become my deliverance." Why does it begin with what seems like a detail: "Horse and rider He threw into the sea?"

Furthermore, we find that after the men had sung, Miriam led the women in song:

> Sing to God, for He is lofty above all that is lofty;
> Horse and rider He threw into the sea.
>
> —Exodus 15:21

The text implies that these are the only words they sang. Evidently, this verse is the essence of the song; the rest narrates the details.[2]

Given the amazing miracle of the splitting of the sea, not to mention the ten plagues, it seems strange that the hurling of horse and rider into the sea is the most important part of the Exodus.

Moreover, it seems from the verses preceding the song that it was the extra surge of faith they experienced upon seeing the destruction of the Egyptian army that caused them to burst into song. "The Israelites saw the great power that God had unleashed against Egypt, and the people were in awe of God. They believed in God and in His servant Moses. Then Moses and the Children of Israel sang this song to God."

But if the song was about the deliverance from Egypt, why did they need to feel more faith in God and in Moses than they had felt when they witnessed the ten plagues and were redeemed from slavery? In fact, why did they not sing then?

The Song at the Sea was not a song of gratitude over the miracles of the redemption from Egypt, or even over the destruction of the Egyptian army and the splitting of the sea. It was rather that in their vision of the Divine Presence they saw the awesome majesty of God's sovereignty, and they burst into song. Like the angels and seraphs who sing in awe of God's omnipotence, the Israelites sang when the radiance of God's light was revealed to them. The sinking of Pharaoh's chariots and army removed the obstruction that prevented them from seeing the Presence of God.

The Ari taught that in the realm of holiness there is a complete system, known as a vehicle or "chariot," through which God governs the world and reveals Himself. There is a parallel system in the realm of evil. The chariots of the power of evil are forces of concealment; they act as a screen that hides the radiance of God's glory. This system is the root of all concealment of God's Presence in this world.

When Pharaoh and his army—the inner essence of the system of evil—together with the angel appointed over Egypt were destroyed, a feeling of fear and dread fell on the surrounding nations as they became aware of God's sovereignty. At that time, the screen obscuring the Source of light was torn asunder, and the radiance of God was revealed to the eyes of all Israel. They immediately burst into song, for they attained the level of angels who gaze at the radiance of God and sing His praises.

"The Israelites saw the great power that God had unleashed against Egypt." They saw that the powers of evil screening God from them had been removed. They were able to gaze at the Divine Presence in a way that later prophets could not, for these prophets came after the sin of the Golden Calf, when the powers of evil again formed a screen blocking the light of God from all eyes.

Upon seeing the complete annihilation of the powers of evil, the Israelites awakened to God's awesome transcendence and were overwhelmed by the radiance of His glory. Their belief in God and in His servant Moses became crystal clear and they burst into song: "I will sing to God for He is lofty above all that is lofty." This was a song upon seeing the essence of God's majesty, that He towers above all that is high, and there is no end to His greatness.

The end of the verse, "Horse and rider He threw into the sea," is the driving motif of the song, for the "horse" refers to the system of evil, and the "rider" represents the Supernal powers that control it. The song is an expression of the appreciation of God's splendor, which the horse and rider had previously prevented Israel from seeing. The song goes on to relate in detail how the different powers obstructing the vision of God were reduced to nothing.

The end of the song, "God will reign forever and ever," is a prayer that the revelation of the splendor of His sovereignty may last forever. That was their intense wish. Indeed, the *Zohar* notes that even after the Israelites finished singing the song, the vision of the Divine Presence continued, since the powers of evil had been annihilated. As they gazed at the Divine glory eye to eye, their souls were filled with ecstasy. In their desire for more revelations of that glorious mystery, they refused to continue on their journey. Moses had to beg the Almighty to transfer His glory from the sea to the desert so that they would allow him to lead them away.

God had been waiting for such a song to be sung, say the sages, for until then no one had done it. It is not just a song of gratitude that He wanted; Adam and the Patriarchs had already sung such songs, and so had the Israelites when they left Egypt. God was waiting for the song of a human being who finds himself gazing like an angel at the awesome greatness of the Presence of God, and this song was only possible after the destruction of evil. As Miriam and the women sang in only one verse, "I will sing to God for He is lofty above all that is lofty"—His greatness is apparent—now that "horse and rider He threw into the sea," and there is no longer a screen that prevents us from gazing at His light.

Our sages say that at the sea, the ministering angels wished to sing, but God objected, saying: "The work of My hands is drowning, and you wish to sing!" The drowning of the Egyptians prevented the angels, but not the Israelites, from singing. The reason is that the angels wished to sing of Israel's deliverance, but Israel sang of the revelation of God's loftiness.

Similar to the Song at the Sea is the "Song for the Shabbat day."[3] Remarkably, this psalm does not refer to Shabbat directly; it sings of the praise of God, the destruction of evil, and the exultation of the righteous. The reason is that on Shabbat, the heavenly realms are elevated to their Source, and God's Presence is no longer hidden by a screen. Israel can then sing, "It is good to thank God, and to sing praise to Your name, Most High. . . . How great are Your works, O God; exceedingly profound are Your thoughts!"[4] And at the sea, Israel sang: "I will sing to God, for He is lofty above all that is lofty." This is the type of song that God had awaited since Creation.

The weekly Shabbat is a taste of the ultimate Shabbat—the world to come. Whoever sings the Song at the Sea in this world, say our sages, will sing it in the world to come. This means that he who sings the song as the Israelites sang it, purifying himself from the grasp of evil to remove the veil that hides God's Presence, feeling that his heart and flesh are bursting in a song for the Living God, will deserve to sing it in the world to come. In this ultimate Shabbat, his vision of God will be on an infinitely higher plane; he will delight in gazing at the light of the Divine Presence.

13

Tefillin:
Remember the Exodus!

T HE MOST COMMON IMAGE that Jewish prayer conjures in our minds is that of a man wrapped in a white prayer shawl (*tallit*), with little black boxes strapped on to his forehead and left arm (*tefillin*).

Although the mitsvah of tefillin is most commonly associated with prayer, for Jewish men must don tefillin every day during the morning services except Shabbat, the mystical purpose of the tefillin is much more encompassing. Tefillin serve to bind the mind and heart to a constant awareness of the Divine Presence. Thus, in Talmudic times, scholars would wear tefillin all day long. Today, most men have discontinued this practice, because the donning of tefillin requires a constant state of purity in body and thought. However, even today, there are Torah scholars who continue to wear tefillin all day long.

Tefillin are small, black leather boxes, set upon the head and tied to the arm with leather straps. The head tefillin is divided into four segments. In each segment is a passage from the Torah. The arm tefillin contain only one section, and all four Torah portions are written together on the same piece of parchment.

TEFILLIN AND THE "BACKBONE" OF THE TORAH

The mitsvah of tefillin is closely connected with the three commandments that underlie the entire Torah: to fear God, to love Him, and to cleave to Him. Each of these basic commandments has various aspects. A person's initial desire to do God's will leads to the fear of the consequences for transgressing it. On a higher level, fear of God manifests itself as awe of the Divine Presence. Various expressions of the love of God are found in the Shema, "with all your heart, with all your soul, and with all your might." Cleaving to God (*devekut*) can mean emulating His attributes, as the Talmud states, "Just as He is compassionate, so you should be compassionate." It can mean associating oneself with the sages of Israel. Or, it can mean developing a deep spiritual attachment to the Source of being. It is important to understand the difference between these last two levels—love and *devekut*.

LOVE AND ATTACHMENT

As we have explained, this world is characterized by a nearly complete concealment of God's Presence, and for all appearances, seems totally disconnected from the Divine. Yet, there is a direct inner connection to God through the Foundation Coronet (*Ateret haYesod*), namely, the Divine source of all blessing and sustenance. For, despite appearances, this world has no independent existence; it is attached to its Maker through an inner dimension—the Foundation Coronet—where the union between the Creator and Israel's soul-roots takes place.[1]

This relationship between God and the Community of Israel is like a tree whose branches are above ground and whose trunk is below. It would seem that the branches are separate entities, but by removing the earth from their base, we can see how they are all connected, extensions of the same tree. This meeting point between the hidden and the revealed is the Foundation Coronet. The People of Israel are like the branches of this tree; as such, they are forever longing to achieve an awareness of the meeting point within their souls.

We can now perceive the difference between loving God and being passionately attached to Him. When we relate to God with love there is no revelation of the soul-roots of the Community of Israel at the Foundation Coronet. Israel and their Maker are then like two separate entities, although their mutual love is like fiery coals, as overwhelming and irresistible as death.[2]

In contrast, attachment to God entails a revelation of the soul-roots of the Community of Israel at the Foundation Coronet. This happened at the Giving of the Torah, when their souls cleaved to the Divine Source. The Israelites then experienced their attachment to the Holy One like a branch connected to its root. This is alluded to in the verse: "They saw a vision of the God of Israel, and under His feet was something like a sapphire brick."[3] Kabbalistically, this "sapphire brick" alludes to the Foundation Coronet.

Such is the level of *devekut*, that goes beyond that of love.

FAITH AT THE FOUNDATION CORONET

Scriptures say about the trait of loving God:

> As water reflects a face back to a face, so one's heart is reflected back to him by another.[4]

It is possible, however, that the love one has in his heart fails to arouse that of the other, since they are two separate entities. Passionate attachment, however, stemming from the revelation of the root, will always be mutual. Both Creator and Creation desire to draw close to one another.

The Torah mentions the haste related to the Exodus from Egypt. But the Talmud asks, whose haste was it: the Egyptians', the Israelites', or the Creator's? The commentators answer that all three were in haste. The Egyptians were in haste to free the Israelites after the plague of the firstborn. In the case of the Children of Israel and the Creator, however, the haste originated in the revelation on the night of the Exodus. The Foundation Coronet was revealed, arousing a powerful desire in Israel to run after their Maker, as the verse says:

> I remember how you were faithful in your youth, your love as a bride, how you followed Me in the wilderness.[5]

And if it can be said, in revealing the Foundation Coronet, the Creator showed that more than anything else, He wanted to draw Israel to Himself, as it is written:

> I have borne you on the wings of eagles and brought you to Me.[6]

A PEEK INSIDE

Let us attempt to determine how the commandments at the backbone of the Torah are connected to the mitsvah of tefillin. The portions of the Torah placed within the tefillin are the very passages that mention this mitsvah. The Torah's first mention of tefillin is found in the account of the Exodus:

> Moses said to the people: "Remember this day as [the time] you left Egypt.... [These words] must also be a sign on your hand, and a reminder between your eyes. God's Torah will then be on your tongue. It was with a show of strength that God brought you out of Egypt."[7]

The paragraph immediately following, concerning the mitsvah of consecrating one's firstborn son in memory of the plague of the firstborn, ends with the words:

> There shall come a time when God will have brought you to the land.... You will then bring to God every [firstborn] that initiates the womb.... You must [also] redeem every firstborn among your sons.... [These words] shall [also] be a sign on your hand, and tefillin between your eyes. [All this is] because God brought us out of Egypt with a show of strength.[8]

The third paragraph referring to tefillin is in the Shema:

> Listen, Israel, God is our Lord, God is One.... These words which I am commanding you today must remain on your heart.... Bind [these words] as a sign on your hand and let them be tefillin between your eyes.[9]

The fourth reference—recited as the second paragraph of the Shema—ends with the words:

> If you are careful to pay heed to My commandments, which I am prescribing to you today.... I will grant the fall and spring rains in your land at their proper time, so

that you will have an ample harvest of grain, oil and wine. . . . Place these words of mine on your heart and soul. Bind them as a sign on your arm, and let them be tefillin between your eyes.[10]

According to the medieval sage Rabbi Yosef Albo, there are three basic tenets upon which Judaism stands:

1. Belief in God as the Creator and Ruler of the Universe.
2. Belief in reward and punishment.
3. Belief in Israel's free choice to serve Him.[11]

This third principle, however, can be divided into two. It implies a relationship between the Community of Israel and their Creator not as separate entities, but in a bond of union, through the Foundation Coronet. Every commandment they observe removes another obstacle toward the revelation of their state of *devekut* and of their bond to the Holy One. The common goal here is a total attachment:

3a. The Holy One's attachment to Israel, and
3b. Israel's attachment to their Maker.

These four divisions of faith correspond to the four different passages of the tefillin.

1. The first paragraph of the Shema explains the first branch of faith, namely, that God is One, and that He is the Creator and Ruler of all created.
2. The second paragraph of the Shema explains the concept of reward and punishment.
3a. The paragraph referring to the Exodus explains the subdivision of faith concerning *devekut*, passionate attachment. First from God's perspective, a reminder that He took us out of Egypt.
3b. The paragraph concerning the consecration of the firstborn expresses the second subdivision, the passionate attachment of the Jews to God. Spiritually, the "firstborn" represents the root of a person's creative ability. By sanctifying the firstborn to God, the people of Israel show that they are passionately attached to the Source of all blessings.

The head tefillin represent the power of the mind, which can grasp and analyze spiritual truths. Therefore, it is made of four separate sections, each one containing a different passage, a different religious principle, just as the mind can understand each principle separately. The arm tefillin, which rest against the heart, represent the power of faith. Therefore, all four paragraphs are in one box, reflecting the basis of faith: God is One, and there is nothing other than His Presence.

By wearing tefillin, the passionate attachment that joins God to the soul-roots of Israel is revealed. A Jewish male who does not don tefillin is therefore denying God's link with the Community of Israel.

Nevertheless, tefillin are not worn on Shabbat, because on that day Creation as a whole ascends to its Source and the Foundation Coronet is revealed to all who have prepared themselves. Shabbat, like tefillin, is "a sign," representing God's love for His people and His intimate union with them.

According to the Talmud, God also wears tefillin. That is, just as the people of Israel give their Creator a tangible proof of their attachment to Him every time they don tefillin, so does God give Israel a token of His love for them by donning "spiritual tefillin." *

* To David, for his courage.

14

The *Tsitsit* and the Splitting of the Sea

Speak to the Israelites and have them make tassels (*tsitsit*) on the corners of their garments for all generations.[1]

LIKE *TEFILLIN*, THE COMMANDMENT of wearing *tsitsit*/tassels also reminds us of the Exodus. In ancient times men would tie these tassels onto the four-cornered garments they usually wore. Even today, a square-shaped garment worn by a man, such as a poncho, requires tsitsit. Furthermore, as in talmudic times, men still wrap themselves during morning prayers in a tallit, a beautiful garment which they don in honor of the encounter with the Beloved. As with all four-cornered garments, the tallit has tsitsit attached to its corners. Also, throughout the day, men can fulfill the commandment of tsitsit by wearing a smaller version of this prayer shawl under their clothes.

The mitsvah of tsitsit is found in the following verses:

God spoke to Moses, telling him to speak to the Israelites and have them make *tsitsit*/tassels on the corners of their garments for all generations. They shall include a twist of *techelet*/ocean-blue wool in the corner tassels.

These shall be your tassels, and when you see them, you shall remember all of God's commandments so as to keep them. You will then not stray after your heart and eyes, which [in the past] have led you to immorality.[2]

In this verse, Rashi finds an allusion to the process that leads to transgression: the eye sees the forbidden object, the heart desires it, and finally the body commits the sin. The commentators add that the injunction not to "stray after your heart" warns against thoughts of separation from God, and "after your eyes" alludes to sexual promiscuity.

The sages stress that the desire to sin preceding the actual sin can cause more damage to an individual's spiritual structure than the sin itself, for the desire to transgress is keener while thinking of the forbidden pleasure than when faced with the source of temptation. The luscious image of the forbidden fruit roves in the mind's eye longer than it takes to eat it. The desire to sin sinks the person into the physical world with greater intensity and more lasting effects than the actual transgression.

Yet, as men see the strings of the tsitsit hanging at their sides, they are reminded to guard their heart against thoughts of heresy and their eyes against illicit desires.

Like the tsitsit, the commandment of donning tefillin also guards men's heart and eyes. The head tefillin are the counterpart of the brain; they are "between our eyes," while the hand tefillin are bound to the left arm opposite the heart.

Why do men need two different commandments as counterparts of their heart and eyes?

The Ari explains that the Divine luminous energy directed upon a person contains two aspects, a Surrounding Light and an Inner Light. As the Divine energy descends, it first surrounds a person from without, and then penetrates within the body, becoming Inner Light enclosed within the main human organs—the brain, heart, and liver.

It is for this reason that men wrap themselves in a tallit each morning before donning tefillin. The tallit clothes the body like the Surrounding Light, whereas the tefillin are in direct contact with the skin, illuminating a person with Inner Light. The tefillin draw down this light into the brain and heart, where most of the Inner Light dwells.[3]

Men must first draw around themselves the Surrounding Light of the tsitsit, and only then don tefillin, drawing Inner Light within their brain and heart. The reason for this order is that the energy of the tsitsit will surround them with a light that will protect them from stray thoughts while they are wearing tefillin.

Furthermore, the light of the tsitsit helps men master their sexual temptations: it was specifically concerning the mitsvah of tsitsit that Rashi commented, "The eye sees, the heart desires and the body sins." The reason is that the tsitsit are in contact with the body's tools of action which allow men to go "after their eyes" and to transgress, prey to illicit sexual desires, whereas the tefillin are connected only with the heart and the eyes.

THE EXODUS FROM EGYPT

This distinction between tefillin and tsitsit is also reflected in the story of the Exodus from Egypt.

As we have seen, the mitsvah of tefillin is meant to remind us of the redemption from Egypt. As the verse says,

> Moses said to the people: "Remember this day as [the time] you left Egypt. . . . And it shall be a sign on your hand, and a reminder between your eyes, so that God's Torah be on your lips; for with a strong hand God brought you out of Egypt."[4]

The relationship between the mitsvah of tsitsit and the Exodus is also clear:

> You will then not stray after your heart and eyes, which [in the past] have led you to immorality, that you should remember and fulfill My commandments, in order to be

holy to your God. I am the Lord your God, who took you out of the Land of Egypt to be your God.[5]

In addition, the four corners of the garment correspond to the four expressions of redemption in the Book of Exodus: "I will draw out," "I shall save," "I shall redeem," "I will take."[6] Also, the tsitsit of each corner are made up of eight strings, alluding to the eight days between the time of the Exodus and the splitting of the sea.[7]

Kabbalah explains that, much like a human being, each nation has its own spiritual structure composed of an Inner Light and a Surrounding Light. All the plagues were inflicted upon Egypt by the means of its Inner Light, including that of the firstborn, as the verse hints to:

> Around midnight I will go out *in the midst* of Egypt, and all the firstborn in the land of Egypt will die.[8]

This alludes to the Divine Inner Light that flooded Egypt with such force that the country's "soul" could not withstand its purity and power. Another allusion to this renewed Inner Light may be found in the plague of darkness:

> The Israelites, however, had light in their dwellings.[9]

On the other hand, the miracle of the Red Sea was accomplished by the means of the Divine Surrounding Light. It took place outside Egypt. Consequently, God's revelation at the sea was much greater than His revelation in Egypt. "This is my God, and I will glorify Him," sang the Israelites.[10] "They could point to the Divine Presence with their fingers," says the Talmud. In Egypt, however, the revelation is only alluded to:

> Has God ever done miracles, bringing one nation out of another nation with . . . terrifying phenomena, as God did for you in Egypt before your very eyes?[11]

"Terrifying phenomena," say the commentators, refers to the revelation of the Divine Presence.

It is for this reason that the mitsvah of tsitsit also alludes to the splitting of the Red Sea, whereas the four paragraphs of tefillin mention the miracle of the Exodus and the plague of the firstborn, but not the miracle of the Red Sea at all.

BEYOND THE PHYSICAL

The preceding helps us to understand the deeper meaning of the eight strings of the *tsitsit* and of the eight days between the Exodus and the splitting of the sea.

In his study of the mitsvah of tsitsit, Rabbi Aryeh Kaplan explains that whereas the number seven, related to Shabbat, represents the perfection of the physical world created in six days, the number eight alludes to a dimension that transcends the physical:

> [The eight strings of the *tsitsit*] indicate that the Jew is bound far beyond the realms of the physical world.[12]

The numerical value of the letters of the Hebrew word *Az*, which begins the Song at the Sea, is eight, a hidden reminder that on the eighth day of the Exodus, we entered the higher dimension of the Surrounding Light.

The Inner Light instills in our hearts a feeling of love and fear of God in our heart, and the Surrounding Light awakens in us the awe of His Presence and dread of His greatness.

This distinction between the function of the Inner versus the Surrounding Lights further differentiates the tefillin, worn on the head and close to the heart, from the tsitsit, which helps men "not to stray after their eyes and heart."

The tefillin are said to help man master the temptations of his heart. Although his heart and thoughts entice him to indulge in the pleasures around him, the Inner Light that spreads within him when he wears tefillin gives him a surplus of energy that helps him overcome his temptations if that is what he wants to do.

In contrast, the Surrounding Light of the tsitsit helps man "not to stray," that is, not to pay attention to the matters of this world, and focus instead on God's greatness and majesty that he is in contact with through the strings of his tsitsit. At this point, anything connected with this world pales in comparison.

The Talmud tells the story of a man who was particularly careful in his observation of the commandment of tsitsit. One day, he was faced with an overwhelming urge to give in to a grave transgression. At that moment, the strings of his tsitsit—whether physically or psychologically—slapped him in the face. He was suddenly shaken into perceiving the magnitude of God's power, and felt his illicit desires waning.[13]

The very word *tsitsit* is related to the Hebrew word *tsuts*, which means "to look." The implication is that by perceiving the Surrounding Light drawn down by the tsitsit and fixing their thoughts on it, men can avoid straying after their hearts and eyes.

One final point: originally, the four tassels tied to the corners of a garment were to include one thread of deep blue. This color, called *techelet*, was produced in ancient times from a die derived from a marine creature known as *chilazon*.[14] This color also served as a reminder:

> Rabbi Meir said: Whoever observes the mitsvah of *tsitsit*, it is considered as if he greeted the Divine Presence, for *techelet* resembles the sea, and the sea resembles the sky, and the sky resembles the Throne of Glory.

Hence, the mitsvah of techelet makes man aware of God's holy Throne, the source of the Surrounding Light. Thinking about God's kingship reminds us that we must guard the honor of the Holy One, which would be damaged should we fall into sin.

ON SHABBAT

All this helps us understand the relationship between tsitsit and tefillin and the mitsvah of Shabbat. The commandment of Shabbat, as the fourth of the Ten Commandments, is recorded twice in the Torah, with a variation in the text:

Zachor/Remember the Shabbat day to keep it holy.[15]

Shamor/Observe the Shabbat day to keep it holy.[16]

Zachor refers to the preparation for Shabbat: sanctifying it through the *kiddush* over wine,[17] the fine meals, and the elegant clothes. *Shamor* refers to refraining from thirty-nine types of creative work defined in Jewish law. On a deeper level, *zachor* reminds us of God's love for Israel, while *shamor* awakens Israel's love for God.

Shamor and *zachor* both represent the tefillin. Throughout the week, the head tefillin draw an Inner Light that reminds us of God's love for man, while the hand tefillin, which rest against the heart, awaken Israel's love for God.

However, tefillin are not worn on Shabbat, for by refraining from the forbidden activities—*shamor*—we can also awaken our love. Furthermore, the Inner Light, integral part of the Shabbat gift, vibrates most intensely within us on Shabbat as we receive our additional soul on this day. Hence, that of the tefillin is no longer necessary.

Tsitsit, however, are worn on Shabbat, for the Surrounding Light has still to be drawn down. Thus, in the Shabbat evening prayers, we ask for God to spread over us the shelter of His peace, suggestive of the Surrounding Light.

I HAVE SANCTIFIED YOU

The process of drawing of Inner and Surrounding Lights can also be found in the Jewish marriage ceremony. The union is first sanctified through the blessing over wine. As with the *kiddush* recited over wine on eve of Shabbat, this sanctification draws down the heavenly Inner Light. The union is then completed with blessings pronounced under the wedding canopy—a tallit spread out over the bride and groom—thus drawing down the Surrounding Light over the newlyweds.

The daily donning of tefillin recalls the sanctification of the marriage union. Indeed, as men wrap the strap of the hand tefillin around the middle finger of their left hand in the form of a wedding ring, they recite:

I will make you My bride forever. I will make you My bride with righteousness, with justice, with kindness and with mercy. I will make you My bride with faith. Then you will know God.[18]

When men wrap themselves in a tallit during their morning prayers they are drawing down upon themselves the shelter of Surrounding Light whose protection will help them reach the soul-union toward the end of prayer. In contrast, the light of the tefillin will help them to hold on to the Divine energy they experience in the union for the coming day.*

* To Gabriel Pinchas, may He always help you to draw the qualities of fire and strength implicit in your name to enhance the honor of His Name.

15

"Seven Perfect Sabbaths"

O N THE SECOND DAY OF PASSOVER, an *Omer*/measure of barley was brought as an offering into the sanctuary of the Temple. The *cohen*/priest would wave the Omer of barley in each direction as a reminder that the whole world is God's, then raise it and lower it as a reminder that the highest and lowest creations are His subjects.

There is a separate mitsvah, in force even today, to "count the Omer"; namely, to count the days from the day of the Omer offering until the festival of Shavuot. We count the forty-nine days to prepare ourselves for Shavuot, the festival that marks the day Israel received the Torah. Each day counted marks a further step away from the defilement of Egypt and a step toward spiritual purity, toward being worthy of receiving the Torah.[1]

> You shall count seven perfect Sabbaths from the day following the [Passover] holiday [literally: the Shabbat] when you brought the Omer as a wave offering, until the day after the seventh Shabbat, when there will be [a total of] fifty days. [On that fiftieth day] you may present new grain [two loaves of bread] as a meal offering to God.
> —Leviticus 23:15–16

The mention of "Shabbat" in the verses about the Omer is puzzling. Why does the Torah refer to the first day of the Passover holiday as Shabbat, and to the seven weeks between Pesach and Shavuot as seven perfect Sabbaths?

The Torah is emphasizing that the beginning of the Omer period, marked by the barley offering, as well as its end, with the offering of the two loaves of bread, are connected to the concept of Shabbat. The purpose of the Omer period is to reach a Shabbat state of consciousness, where the Divine Presence can be clearly discerned by our senses.[2]

UPROOTING EVIL

The *Zohar* teaches that on the first night of Passover, the Israelites did not yet reach a total state of purity. Some degree of the defilement of Egypt was still attached to

76

them. They therefore had to count seven weeks to prepare themselves for the soul-union that would take place on Shavuot, just as a woman whose menses have ended counts seven days of purity before she immerses herself in a *mikveh*/ritual bath and be permitted to her husband.

We may ask, How is it possible that the Israelites were not sufficiently pure? Surely there was no impurity in them on Passover night when they came into direct contact with the very Source of purity!

True, as long as the Divine splendor reigned manifestly, no defilement could be present. Still, the only reason evil lost its grip on Passover night was the overwhelming power of the Divine revelation. Thus, God revealed His Divine Light to Israel in a gesture of lovingkindness, not because Israel had merited it, but the moment the revelation ceased, evil was able to regain its grip.

Such is the power of free will that God built into Creation. To allow us to recover from the Egyptian ordeal, God temporarily removed the power of evil. God then allowed evil to return, for the only way to obliterate evil permanently is for us to fight and conquer it. Although the holiness the Israelites reached on the night of Passover was complete, it evaporated after that moment of passionate attachment because the holiness came as a gift and there was no inherent base of personal effort to hold it.

The purifying effect of Passover is similar to that of Shabbat. Both have the purpose to bring holiness to the Community of Israel, as it is written, "Keep My Sabbaths, for it is holy to you,"[3] namely, "for it brings you holiness." The light of Shabbat shines down so intensely that its holiness disperses the power of evil. The light forces the evil to lose its grip on Israel despite the defilement that still clings to us if we have not yet completed our self-improvement.

However, to retain this light after Shabbat requires more than the most meticulous Torah observance. As long as a person has not completed his work of self-growth, he is unable to experience God's splendor. It is important to realize that rejecting the promptings of our evil impulse without actually getting rid of the impulse is like pressing down on a springboard: the root of the defilement remains and has the power to regenerate itself.[4]

The festivals give Israel the special energy needed to uproot the source of defilement and evil within us. The festivals are referred to as "days appointed for holiness" because they are the means of having the holiness dwell on us perpetually. The holiness of Shabbat that comes after a festival will not have to leave with the onset of the weekdays; it will remain to inspire us permanently. A person can then build up his level of holiness and consequent closeness to God from Shabbat to Shabbat without limitations.

The sages say that those who desecrate the festivals, thinking that they get enough holiness through Shabbat, are like those who ask for water when they lack a vessel to contain it. Only with the special energy of the festivals assisting us to remove the spring-back effect of impurity will we be able to create space inside ourselves and be able to absorb the holiness that God gives on Shabbat.

The holiness that we feel on Passover is, like that of our ancestors at the time of the Exodus, fleeting, because it dwells within us together with the roots of our character flaws, which are ready to spring back at any moment.

On the first day of Passover, the day of the Exodus, the power of holiness shone in all its splendor: God had removed the source of concealment of His Presence in the world in order to establish His love relationship with Israel.

He did, however, leave a residue of these negative forces inside Israel, so that the people themselves would work on uprooting evil throughout the Omer period between Passover and Shavuot. They had the opportunity of removing a different part of these forces on each day of the Omer period with the help of a special energy available on these days.

The Ari explains that the light which flooded Israel on the first day of Passover with a total revelation is the source of the Divine luminous energy that we may draw on each of the forty-nine days of the Omer period. Its initial concentrated form, deployed for the redemption, was due to the opening on that first Passover day of the fifty gates of understanding. The fifty gates represent the highest level of human perception.

Although each of the fifty Sabbaths of the year opens one of these gates, on the festival of Passover, which has the characteristics of Shabbat, all fifty gates open. Hence, it is precisely as the Torah gives us the commandment of the Omer that it informs us of the Shabbat quality of Passover. We are reminded that on each of the forty-nine days it is within our reach to open one of the fifty gates by working on our character flaws.

We explained earlier that Shabbat is the root of the six days that follow; the amount of holiness that we have gathered on Shabbat—product of our Divine service of the previous week—will be our reserve of Divine energy for the coming weekdays. Kabbalah stresses that in the same way, each of the days of the Omer period is the root of one of the Sabbaths of the year.

Since Shabbat is the source nourishing the six weekdays, we can say that the days of the Omer period are the root of the entire year. The level of Torah observance and self-improvement we exhibit during the Omer period will therefore be a determining factor in the goals we attain throughout the following year.

Consequently, the Omer period is for us, as it was for our ancestors, the most appropriate time for introspection. We must first attempt to identify and then to rectify our character flaws. We want to empty ourselves of our negative traits in order to become vessels for the Divine light.

The purification we undergo works on four levels. Physically, we are no longer slaves to our base instincts. Emotionally, we are no longer filled with negative and destructive emotions. Intellectually, all confusion is gone, leaving us with clarity of mind. Spiritually, we feel the closeness of God in all facets of our lives.

INHERITING THE LAND

Our sages taught:

Do not underestimate the mitsvah of Omer, for it is through this mitsvah that Abraham merited to inherit the land, as it is written, "[I shall give . . . the whole land of

Canaan . . . to you and your descendants after you. . . .] As for you, you shall observe
My covenant" (Genesis 17:9). This refers to the mitsvah of Omer.
                                                    –*Vayikra Rabbah* 28:6

A question arises. The verse quoted is clearly referring to the *brit milah*/covenant of
circumcision. Why does the Midrash say it is referring to the Omer?

The purpose of circumcision is to remove from ourselves the capacity to sin, represented by the foreskin. The essence of *milah*, like Omer, is uprooting the sources of
defilement in our nature.

Through the mitsvah of circumcision, Abraham acquired the land of Israel,
whose unique holiness distinguishes it from the rest of the world. "You are a land not
cleansed, nor rained upon in a day of wrath."[5] When the Great Flood of Noah's time
uprooted the material tendencies that led man to sin, the waters of Divine wrath did
not submerge the Holy Land, for the roots of evil were not to be found there.

Kabbalah teaches that the commandment of the Omer is a subtle warning against
the misuse of sexual energy, referred to as *pegam habrit*/flaw of the circumcision. The
proper use of sexual energy involves the sanctity of the marriage bond and abstinence
from all forbidden relationships, including those not sanctified by marriage.

Through *milah* God was establishing the fact that the history of this nation would
transpire on a level that transcends the mere physical. Rabbi Kaplan teaches:

> Ultimately, the greatest aphrodisiac between a man and a woman is love. What cre-
> ates the greatest pleasure between spouses is a very deep emotional and spiritual love
> between them. This is the one thing that the foreskin diminishes, the capacity for
> spiritual love, but the circumcision enhances that very much. In the end, the physical
> aspect of the relationship is also heightened, but it becomes much purer.

> [Sex] represents one the greatest human pleasures that exists. Pleasure can be good
> or evil, as it can lead into either direction. Through the *milah*/circumcision, we
> remove the [physical] barrier from our pleasure experience, and therefore our desire
> for pleasure becomes pure holiness. Sexual desire is the one thing that is most often
> responsible for leading a person away from God.[6]

On the other hand, when it is sanctified by marriage and by observance of the laws of
family purity, sex becomes Godly.

Approaching Shavuot

We have seen how with the Omer, as with *milah*, we cut away the roots of evil within
us. When we fulfill God's will by making good use of the Omer period, we create
space within ourselves to receive the gift of holiness that He longs to give us. For when
a person struggles to uproot his personality flaws, God grants him His holiness as a
gift.

In the end, God leads him upon the path that he desires to follow; causes His holiness to rest upon man, thus enabling man to maintain a constant intimacy with Him.
Where man's nature hinders him, God will assist him.[7]

If, during the *Omer* period, we struggle to purify ourselves from the shell of impurity that blocks God's radiance, on Shavuot the screen will be torn asunder, as it was for our ancestors at the foot of Mount Sinai.*

* This chapter is dedicated to the memory of Eliezer Shlezinger, z"l, whose eighteenth and last birthday was on the forty-third day of the Omer. Eliezer was murdered by an Arab a few days after Shavuot. Despite his early age, Eliezer had grown to a degree of piety that is rarely seen in our time. Shortly before his death, he inscribed in his journal where he gave himself grades for his Divine service of each day: "Shavuot is coming; I am not ready yet."

16

"We Will Do and We Will Hear"

> Behold, days are coming, says the Lord God, and I will send famine into the land, not
> a famine for bread nor a thirst for water, but to hear the word of the Lord.
>
> —Amos 8:11

NAME OF THE FESTIVAL

THE FESTIVAL CONCLUDING THE FORTY-NINE DAYS of the Omer is most commonly known as *Shavuot*/the Festival of Weeks.

It is important to note that this name, Shavuot, seems not to to be related to the essence of the day, as it the case with other holidays. For instance, we refer to Passover as the Festival of *Matsot*, because the mitsvah of the day is to partake of the bread that our ancestors ate when they left Egypt. *Sukkot* literally means "booths," for during this holiday we dwell in booths as did our ancestors in the desert. *Rosh Hashanah,* the New Year, is known as a day of *Teruah*/Calling, because of the commandment of blowing the *shofar*/ram's horn. *Yom Kippur* owes its name to the atonement that occurs on that day.

The name *Shavuot,* however, refers to the time period *preceding* the festival and the counting of seven weeks; whereas the names *Atseret*/Assembly, or *Bikurim*/"Day of First Fruits," which describe the day itself, are less common.

There are two points to consider:

1. The Torah does not describe Shavuot as the day of the Giving of the Torah.
2. The Torah sets no specific date for the holiday. It only describes it as occurring on the fiftieth day after Passover.

From all this, we can conclude that the most important aspect of Shavuot is that, on this day, we finish counting the period of seven weeks. Therefore, the holiness of the day is related to the end of the counting period. What, then, is the spiritual significance of these seven weeks?

MEANING OF THE FESTIVAL

The *Zohar* compares the period of seven weeks from Pesach to Shavuot to the seven clean days that a woman must await after her monthly menses. These days are concluded by her immersion into a *mikveh*, a gathering of pure water that reestablishes her link with the Edenic state. Afterward, she is reunited with her husband. The separation from the beginning of her menses until immersion in a mikveh is as important for the marriage bond as the days of reunion themselves, in the sense that the longing for each other during the time brings about a monthly renewal of their relationship.[1] Furthermore, it is an earthly model of the longing that the Community of Israel experiences for her Companion of the soul.

The period of Israel's purification that enabled them to experience the Sinaitic revelation exactly reflects this process. Only after the Jewish people counted seven weeks from the time they left Egypt could they be united with their Beloved. On the fiftieth day they were as pure as the ministering angels; they had reached the level of "godlike beings" over whom the Angel of Death had no control.[2] At this time, they were lifted up to the level of "children of the Most High."

Therefore the name Shavuot is related to the seven weeks Israel counted before experiencing union with the Holy One. It captured the essence of the festival, for this period of time was needed by the Community of Israel to cleanse itself of the impurity of Egypt that had prevented their bond with the Source of Light.

LEAVEN IN THE DOUGH

The *Zohar* teaches that the Egyptians' domination over the Israelites subjected the latter to the temptations of their evil inclination. Like leaven in the dough, the evil inclination enters man's consciousness and slowly spreads until all of a person is dominated by its influence. Hence, the leaven symbolizes the body and its temptations to indulge into illicit pleasures. For this reason, it was forbidden to bring leaven into the Temple as an offering.

On Shavuot however, two loaves of leavened bread were brought to the Temple, a tangible proof that even the leaven of the Israelites—their physicality—was now perfectly pure as a consequence of their efforts of self-improvement during the Omer period, and that no evil could hold sway over them. Hence, Shavuot's name of "time of the first fruits of the wheat harvest."

Therefore, on Shavuot, Israel rejoices in their spiritual achievement by ceasing from work and enjoying festive meals. This is hinted at in the name *Atseret*/general gathering. Thus, the Torah does not refer to Shavuot as the festival of the Giving of the Torah because the fact that Israel received the Torah on this day was a consequence of the high level of purity they had achieved.

Let us pay closer attention to the process of purification the people of Israel underwent in the wilderness, as well as to the fruits of their labor.

PERCEIVING THE TORAH

Our sages taught that at the time of the Exodus the Israelites had fallen into a state of impurity so dense that, had they remained there another moment, it would have been impossible for them to ever escape. The power of evil would have had such a grasp on them that they would have been unable to repent.

At the beginning of the redemption, God dealt a powerful blow to the system of evil that Egypt embodied. The first stage was the death of the Egyptian firstborn. The second stage was the destruction of Pharaoh and his army at the Red Sea.[3] The clouds of impurity that blocked Israel's perception of God were now removed, and they were able to experience spiritual revelation.

However, in order to merit the ecstatic intimacy with God that awaited them at Sinai, they had to further purify their bodies during the seven weeks of the Omer. An essential part of this purification involved the food they would eat. They would have to eat and drink in a state of holiness like that of the Patriarchs, who experienced deep spiritual insights even before the Torah was given. It is said of Abraham that his kidneys were like two wellsprings of Torah wisdom. Later, King David was to sing, "Your Torah is in my innards."[4]

To eat in holiness, one must maintain a level of God-consciousness throughout the meal. This is done by thinking that the holy sparks of life which give existence to the food or drink, as well as the pleasure of our taste buds, stem directly from the Creator. When we intend to serve God with the energy we acquire, these Divine sparks become released into our system as we consume our food. We can then elevate the spark to its source through the blessing we pronounce before partaking of the food.

As the sixteenth-century kabbalist Rabbi Eliahu de Vidas expounds in his *Beginning of Wisdom*, because of the screen of the liver where it dwells, the *nefesh* soul is deprived of its former enjoyment of the Divine radiance. The blessing man pronounces before eating gives spiritual sustenance to his *nefesh* soul, so that it can absorb the heavenly energy he draws down to himself as he eats.

A person who eats and drinks in this manner is serving God with all his being. Needless to say, it requires extensive efforts to refine one's physicality. Israel, after many generations of bondage, was not able to perform this task. God helped them by sending heavenly *manna* and providing water from a miraculous well known as Miriam's well, since its life-giving waters were in her merit.

After seven weeks in the desert, the Israelites reached a level of purity that made them fit to receive the Torah. Thus, we say in the Passover Haggadah:

> If He had brought us to Mt Sinai without giving us the Torah it would have been enough.

The kabbalists understand this as an expression of gratitude to God over Israel's newly acquired ability to perceive the Torah. For the Torah was not given until they had acquired by themselves the necessary level of consciousness. Nevertheless, at the very moment when their perception of Torah spontaneously arose from within themselves, God gave it to them as a gift.

"WE WILL DO AND WE WILL HEAR"

Thus there are two pathways to the Torah—perceiving it from within, or receiving it from above. According to the Ari, these define the relationship between the days of the Omer period and Shavuot. On each of the fifty days, the Israelites purified their minds another level in order to draw an additional measure of the lofty state of *mochin*/consciousness needed to perceive the Torah. On the other hand, by counting seven weeks, corresponding to a woman's seven pure days, they prepared themselves to receive the Torah from above, as a gift.

In the soul-union that occurred on the fiftieth day, God gave them the twenty-two Hebrew letters that had served to write the Torah, enabling Israel to internalize them. Hence the two wheat loaves Israel that would later on offer at the Temple on this day, for the numeric value of the Hebrew word for wheat, *chitah*, is twenty-two, the number of letters of the Hebrew alphabet.

How does the perception of the Torah differ from its reception?

When a man sanctifies the various aspects of his physicality—eating, drinking, sexual impulse—his intellect is naturally sharpened and he can draw illumination from the spiritual realm. As a result, he gains ever deeper Torah insights and is able to understand the inner reasons behind the commandments. He can then come to observe them as a result of his perception alone.

In contrast, the Torah was given as a result of the soul-union between God and the Jewish people. Even though the receiver has already acquired the perception of the Torah, a new aspect of this wisdom is given to him through *devekut* and soul-union.

Rashi explains that before the Ten Commandments were given, God asked Moses to come up to the mountain. Upon his descent, Moses wrote on a scroll the "Book of the Covenant," all the commandments from Genesis until this point in the Book of Exodus, as God had explained to him. The following morning, Moses gathered the Israelites to read it to them. Yet, *before* the actual reading, Israel exclaimed, "We will keep every word that God has spoken."[5] For, although they had not yet heard the Divine message, they were already aware of its contents because of their direct perception of the Torah.

After reading this book, Moses brought the people into a covenant with God. He asked twelve young men, one from each tribe, to sacrifice oxen according to God's instructions.

The biblical account continues,

> Moses took half the blood [of these offerings], and put it into large bowls. The other half he sprinkled on the altar.[6]

The blood of the Covenant was split exactly in two, half to be sprinkled on the altar and half on the people. The equality of the halves hinted at the love bond that was to be formed: the bond was to be on an equal basis. The Israelites then understood that there was something higher than merely intuiting the Torah; they realized that the Torah is a gift, resulting from the soul-union between their collective souls and the Creator.[7]

We find in the biblical text allusions supporting the distinction between the level of Torah wisdom stemming from perception and that which is the product of the soul-union. The laws that Moses was given to set before the people as recorded in the Book of the Covenant are devoid of any suggestion of intimacy and merely show the aspect of Torah perception.[8] In contrast, the biblical references to the ensuing ceremony in which this Covenant was sealed with blood and recorded for future generations do justify the kabbalists' reading of *devekut* and *yichud*/soul-union.[9]

The kabbalists thus infer that the Israelites' "We will do and we will hear all that God has declared" means that rather than focusing on receiving a Torah they were already able to perceive, they desired to have access to the Torah from the aspect of soul-union, where the main goal longed for is the passionate attachment to the Creator.

Another goal, mentioned by the *Maggid*, the angel who came to teach Rabbi Joseph Karo (1488–1575), compiler of the *Code of Jewish Law,* is that "hearing" what they already knew would help them submit their bodies to the discipline of Torah observance.[10]

We can hear the same yearning in King Solomon's Song of Songs:

> O that He would kiss me with the kisses of His mouth! Your spiritual love is far more precious to me than wine [all the bodily pleasures and stimulants].[11]

The people Israel of all generations want to hear from God once again the innermost secrets of His Torah as they did at Sinai, namely, in the form of "a kiss," a revelation stemming from their passionate attachment, and not only as an intellectual perception. Hence the statement "For Your spiritual love is far more precious to me than wine"; in other words, "the delight experienced from the passionate attachment to God is far more intense than that derived from Torah study as a mere intellectual stimulation."

As he heard their exclamation, "We will do and we will hear," Moses sprinkled over them half the blood to show them that they would indeed become the "Community of Israel, His Companion of the soul." In order to reach that level, however, they had purified themselves over the previous seven weeks by letting go of anything that would prevent them from experiencing the direct contact with their Creator.

This helps us understand a talmudic teaching:

> When Israel declared, "we will do and we will hear," a heavenly Voice asked: Who revealed to My children this secret safeguarded by the ministering angels?[12]

Up until the Giving of the Torah, the secret of the soul-union had been known only to the ministering angels and to those individuals who had reached that lofty level. Yet now there was an entire nation who, not satisfied with a mere intellectual perception of the Torah, longed to experience the intimacy of "hearing" their Creator.

THE FESTIVAL OF SHAVUOT

As we have seen, there are two ways of receiving the Torah: (1) by drawing upon oneself ever higher levels of consciousness throughout the Omer period, and (2) receiving it as a gift by experiencing a soul-union after counting seven weeks of purity.

We can now see why the Torah does not explicitly call Shavuot the time of the "Giving of the Torah." The Torah was both given and received. Yet, since the gift was the product of the intimate union between God and Israel, it had to retain an aura of secrecy and could not be mentioned openly. Consequently, this is one of the mysteries of the Torah that the sages have only alluded to in their oral teachings.

The Torah has the power to purify a person to the degree that he can become like an angel. Then he is worthy of receiving the Torah as a gift and of gaining access to its deepest secrets. For even though the Torah was already given to us at Mount Sinai, still, the illumination returns every year at this time. If we use the days of the Omer period to rise beyond ourselves in holiness and purity—each person according to his efforts—we can receive the light of the Torah as our ancestors did at Sinai.

17

Children of the Living God

I N CONTRAST WITH THE SHABBAT AMIDAH, which is different in the evening, morning, and afternoon, in the three festivals—Pesach, Shavuot, and Sukkot—the same Amidah is repeated in the three prayers of the day. Each festival Amidah includes one phrase that can attune us to the special time being celebrated: Sukkot is identified as the "time of our rejoicing," Pesach as the "time of our freedom," and Shavuot as the "time of the Giving of our Torah."

The commentators wonder about the discrepancy between the prayer book and the Torah, since the latter does not link Shavuot with the Giving of the Torah while the former does.

THE ESSENCE OF THE TORAH: THE MITSVOT

After Israel heard the Ten Commandments, God said to Moses,

> Come up to Me, to the mountain, and remain there. I will give you the stone tablets, the Torah and the commandments that I have written for [the people's] instruction.[1]

Moses was to spend forty days on the mountain in order to learn every detail of the 613 mitsvot/commandments, the Written Torah, and the Oral Law (later recorded as the Talmud and the Midrash). In the end he would bring down the Tablets containing the Ten Commandments. These Tablets that God gave to Israel were to teach them what they needed to do in order to establish their intimate relationship with Him.

All 613 mitsvot are included in the Ten Commandments,[2] and each of the 613 has its root in a word of the Ten.[3] The Zohar's teaching that the 613 mitsvot are as many ways of acquiring passionate attachment to the Most High explains the meaning of the Mishnah,

> The Holy One, blessed be He, wishing to purify Israel, magnified for them the Torah and its commandments.[4]

The goal of God's wish to "purify Israel" is not to increase their reward in the world to come, but rather to help them reach the level of *devekut* in this world.

We have seen that the Hebrew word *mitsvah* comes from a root that means "to bind." A mitsvah is a type of joining in the sense that it is a means of integrating the physical world with the higher spheres. When we observe a commandment, God reaching out for us comes together with our ability to experience Him.[5] To that end, God gave us a number of commandments that equal the number of parts in the body. Of the 613, 248 mitsvot relate to physical activities that parallel the parts of the body performing them, and 365 mitsvot involve transgressions to be avoided, that are counterpart of the nerves and sinews.

Linking body parts with commandments seems like a radical idea, but so did the interconnection between mind and body or the effects of mind states on illnesses which were a "scientific heresy" until fairly recently. And yet, currently, the field of mind-body medicine is a rapidly expanding subject of research and practice. The theory of organ consciousness prevalent in "alternative medicine" takes on a new light when we understand the kabbalistic teaching that when man engages himself to observe the mitsvot with love, and sees the transgressions as acts that disrupt the union with the Beloved, his body parts become vessels so refined by God's light that their physicality itself acquires the quality of light.[6]

One may object, however, as Maimonides does, that man cannot be held responsible over something he has not taken upon himself consciously. How did Israel's spontaneous outburst "We will do and we will hear" make them accountable for the mitsvot since they did not know what they were accepting?

The *Zohar* clarifies that through their exclamation the people of Israel were engaging themselves to nurture the flame of their passionate attachment to Him, and be "a kingdom of priests and a holy nation,"[7] in accord with the Divine wish. To them, the mitsvot were not unwanted yokes, but tools that would help them fulfill their yearning for *devekut*. As such, they welcomed their large number: the more mitsvot, the higher their chance to regain access to this treasured bond.

We derive from the *Zohar* that the culmination of Shavuot is Israel's *devekut* with the Most High. Thus, Rashi explains that the Song of Songs' reference to "His wedding day"[8] points to the Sinai experience—that is, Shavuot.

Through marriage, a man and a woman get close to each other in a bond in which one completes the other. Similarly, in the spiritual dimension, the Torah was given to Israel in Sinai on the sixth of the month *Sivan* as a series of instructions to help them maintain the passionate attachment of their bond.

Given this aspect of Shavuot, how can one think that the sages instituted the festival in order to commemorate the giving of the instructions that permitted Israel's bond to their Creator?

We may understand the sages' decision to refer to the covert meaning of Shavuot only by allusion. Yet, if Shavuot was really "His wedding day"—the day in which the Community of Israel became His Companion of the soul—why did they identify the festival with the Giving of the Torah in the Amidah prayer?

HEART VERSUS INTELLECT

Before receiving the Torah, the Israelites had purified their essence throughout the days of the Omer. Their physicality was so refined that they could now attain an intimate bond with the Creator, as it were, on an equal basis.

The two aspects of the state of *devekut* attained by the Israelites at the Giving of the Torah have two expressions: one is centered on the heart and the other is based on the intellect. The *devekut* of the heart's thoughts allows one to cleave to the Holy One with a "fiery love, a flame of the Divine." In this case the 613 mitsvot are instructions on how to hold on to this ethereal bond. It is important to clarify, however, that only one who has invested many years in his Torah studies can reach this *devekut* of the heart and be aware of all the nuances involved in the fulfillment of each commandment.

The early kabbalist Rabbi Joseph Gikatalia (1248–1323) explains that one who attains this quality of bond is assured that it will continue to grow beyond the physical death of his body. The talmudic sages ask, "Is it possible to bind oneself to the Living God? Isn't God like a consuming fire?"

It is indeed possible to refine the physical body until it acquires the purity of the sapphire of the Second Tablets on which were engraved the Ten Commandments hinting to the 613.[9] When man's entire body has become a pure vessel ready to contain the light, he is now able to cleave to his Maker. For him, God's "consuming fire" is the ecstatic *oneg*/delight spreading in all the parts of his body, reaching beyond the body to the soul.

This is the *devekut* of the soul for the Holy One in which the person is consumed by love. The fusing of body and soul experienced by one who feels sick with a longing that burns like a fire blazing within may be referred to as "Heaven on Earth." Indeed, what is the idea of the Garden of Eden other than a space where the delight of the body is that of the soul, a space where one can hear the angel's song?[10]

Not every person merits attaining the full level of *devekut* of "my soul is sick for your love," however.[11]

Hence, one who does not feel the *devekut* of the heart through the way in which he fulfills the commandments may aim for the *devekut* of the intellect by resorting to his Torah studies. In the *devekut* of the intellect, one whose mind dwells on his Torah studies day and night draws close to the Creator through His attachment to the wisdom of the Torah and to the sages and their disciples who expounded upon it.

When Torah study forms the basis of one's *devekut*, the person cleaves to the Torah as the product of the Divine intellect, and as a result, becomes attached to God Himself. Thus, while all 613 are instructions on how to maintain one's level of *devekut*, Torah study has in this case an end in itself.

One may study Torah to acquire knowledge. Even though such study will not lead to the inner dimension of the Torah, one is still fulfilling the commandment to study. Yet, if the study itself leads to *devekut*, one enjoys the effort involved in understanding the Torah's depth, knowing that the fruit of this mental struggle will be greater attachment to the Divine.

When the angels realized that God wanted to give man the Torah, they complained:

> What is man that You should remember him, and the son of man that You should be mindful of him?[12]

The angels claimed that the Torah, due to its lofty essence, was fit only for angels, not for lowly man.

Moses was aware of the intrinsic nature of his flock as only a faithful shepherd could be, and thus knew that the possibility of their fall was very real. He therefore answered the claim of the angels by showing them that the Torah had to be given to Israel even if they fell from their present state of consciousness, for only through the Torah would they be able to elevate themselves and cleave to the Source of life, returning to their level as angels.

This understanding of the two forms of *devekut* explains the discrepancy between the definition of Shavuot found in the Torah and of that in the prayer book. We have seen that the name *Shavuot*/weeks was ascribed to the festival as a hint leading to the counting of seven weeks of purity after which Israel became God's Companion of the soul.

Foreseeing that in later generations it would become increasingly difficult for the Jewish people to attain the level of *devekut* of the Israelites at Sinai, the sages identified Shavuot with "the time of the Giving of the Torah" in the Amidah prayer. This new definition of the festival was to remind Israel that delving into the intricacies of the Torah would help them regain their former closeness.

ENTERING THE "HOUSE OF WINE"

Love-sick Israel exclaims in the Song of Songs:

> He has brought me to the House of Wine, and His banner over me is love.[13]

The "banner of love" found in the "House of Wine" hints to the *devekut* Israel experienced at Sinai at the Giving of the Torah, which they ever try to recapture. The Hebrew word for wine, *yayin*, has the same numerical value as the word *sod*/mystery, leading us to understand that by dwelling in the mysteries of the Torah we may attain an experiential perception of God's love.

During the times in which man's evil inclination cools his love for God, making it harder for him to perform the service of the heart, he should dwell in the mysteries of the Torah; this particular form of Torah study infuses the heart with a fire of love of such intensity that the water of the delights offered by the evil impulse is unable to dim it. As the verse says,

> Love is strong as death. . . . Love's sparks are fiery coals, a flame of the Divine. Many waters cannot extinguish love.[14]

Commenting on the *Zohar*, the Ari teaches that the inner teachings of the Torah reveal the love and closeness binding the Creator and the Community of Israel, His Companion of the soul.

As long as the Temple stood, man had a direct contact with the Divine Majesty that constantly increased his awe of the Creator. After the destruction of the Temple, however, this direct bond would have to be recaptured by allowing man to "become intoxicated" by peeking into the depths of the Divine love as revealed by the esoteric tradition.

Hence, immediately after the destruction, Rabbi Shimon bar Yochay received the permission to divulge some of these mysteries,[15] in particular that of the soul-union between the Creator and the collective souls of Israel caused by each mitsvah and festival. It is the knowledge that each mitsvah observed brings about the desired soul-union that sets the heart of each member of the Community of Israel ablaze with a love of "fiery coals, a flame of the Divine."

A PEOPLE OF EXTREMES[16]

The Sinai experience led Israel to understand that beyond the Torah's revealed aspect, there was a secret tradition mapping its inner dimension. They expressed their yearning to receive this other aspect of Torah as well, since it was there that they would always find access to God's love. The Holy One then opened their eyes to the light of the Torah mysteries, which prompted them to exclaim,

He has brought me to the House of Wine, and His banner over me is love.

The Talmud teaches that a transgression annuls a mitsvah, but does not cancel the Torah: as it is written, "many waters cannot extinguish love." Rashi explains that the "many waters" of sin may not extinguish the fire of the Torah, referred to as "love."

The bond of love between the Most High and the Community of Israel cannot be broken, for the house of wine of the Torah mysteries reveals God's love to Israel, and as a result, their own love for Him is aroused. This double bond of love is so powerful that no transgression can break it. As the verse says, "love covers all transgressions."

A person who commits a transgression is invaded by a sense of shame toward his Maker that turns into fear of Divine retribution. He becomes despondent, as we can understand from the reaction of the Israelites when faced with the Divine wrath:

The people began to mourn. They stopped wearing jewelry.[17]

Kabbalah explains that the reason the evil inclination wants to cause Israel to fall away from truth lies in the depression that overcomes the person as the immediate consequence of a transgression. This depression occurs only in the initial stages, however; a person who continues to transgress soon becomes invaded by an insensitivity to the spiritual dimension. He no longer feels the harm that the transgressions inflict upon his soul and as a result may continue his present behavior because he is oblivious of the consequences.

Israel is traditionally compared to the moon; as such the people's rising and falling is determined by their degree of closeness to the Creator. When they struggle to elevate themselves, they are illuminated by the radiant light of the Giver and can rise to the very heavens, but by the same token, when they fall, they can reach rock bottom with record speed. A vivid example of Israel's ability to fall is the Golden Calf, made a mere forty days after the union of Sinai.

This tendency for extremes can be understood in terms of the nature of the covenant to which they bound themselves. When the Knower of all secrets sees that they are struggling to get close to Him in His unequivocal terms, He allows His light to shine unrestrictedly.

In contrast, when their efforts diminish and they begin to slip, God, to the same extent, begins to hide His face, to conceal His light. They become subject to the influence of their evil inclination. At this point, Israel falls to the dust.

Yet, if a person falls into error, but reacts before his feelings start to deaden and enters the "house of wine" where he is exposed to God's love, his own love for the Holy One will be aroused once again. As a result, he will no longer be prevented from approaching the Beloved, even though he still feels tainted by the error he committed.

When a person is in contact with the immensity of God's love, it is impossible to remain estranged, for while in this space, one realizes that life without passionate attachment to the Living God may not be called living. This is the secret teaching of the verse,

Only you, the ones who remained attached to God your Lord, are all alive today.[18]

By toiling to reveal the inner dimension of the Torah, one is able to perceive the awesome closeness of the Community of Israel, children of the Living God, to their Divine Companion of the soul. At this point, one is dwelling under the "banner of His love," in the "love stronger than death" of the Song of Songs.

PART THREE

THE SECOND TABLETS

18
Servant, Child, or Soul-Companion?

O N SHAVUOT, THE PEOPLE OF ISRAEL chose to receive the Torah as "the Community of Israel, His Companion of the soul," rather than as servants or children. As the New Year approaches, each one of us must choose the level of his Divine service anew.

THE SERVANT[1]

Rosh Hashanah is not only the first day of the new Jewish year; it is the day on which we reestablish our relationship with God. Thus, we must decide what kind of relationship we want and aim our Divine service at attaining it.

There are three basic levels of relationship: as servant, child, or Companion of the soul. A *tsadik* relates to God on all three.

The faithful servant does what his master requests with utmost efficiency, whether fulfilling commandments or avoiding transgressions. Nevertheless, because he is a servant, his main motivation is to fulfill his obligation to his master. As God's servant, our Divine service is in the same manner a fulfillment of our obligation, even though we dedicate ourselves with utmost good will.

The level of dedication that we devote to our service determines the quality of the latter. For instance, a man may fulfill his duty to study Torah by sitting at home after work, even though he may feel his attention waning. In contrast, he may make an attempt to improve the quality of his Torah study by going in the evening to a talmudic academy despite a tiring day, so that he can benefit from the exchange with a study partner.

A woman who sees herself as God's servant will observe the Jewish laws of modesty that call for her to wear clothes covering her collar-bone, elbows, and knees and

95

to cover her hair if she is married. Yet, she may adopt this gear as a uniform one wears in order to avoid incurring the master's wrath, or as a projection of her real "self," the luminous Divine energy she draws down with her intention to give pleasure to the Beloved through her style of dress.

In the case of the latter, the woman's careful selection of clothes elevates her beyond the level of servant and constitutes a precious offering of love to her Maker. The initial feeling of frustration caused by her long-sleeved summer dresses and high-necked evening gowns will soon give way as she begins to experience God's promise of dwelling within those who offer Him their very essence.

The levels of child and Companion of the soul are higher than that of servant, but there is an aspect of the servant that is absent in the other two levels: God's servant lowers himself to the place of evil and from there dedicates himself to work for his Maker. Hence, the higher levels can be developed even after departing this world, but the level of servant can be fulfilled only in this world.

As a servant, your energy is directed toward the active part of your Divine service through the commandments that you observe as your duty. Knowing that left to their own, your physical impulses will pull you away from your desired goal, you will struggle to master them and to elevate them into desire to cleave to God. The extent to which we become God's servants in our lifetime determines our ability to get ever closer to Him in the levels of child and soul-companion in the afterlife, when we are no longer bound by a physical body.

The Shabbat song *Yedid Nefesh*/Soul's Beloved captures the anguish of the true servant of God, aware that he should only "run swiftly" to do God's will rather than his own:[2]

> Soul's Beloved, Merciful Father, draw Your servant to do your will. Your servant will then run, as swiftly as a deer, to bow down before Your Majesty. Your love is sweeter to him than the drippings of the honeycomb and any other worldly delights![3]

In this stanza, the servant, aware that he is easily drawn by the forces of evil, fervently asks the Creator to draw him instead to the Divine will. A person may have the inner belief that God has not stopped loving him, but during the time that he is aroused by a physical temptation, he cannot be permeated by the keen delight of experiencing God.

Despite the struggle involved in controlling one's passions, "your servant will then run, as swiftly as a deer," and, as a result, "Your love will be sweeter to me than the drippings of the honeycomb and than any other worldly delight." The servant has attained a higher state of consciousness in which he is no longer slave to his evil desires and is able to experience the Divine love.

Thus, the Torah refers to Moses as a "servant of God," even though he clearly attained much higher levels of Divine service, to show the ultimate achievement of the servant. It is no wonder that when Moses died, God said to Joshua, "Moses My servant is dead," rather than identifying the Faithful Shepherd as "My brother and friend,"[4] alluding to the higher levels of relationship. Moses' aspect of servant was finished; he had refined his physicality to such an extent that the people could perceive the Divine glow emanating from him.[5]

THE CHILD

A person is considered completely righteous if he observes the commandments with the purpose of fulfilling God's will. Yet, it is also possible that you will long for a higher level of relationship. You may feel yourself as God's child. In this case, your sense of duty is transformed into one of profound love. Aware that the root of your soul is bound to your Father in Heaven, you will want to observe every commandment out of love and desire to attach yourself to your Father.

Like a child who appreciates his father and desires to please him, you draw on your intellect to internalize the subtleties of Torah observance, and use your emotions to do your service out of love rather from feeling a duty that could turn into routine.

Yedid Nefesh amplifies Israel's voice as God's child:

> Distinguished, Ancient One, may Your mercies be aroused now to pity the child of Your beloved [nation].

Even though I believe that You are loving and compassionate, I am unable to feel Your love as a Merciful Father. Nevertheless,

> I have yearned and hoped for so long to behold Your power in all its splendor! This is the sole desire of my heart, so please take pity now and do not conceal Yourself any longer!

The stanza ends with the poet's cry for God to let him feel the fatherly mercy for which he yearns.

THE COMPANION OF THE SOUL

You may long for a relationship with the Almighty even closer than that of a child: to be God's Companion of the soul." This is the highest level mentioned in the Torah: "You are a nation consecrated to God your Lord; . . . and God chose you . . . because of His love for you."[6] Our yearning for God is caused by God's very yearning for us. Kabbalah refers to this level of relating as the "Community of Israel, His Companion of the soul." We are wont to choose how close we want to be to God and to what extent we are ready for the consequent scrutiny, but from the Divine point of view, the choice is always the same: God can relate to His beloved people from the lofty third level only.[7] The special love with which God relates to Israel among all other nations is not the natural love that grows out of contact and sharing, but rather the choice love originating in the will of the One who loves, with no particular cause to explain it. It is a love that grows out of desire:

> It was not because you had greater numbers than all the nations that God (*chashak*) desired you and chose you; you are among the smallest of all the nations. It was because of God's love for you.[8]

In human terms, this is like a man's love for a woman, though there may be others more beautiful and finer than she. So is God's love for Israel, born of a simple desire for them. This feeling is expressed in the Song of Songs, which captures the love between the Holy One and the Community of Israel.

In contrast, the feeling of unrequited love is expressed in the Book of Hosea, the prophet who was told to marry a prostitute so that he could fully understand how it is to be filled with love for one whose thoughts are elsewhere,

> Go, love a woman, who although beloved to her companion, cheats on him.[9]

"Such is God's love for the Israelites," finishes the prophet, that is, if it can be said, such is God's anguish in His love for one who is willing to look into any spiritual tradition rather than her own.

There are times in which God relates to His people as servants, as during the Egyptian exile.[10] In other instances, God refers to them as His children, denoting the unconditional love of the father irrespective of the behavior of the child. Later, when they grew as a nation, toiling in prayers and Torah study for the sake of His love, God referred to them as "My brethren and companions,"[11] alluding to the third level of Companion of the soul.

These three levels are hinted at in the book of Deuteronomy:

> If you . . . love God, walk in all His ways, and attach yourself to Him.[12]

The commentators Ramban and Ibn Ezra point out that the verse mentions the level of attachment to God only after that of love. Hence, as servants, the people of Israel relate to their Maker with fear of Divine retribution; as children, with the love shared between father and child, and as the Community of Israel, His Companions of the soul, with passionate attachment.

Although the level of relating as "the Community of Israel, His Companions of the soul" is not clearly indicated in the five books of Moses, it is nevertheless alluded to. Whenever the text uses the word *cheshek*, denoting an emotion beyond love, it is referring to the bond of Companions of the soul.

We find in Deuteronomy:

> The heaven, the heaven of heaven, the earth and everything in it, all belong to God! Still, it was only with your ancestors that God *chashak*/developed a closeness. He loved them, and therefore chose you, their descendants, from among all the nations, just as the situation is today.[13]

The love between father and son is a strong, unconditional love, based upon pure lovingkindness. In contrast, the love between God and Israel is "strong as death, jealousy is cruel as the grave. Love's sparks are fiery coals, a flame of the Divine."[14] The fiery emotion binding soul-companions calls for a response in kind. God's words to the people, imparted by Moses before the nation entered the land, indicate His wish that they rise above the level of child to that of soul-companion.

The level of "the Community of Israel, His Companion of the soul," involves what is not specified in the Torah. Thus you are not a servant doing a job, nor a child acting out of love for his father; your motivating force is a love fused with *cheshek*/passion.

When striving to attain this highest level, you are no longer concerned with the notion of "self." You distance yourself from anything that will stress your material nature, such as any physical dependence. You want to purify all the parts of your body by exercising restraint, even regarding what is normally permitted but is known to bring man's physical lusts to the surface.

At this level, you will do anything to please God, Whom you love; you will go above and beyond what He asks of you. You will endeavor with all your might to learn from the sages, who have already reached that level of closeness and can teach how one pleases God and what distances Him.

As *Yedid Nefesh* puts it:

Please reveal Yourself now, My Beloved, and spread Your shelter of peace over me.
Illuminate the earth with Your glory so that we may delight and rejoice in You alone.
O Beloved, hurry, for the appointed time has come [to redeem us]. Be gracious to us
as in the days of old!

God's shelter of peace is the Divine Surrounding Light, whereas the earth is a symbol for the body. After man has succeeded in his struggle to be free, he is no longer the slave of his physical drives but God's servant by his own choice. As a result, he is able to experience the Divine love of a merciful father and of a Beloved of the soul, and he "delights and rejoices" in God alone. In this space, nothing matters other than the bond with the Beloved.

In response to those who do not limit themselves to what is explicitly asked of them, the King opens His treasures, bestowing both physical and spiritual wealth, "as water reflects a face back to a face."[15] Even the natural cravings of the body are silenced in the intensity of a person's search for God.

You Will Call Me *Ishi*

The level of Companion of the soul has two ramifications, one higher than the other. Hence, within the closeness of Companions of the soul, there is an even higher level, mentioned in God's message to His people through His prophet Hosea:

God said: "At that time you will call me Ishi and no longer will you call me Baali."
—Hosea 2:18

You shall worship Me out of love, not out of fear.

—Rashi

Ishi alludes to such a high degree of intimacy with the Divine that it cannot be expressed in any language other than Hebrew. It denotes a partnership in an ideal love relationship expressed by total devotion and commitment, where the intensity and excitement of the first encounter remain undiminished and the notion of self is no longer important. *Ishi* is the ultimate bond God seeks with Israel.

Baali literally means "my husband," but it may also be translated as "my master."

With His promise, "no longer will you call me *Baali*," God is alluding to the equality that was in potential since the offering of the blood halves at the Giving of the Torah.

The closest relationship that we may have in this world is one of passionate attachment, but there is always the threat of estrangement, like the union of a married couple that could possibly end with a divorce. In the *Ishi* relationship, however, there is no possibility of separation. Israel becomes part of God's essence forever.

The key to the *Ishi* relationship is connected with the concept of the reward as stated in the Shema, the prayer declaring God's unity, reminding him of the imperative to subordinate his very life to the Divine will.[16]

Paragraph 1:

Each one of you shall love Hashem your God with all your heart, with all your soul, and with all your might.[17]

Paragraph 2:

If all of you carefully obey My commandments, to love Hashem your God and to serve Him with all your hearts and with all your souls, then I will grant the fall and spring rains in your land at their proper time, so that you will harvest your grain, oil, and wine . . . and you will eat and be satisfied.[18]

There are several differences between the two paragraphs. In the first, we find the expression "with all your might," whereas in the second paragraph the phrase is missing. Also, the first paragraph is worded in the singular, the second in the plural. Finally, the second promises an earthly reward for serving God; the first does not.

Whereas both paragraphs express the way Israel attaches itself to God, the second addresses the entire people of Israel who were created to fulfill the Divine purpose of Creation. Rabbi Moshe Chayim Luzatto explains this as follows: God created the universe in order to bestow His goodness upon man. However, this goodness needed to be earned by man as a reward; for to receive it as charity would dampen man's delight.[19]

God therefore created the forces of evil to tempt man. By overcoming his evil inclination, man earns his spiritual reward. If he gives in to temptation, however, he denies God the pleasure of rewarding him. Israel's love of God and their Divine service brings about the fulfillment of God's desire to benefit Creation. It follows that God will "grant the fall and spring rains."

In the first paragraph of the Shema, however, God addresses the few individuals who are able to give themselves fully, with all their might, to the intimate bond with God, without any concern for reward. Their only goal is the passionate attachment to God.

An anecdote from the life of the Baal Shem Tov (1698–1760), founder of Chasidism, provides an illustration. An action of his inadvertently caused damage in the heavenly realms. He soon became aware that, as a result, he had lost his share in the world to come. His reaction was one of boundless joy. "Now," he said to his disciples, "I can truly serve God for the sake of my love for Him, without thought of a reward."

The fact that a reward does come in the end is not the point, as we can see from the example of Ephraim, who is mentioned in the *Haphtarah*/Prophetic portion of the second day of Rosh Hashanah:[20]

> I have heard Ephraim lamenting: "You have afflicted me and I have been afflicted, like an untrained calf. Return to me and I will return, for You are God my Lord. Indeed, now that I have turned back, I am filled with remorse. I slap my thighs now that I am aware [of my sins]. I am ashamed and humiliated for I bear the shame of my youth."[21]

Through his repentance, Ephraim rose to the lofty level whereby God speaks of him in terms of "My favorite son," as the next verse indicates. The commentator known as Radak explains that a *ben yakir*/"favorite son" is one who never sinned in his life.

The repentance that wipes away transgressions in a way that it appears that we never committed them is related to the notion of reward.

If you do something that gives great pleasure to one of your friends, and he gives you a present to express his gratitude, he will eventually forget that you ever did him a favor, for, in his mind, he has already rewarded you for your effort. If, in contrast, you refuse to accept his gift, the good that you did to him will be forever present in his thoughts.

The preceding describes the attitude of "Ephraim, my favorite son." The first talmudic sages question why the children of Israel are sometimes referred to as Ephraim. In their answer, they highlight the word *epher*/ash alluded to in the name *Ephr*aim, reflecting the attitude of one who, like the Patriarch Abraham, exclaims, "I am mere dust and ashes."[22]

Such a person fulfills the commandments and observes the Torah out of a profound love for the Creator, without concern for a final reward. God is alluding to this high level of Divine service in His message: "I have indeed seen Ephraim lamenting." Namely, even though Ephraim bitterly regretted his past, he still bemoans and laments, unable to find comfort from the fact that he transgressed against the Holy One.

Of one who attains this quality of repentance, God says:

> Isn't Ephraim My favorite son, a beloved child? Indeed, whenever I speak of him, I remember him fondly. Therefore, I yearn for him, and I will have mercy on him.[23]

One who rectifies his past to this extent is forever present in the Divine love and thoughts.

For those who have the strength of character and Divine help to follow in Ephraim's footsteps, the unique driving force is to give pleasure to the Beloved, as we can read between the lines of the Shema.

Toward the beginning of the Torah portion *Vaetchanan*[24] a few verses before the first paragraph of the Shema, we have, "Only you, the ones who remained attached to God your Lord, are all alive today,"[25] hinting that this attachment was the reason for their very existence.

In contrast, in *Ekev*,[26] the following Torah portion, in which the second paragraph of the Shema appears, the opening verse reads:

> If only you listen to these laws, safeguarding and keeping them, then God your Lord will keep in mind the covenant and love with which He made an oath to your fathers.[27]

As later, in the second paragraph of the Shema, a reward is mentioned, and it is conditional: if all of you carefully obey My commandments.

We now understand the Divine message, "At that time, you will call me *Ishi* and no longer will you call me *Baali*." *Baali* suggests a traditional relationship of Giver and receiver in which the Giver has the leading role and sustains the receiver. In contrast, in the *Ishi* relationship there are no more "ifs." God no longer rewards Israel according to what they perform. He begins to give unconditionally, infinitely, because they are now able to receive His infinite bounty on an equal basis.

This, the *Ishi* level, cannot be asked of an entire nation until the messianic age, as Hosea says, "at that time." And yet, even though the full measure of the *Ishi* relationship is beyond our reach, in the month of Tishri, we can aim for this quality of relationship.*

* To Geoffrey Ephraim.

19

Elul: "He Placed His Left Hand under My Head"

Intimacy between God and Israel

WE HAVE FOLLOWED THE DIVINE COURTSHIP of Israel from the time of the Exodus until the exchange of vows between God and Israel at the foot of Mount Sinai. As God uttered the Ten Commandments Israel acquiesced and said *Naaseh veNishma*/"We will do and we will hear."[1]

The passionate union with God was to take place forty days later, on the seventeenth of Tammuz, when Moses brought down the Tablets of the Law. But when he found Israel worshiping the Golden Calf, he broke them in anger, and the union was lost.

"Shame on the bride for playing the harlot right under the wedding canopy!" the sages commented. The vows exchanged between Israel and God were now damaged. It is no wonder that the three-week period from the seventeenth of Tammuz through the ninth of Av eventually became a time of mourning for Jerusalem, the Temple, the exile, and the suffering of Israel.

To repair the damage they had caused, Israel had once again to accept the yoke of Heaven over themselves. Moses ascended Mount Sinai for the second time, staying forty days, from the eighteenth of Tammuz until the end of Av, praying for mercy. At the end of this time, God agreed to take Israel back. The flaw of the vows was rectified.

Immediately thereafter, on the first of Elul, Moses again ascended Mount Sinai for forty days in preparation to receive the Second Tablets, which would seal the union once more. On this third ascent, Moses was also to reinstate the people's total surrender to the Creator. This was the highest level of repentance, aiming for the closest bond.

The essential difference between the oral and written aspects of the union is that only after the exchange of vows at Sinai was ratified by the contract of the Tablets could we have a relationship of passionate attachment to God.

On Yom Kippur, after Moses' third ascent, God gave Israel the Second Tablets. God's message to Israel, "Of all the nations of the earth, I knew only you,"[2] comes into effect only at this second level. The Hebrew expression used is *yada'ti*, from *da'at*, the intimate knowledge of love. This moment was the sealing of the intimate relationship that God and Israel would share always.

And yet, we lost something. The Second Tablets cannot be compared to the first, because the first were carved and engraved by God Himself, whereas the second were carved by Moses and engraved by God. This means that the union that took place on Yom Kippur does not have the same level of intimacy as the union that would have taken place on the seventeenth of Tammuz.

The First Tablets were to have brought Israel the Infinite Light of Creation. Had the First Tablets not been broken, says the Talmud, no nation would have been able to rule over Israel. There would have been no exile; we would have already entered the messianic era.

Yet our loss has a silver lining. God gave us the First Tablets, though we did not receive them. The First Tablets are in this world. We do not have direct access to them, but through the intense study of Torah, sparks of light are sometimes revealed to us. We will regain full access to the original Tablets, and to complete intimacy with the Almighty, with the coming of the messianic age.

LOVE OR CONSTRICTION?

Today, the forty days from the beginning of Elul until Yom Kippur continue to be a time when God is especially close and approachable. God is waiting for us to purify the tablets of our hearts and come back to Him until we achieve the intoxicating emotion suggested in the verse, "I knew only you."

The "magical" month of Elul and the Ten Days of *Teshuvah*/repentance between Rosh Hashanah and Yom Kippur are impregnated with an atmosphere that makes it easier for us to feel an overwhelming longing for attachment to God. We become charged with energy to rectify the past and fulfill Elul's message, "I am my Beloved's and He longs for me."[3] The service we aim for in Elul is hinted at in the Hebrew letters of the word *Elul*, an acronym of *Ani leDodi veDodi li*/"I am my Beloved's, and my Beloved is mine."[4]

The closeness hinted at in this verse may be seen as limiting, if we compare it to two people who focus their awareness totally on each other to the exclusion of everything else. The only thing existing in the world at this point is the Most High's love for Israel, as the verse says, "I knew only you," and Israel's exclusive love for the Most High. Nothing else matters, as if the verse said, "I *alone* am my Beloved's and my Beloved is mine *alone*." This is the rectification that the Second Tablets brought to us. To the eyes of the world, our vision seems constricted, but from Israel's point of view, our love is in concealment at this time.

This blend of love and concealment is the hidden message of the shofar, sounded throughout the month of Elul until Yom Kippur:[5]

> Fortunate is the people
> who know the *teruah*/shofar blast, God;
> in the Light of Your countenance
> they walk.[6]

The *Zohar* notes that the verse does not say "who blow the call of *teruah*," but rather "who know the *teruah*," that is, who understand the mystery of *teruah*. This secret lesson is that the concept of *teruah* has a connotation of concealment and strict justice, in contrast with the calls themselves—the different sounds emitted from the ram's horn—that allude to love. Fortunate are the people who are able to understand that this concealment of the Divine light is not intended to bring strict justice upon the world, but rather to cause Israel to call out to their Father in Heaven with the shofar. These calls will draw God's fiery love onto Israel.

Therefore, at the end of the days of judgment, at the close of Yom Kippur, we proclaim seven times that the holy Name Tetragrammaton is equivalent to the Name *Elohim*, hinting that we cannot have one without the other. The Tetragrammaton, or *YHVH*, represents pure lovingkindness, whereas *Elohim* denotes strict justice. It is only through the combination of the two that we can reach the level of

> Of all the nations of the earth, I knew only you, for just as a loincloth clings to a man's hips, so did I make the entire House of Israel . . . cling to Me.[7]

The word *teruah*, in the Book of Psalms, expresses not constriction, as the *Zohar* teaches, but joy:

> Sing Him a new song, play skillfully with *teruah*/jubilation.[8]

Another example is:

> With trumpets and the sound of the shofar
> shout for joy before the King, *Hashem*[9]

and

> Shout for joy to *Hashem*, everyone on earth.[10]

The Hebrew word used for "shout for joy" is *hari'u*, which comes from the same root as *teruah*. Even more puzzling is that the *Targum*, the accepted Aramaic translation of the Bible, renders homiletically all three variants of the word *teruah* in the psalms as *yababa*, an expression indicating lament.

The kabbalists explain that true joy stems precisely from blowing the shofar with the lamenting sound of *teruah*, for by calling out with the shofar, we draw God's love to ourselves, while through the sound of *teruah* comes the constriction. The Divine love is directed onto His people to the exclusion of anything else, as the verse says, "I knew only you."

One usually cries of sorrow, but tears can also express joy. Like pain, joy may be constricted and released by shedding tears.

Let us examine the nature of this concealment.

A Seal upon Your Heart

After the closeness of Elul, God rises up to sit as our King. On Rosh Hashanah, He judges us, and at the close of Yom Kippur, He seals the verdict. Yet the verdict can still be overturned. The second and irrevocable sealing of the verdict occurs on the last day of Sukkot, known as Hoshanah Rabbah. In order to execute judgment, He must conceal His love from us. At that point, lovesick Israel prays that, though God hides His love, its impression remain in our hearts like a seal, and that the imprint of our love remain in God's heart (as it were) so that He will not forget us.

> Place me as a seal upon Your heart, a seal upon Your arm.
> —Song of Songs 8:6

> For the sake of my love, seal me upon Your heart so that You do not forget me, and You will see that my love for You goes beyond death itself.
> —Rashi

Just as seals were once used to stamp an impression in wax, so Israel asks God that His love for them be as everlasting as a seal, whose impression remained in an envelope. "Just as we place You as a seal upon our arm through our *tefillin*, which leave an imprint in our skin, so should You place us as a seal upon Your heart."

Elul is a time where we can feel God's love for Israel. Immediately following Elul is Rosh Hashanah, the only Jewish holiday on which the moon is hidden. The darkness hints to the constriction of God's love on the Day of Judgment. However, Israel says, "For strong as death is my love . . . its sparks are fiery coals, a flame of the Divine."[11] During the time Your love is revealed to us, our own love for You is such that its sparks are fiery coals from the flame of God; its imprint will remain with us when the lights are concealed.

The month of Elul is the most propitious for repentance out of love, to feel in our hearts a love for God that is stronger than death itself, so that its light remains even during the days of concealment and judgment. This is the preparation we need for the climax of the love relationship that is to take place on Yom Kippur.

During these ten days of concealment in which we are distanced from God's light, the Divine love that is revealed to us is the everlasting brotherly love that precludes separation. This steady love is crucial now, when the accusers are attempting to cause hatred between Israel and their Father in Heaven. At the same time, we express our yearning for intimacy with the Beloved by focusing all our interests and energy on the reestablishment of a close relationship to the exclusion of all else.

The awe of God that permeates these times increases our awareness of His Presence. The concealment of His light facilitates our task during these days, at the climax of which we become "His Companion of the soul" on Shemini Atseret.

"He Placed His Left Hand under My Head"

The Ari teaches that the month of Elul, as well as the ten days of Repentance that follow, are impregnated with the luminous energy of the thirteen attributes of mercy. On the other hand, as we have seen, this is a time of awe of the coming judgment, a time beset with the personal problems resulting from the concealment of light that we have mentioned. How can these two teachings be true within the same period of time?

This seeming contradiction in terms is found in the psalms:

> O God of vengeance, Hashem
> O God of vengeance, reveal Yourself.[12]

The Baal Shem Tov points out that the Divine Name used in this verse, *El*, denotes lovingkindness, whereas the word "vengeance" points to strict justice.

The combination of justice and lovingkindness in a Divine revelation may be understood at the level of the servant, the child, or the soul-companion. Let us say that a person who considers himself God's servant gives in to a forbidden pleasure and finds himself engrossed in his action. If the Divine attribute of strict justice acts at this moment by sending him a sudden illumination reminding him of the greatness of the King of kings, Whom he is serving, he will understand the gravity of his transgression against the Divine will. Although the shame he will feel upon returning to his senses might be felt as a Divine vengeance, it is really a kindness, for this revelation prevents him from slipping farther away from the role he has chosen for himself.

Another situation might be as follows: a transgressor might receive a flow of Divine energy that makes him realize that all the good he is enjoying in his life is due to the kindness of his Father in Heaven. As he becomes aware of the extent to which he was being ungrateful by rebelling against his Maker, he will be filled with pain. This is the level of God's child.

Yet another situation that involves just as much struggle but at a much higher level is that of the person who has an illumination of the awesome closeness of the Holy One with the Community of Israel, who are not just His children, but His Companion of the soul. At this point an intense bitterness invades the transgressor; his heart is torn with mental anguish at the thought of the intimacy that he lost in exchange for an empty physical pleasure.

Such a person brings strict justice upon himself of his own volition. He is ready to expiate his sin and afflicts himself—according to his source of Torah guidance—in order to regain the full force of the Divine love that he once had.

These three levels of Divine revelation—of the servant, the child, and the soul-companion—define the special judgment of the people of Israel on Rosh Hashanah, which is in addition to the general judgment God metes to the entire world at this time. The general judgment is described in the verse,

> Through justice a king establishes a land.[13]

However, the judgment to Israel stems from the attribute of lovingkindness that is revealed during this time of the year, as the verse says,

> The world is built on kindness.[14]

This type of lovingkindness couched in a shell of strict justice is what Kabbalah calls "embrace of the Left." God's "left hand" is a term for justice and concealment, whereas the "right hand" represents love and tenderness. Hence, the revelation begins gradually, in the midst of the problems associated with the concealment of Divine energy, as the verse says, "He placed His left hand under my head."[15] Initially, there cannot be a powerful revelation of the love and attachment in potential between the Most High and His people Israel.

Beholding the full radiance of the overwhelming love they have missed, at the time that Israel has sinned, would be too bitter an experience for them to bear. The pain and sorrow that would follow at the thought that their sin had destroyed this precious bond would be too intense.

The initial "embrace of the Left" is evocative of the verse "At that time you will call me *Ishi* and no longer will you call me *Baali*," for as we have seen, *Baali* indicates a lower level of closeness within the bond of soul-companion. *Ishi*, however, is the tempestuous love that, in the words of the Song of Songs, is as irresistible as the power of death itself.

The gradual revelation of the level of *Baali* and of "His left hand under my head" prepares Israel to repent in order to regain the higher level. The special nature of the strict justice that comes through during these days stems precisely from the levels of revelation we have discussed. There is no greater sin than receiving an illumination that makes one aware of a flaw one has caused and not feeling regret for it.

After the repentance of Elul, of "He placed His left hand under my head," Israel is ready for that of Yom Kippur, of "His right hand embraces me still."[16] This higher bond gives us a glimpse of *Ishi*. The word *Ishi* stems from the expression *shalhevet esh/* flames of fire. The purifying influence of Yom Kippur leaves the Community of Israel ready to repent once again, now for any errors committed that might have affected this highest level.

20

Drawing Down
the Hidden Light

IN THE MONTH OF TISHRI, which includes the holidays of Rosh Hashanah, Yom Kippur, Sukkot, and Shemini Atzeret, there is an energy available to help us alter our relationship with God, within the level of Companion of the soul, to *Ishi*. The tool we have to achieve this is hearing the sound of the *shofar*/ram's horn on Rosh Hashanah. The shofar can help a person become passionately attached to God when he knows how to take advantage of it.

Rosh Hashanah is known as both the Day of Judgment and the Day of *Teruah*/sounding the shofar. Strangely enough, the Torah, which transmits the essence of each festival, does not link Rosh Hashanah with judgment. The Torah describes Rosh Hashanah only as a day of sounding the shofar:

> The first day of the seventh month . . . shall be a day of *Teruah*/sounding the shofar.[1]

In fact, the Midrash relates that the angels asked God why Israel doesn't sing *Hallel*[2] on Rosh Hashanah. God replied, "The ledgers of who will live and who will not are opened before Me."

According to this Midrash, the angels did not know that Rosh Hashanah is the Day of Judgment until God told them so! This is because the angels are aware of the *inner purpose* of the day, which is *not* the judgment of Israel but its desire to relate to God in the deepest possible way. Why shouldn't Israel say *Hallel*? God had to explain to them the purpose of the day: even though it is the renewal of love, judgment is nevertheless present. Thus it is a time of fear, when songs of praise are not appropriate.

The only Scriptural reference to judgment on Rosh Hashanah is the verse:

> Blow the shofar at the moon's renewal,
> at the time appointed for our festive day.
> Because it is a decree for Israel,
> a judgment for the God of Jacob.[3]

THE MYSTERY OF *TERUAH*

We have seen the *Zohar*'s teaching about the blend of love and constriction at the basis of the call of *teruah*. Let us look into the etymology of the word, in order to gain further insights into this mysterious concept.

The Hebrew word *teruah* is related to the word *reut*, which means friendship, connection, and binding. Hearing the sound of *teruah* with proper intentions forms a special bond between God and the Jewish people. Through this, we can merit the hidden light of Creation, and the soul-union that is at the level of *Ishi*.

The key to the mystery of *teruah* lies in the verse, *Teroem beshevet barzel*—"you will smash them with an iron rod."[4] The word *teroem* comes from the same root as *teruah*. The sound of *teruah* helps us break the powers of evil so that we can bind ourselves to God.

We have seen that from the beginning of Creation, it was God's will to delight in Israel, to bind us in a relationship to Him in love. However, as long as the forces of evil exist in the world, and in our own unrefined selves, such a relationship is impossible. There is no room in us for the Divine. Yet, when through self-restraint we purify ourselves of our negative traits, we are preparing ourselves for the love bond God longs to have.

Self-restraint is the rod of iron with which we break the powers of evil. It is a tool to help tie the close bond of *Reut*/friendship for which we yearn. Fortunate is the people that understand that *teruah* is a means of achieving the intimate relationship with God and to walk in the light of His Presence.

> God is my light[5]—on Rosh Hashanah.
>   —Midrash

The Day of Judgment is in essence a day of light for Israel, who desire to arouse their love of their Creator, which is temporarily hidden.

JOINING LOVE AND AWE

The *teruah* is not only God's call to Israel; it is also Israel's call to God. According to the Ari, our intent during the prayer service on Rosh Hashanah is to arouse God's loving relationship with us through the shofar blast.

The term *teruah* is a general expression for three different sounds of shofar: *tekiah*, a long, unbroken blast; *shevarim*, three medium blasts; and *teruah*, nine staccato blasts. The *Zohar* describes these sounds as follows:

Tekiah—representing the sigh of love.
Shevarim—representing the prolonged groaning that precedes tears.
Teruah—similar to uncontrollable sobbing.

Thus, Kabbalah sees the different sounds of the shofar as reflecting different stages of the love bond.

In the first stage, represented by *tekiah*, Israel expresses its love and awe of God, the fusion of which inflames Israel with passion and causes them to sigh of desire for the King of the world.

In the second stage, represented by *shevarim*, the fire of God's love is aroused toward Israel, and it is much stronger than His original love, thus preparing the way for the ultimate union. Israel responds with the groans that precede tears.

In the third stage, represented by *teruah*, Israel feels God's burning love inside them. Their own emotions are intensified in response, renewing the cycle. The arousal of love from below causes an awakening of love from above, which in turn produces an even more intense upsurge of passion below.

The *Musaph/*additional prayer of Rosh Hashanah includes three sections, each accompanied by a set of shofar blasts, which reflect these three stages:

*Malchuyot/*kingship—God's light and love are concealed from us, yet we declare our wholehearted acceptance of God as King. Our initial feeling of abandonment turns into a deep longing.

*Zichronot/*remembrance—God's love is aroused. In response to our arousal, it becomes accessible and intensified. We ask God to remember the great love of our original union, thus we recite the verses:

> I remember how you were faithful in your youth, your love as a bride, how you fol-lowed Me in the wilderness, a land not sown.[6]

> Isn't Ephraim [i.e., Israel] My favorite son, a beloved child? Indeed, whenever I speak of him, I remember him fondly. Therefore, I yearn for him, and I will have mercy on him.[7]

Shofarot—our longing deepens as we experience a spark of His love. We yearn to be face-to-face with Him. Recalling God's love awakens in us the ability to feel it. The veils of concealment are somewhat lifted. The yearning to experience His Divinity—as we did in Sinai, when the revelation was also accompanied by the shofar blasts—is now painful in its intensity. As we become immersed in the *Shofarot* section of *Musaph*, we experience a taste of the soul-union that occurs only once a year, on Shemini Atseret.

LOVE AND BINDING

Although the sound of the shofar can arouse in us love, traditionally the powerful blasts are understood to produce a fear that can move a person to repent.

> If a ram's horn is sounded in the city, can the inhabitants fail to be alarmed?[8]

"Do you think that occurrences are accidental?" says God. "Respond when you hear My clarion call!"

According to Maimonides, the sound of the shofar awakens those who are spiritually asleep and motivates them to rectify their deeds.[9] But this reason seems to be the very opposite of the one given by the *Zohar*, that the shofar blasts lead to the revelation of light. Nevertheless, to establish an intimate relationship with the Divine, we need both love and awe.

The kabbalist Rabbi Joseph Gikatalia (1248–1323) distinguishes between external fear, or fear of Divine retribution, and internal fear, which is an awe of God's greatness.[10] The Baal Shem Tov explained that external fear can bring a person to internal fear. As Rabbi Kaplan puts it,

> The internal fear also involves a loss. It is the loss of existence that one has when he attaches himself to the Life of all life.[11]

A person who stands constantly in God's Presence has no individual existence. His natural traits are nullified in his awareness of God. How can one become angry, fall into base desires, or sink into depression when the Divine Presence is right in front of him?

This is the meaning of the Mishnah: "Make your will His will"[12]—give up your will so that you want what He wants. As Rabbi Tatz stresses, "This does not mean becoming a passive, lifeless individual; on the contrary, one must passionately want what God wants."[13]

Internal fear is an awe that leads to the love of God, as in the words of the old Chasidic song, "Out of fear of You, I flee to You." This is why, every day, we pray at the end of the Amidah:

> May it be Your will that the Temple be rebuilt speedily in our lifetime . . . and there we shall serve You with fear as in the days of old.

We say "with fear" rather than "with love" because our aim is to love God so intensely that the thought of separation from Him is unbearable and we fear to do anything that may remove us from His Presence.

When the passionate love of God is imbued with this internal fear, the heart faints, for the love burns like fiery coals: "for I am sick with love."[14]

The goal of our Divine service in the month of Tishri is to move from the Divine service in which we look to God as a Father, to grow into the more mature relationship of "the Community of Israel, His Companion of the soul." We must allow the powerful sound of the shofar to fill us with awe of the Divine, for when this feeling mixes with our longing for attachment, the result is a love that burns like fire. The relationship with God is then "face-to-face." The numerical value of the Hebrew letters of *Yom Teruah*/Day of Teruah—737—is the same as that of *shalhevet*/flame, hinting to the type of relationship with God with which we want to start the year.

If we understand the call of *teruah*, we realize that the shofar has the power to arouse in us the fear of alienation from the Beloved, with the final purpose of drawing down the hidden light of Creation. Rosh Hashanah is a day of *teruah*, of *reut*/binding, with the potential to elevate us to the level of *Ishi*.

JUDGMENT AS RESTRAINED LOVE

In His desire to help us merge the two emotions of awe and love, God restrains His own love. The Divine restraint, so to speak, blows on the coals of our love so that we first come to Him from our own efforts rather than drawn by the irresistible magnet of His love. Our love will then be weathered and matured in a way that would not be possible had the Divine love been immediately revealed. God therefore first reveals His love during Elul, and then restrains it, thus creating in His Companion of the soul, Israel, a thirst and a passion for that first love, an overwhelming desire for union with the Beloved.

God does not satisfy Israel's longing immediately. Rather, He stirs the embers of this pining through a waiting period in which the intensification of His concealment is painfully felt within. Afterward, the arousal from below is echoed by an arousal from above. Just as at Sinai, the burning passion that consumed Israel aroused God's love for them, as Rashi notes on the verse, "Under the apple tree I awakened You."[15] As water mirrors a loving look, God comes back in a face-to-face relationship, allowing the higher Divine Providence to be stirred with the fire of love for the Community of Israel.

The painful concealment of the Divine Presence lasts throughout the prayers of Rosh Hashanah until the blowing of the shofar. The first powerful sound, voicing our longing for our beloved Companion, mingles with our heartfelt prayers in which we pour out our souls to the King of the world. As our consciousness is heightened, we begin to experience God's love reaching out to us, and His immediacy permeates us with a profound love that is fused with awe of His Presence. The second call of the shofar expresses our longing for Him, which is now overpowering. With the third call, our state of consciousness reaches its peak. The fusion of our love with the fear of God enables us to experience God's incandescent love of "fiery coals, a flame of the Divine." Our resulting state of *devekut* is the preparation we need for the soul-union that follows.

The separation that God imposes on us after the closeness of the month of Elul is necessary so that there can be a stronger union afterward. Estrangement and distance from the Beloved intensify desire, and the ensuing reunion is then more intense than it could have ever been. That is why repentants at any level are very precious to God, for the longer the separation, the sweeter the reunion.

The purpose of Rosh Hashanah, then, is to renew our intimate bond to God. The role of judgment and concealment is only to enable us to feel the fear that leads to an overpowering love. In a way, we ourselves bring strict justice into play through our very desire to attain the "face-to-face" *Ishi* relationship. Our sense of awe creates the intimate bond of *Reut*, which allows us to draw God's hidden light down upon us. Then our love breaks through God's concealment, leading the way to the soul-union of Shemini Atseret.

21

King Above, King Below

THE JEWISH CONCEPT OF KINGSHIP is deeply connected to that of repentance. During the Ten Days of Repentance, from Rosh Hashanah until Yom Kippur, we recite the words, "Blessed are You, the holy King" in the third blessing of the Amidah, rather than the unusual ending, "the holy God." And every year, on the first Shabbat of Elul, we read the Torah portion concerning the appointment of a Jewish king:

> When you come to the land that God your Lord is giving you, so that you have occupied it and settled it, you will eventually say, "We would like to appoint a king, just like all the nations around us." You must then appoint a king whom God your Lord shall choose. You must appoint a king from among your brethren; you may not appoint a foreigner who is not one of your brethren.[1]

Appointing a king was one of the three injunctions that the Israelites were to fulfill upon entering the Holy Land. And yet, at the time of the Prophet Samuel, when the Israelites asked for a king, God became angry with them. The problem was not in their request, but in the type of king they wanted.

> Appoint a king to rule over us! . . . We shall be like the nations, and our king will judge us and wage our wars.[2]

Maimonides explains that the Creator's displeasure at Israel's request for a king grew from the fact that this request was really a voicing of their grievances against Samuel rather than a desire to fulfill the commandment of appointing a king.[3] God therefore expresses to Samuel the implications of their complaints:

> They did not reject you, but Me![4]

It would have been the prophet's duty to appoint a king, even had the people not asked for this. But what the people were unhappy about was Samuel's role as prophet, which was similar to that of the king. The people had no desire for the Divinely conceived relationship with the prophet/king that was demanded of them, and therefore asked for a sovereign ruler "just like all the nations around us." Let us examine the concept of a Jewish king in order to understand the people's objection.

THE HEART OF THE NATION

A Jewish king is not like the kings of the nations. He does not reign over the people as a distant and sometimes demanding ruler. Rather, his soul has the ability to embrace within it the souls of the entire Jewish people. From the moment he is anointed, he becomes the heart and mind of the nation. The Hebrew word for king is *Melech*, an acronym for the words *moach*/mind, *lev*/heart, and *caved*/liver, the dwelling places of the *neshamah*, *ruach*, and *nefesh* souls.[5] When the people accept him as king, they surrender not only their bodies as faithful servants, but they surrender the three aspects of their souls, that he should direct them too in the service of God.

Seen in this light, it follows that the commitments that the king asks of Israel are more natural requests that coincide with the needs of their intellect or emotions, rather than impositions to further his own needs. If he decides to impose a decree upon them that is difficult for them to obey, they have to understand that he is in the position to know what they need to do because their essence is part of his own. Hence, their best interest is his primary consideration, for it is also his own.

The king **is** their *nefesh*, *ruach*, and *neshamah* souls, and therefore he immediately feels within himself everything that the people do relating to his kingship, just like the mind, heart, and liver feel all that happens to the body. We see an example of this in a story from the Bible.

The first king of Israel was Saul. Appointed by the prophet Samuel, he reigned for only two years. Among the reasons for his dethronement was his failure to destroy the nation of Amalek, as God had commanded. A short time after this incident, God spoke to Saul and commanded him to anoint David as the new king of Israel:

> Then God said to Samuel, "How long will you mourn over Saul, whom I have rejected as king over Israel? Fill your horn with oil and go. I will send you to Jesse the Bethlehemite, for I have seen a man [worthy to be] king among his sons."
> But Samuel said, "How can I go? If Saul hears, he will kill me!"
> God said, "Take a calf with you, and say, 'I am coming to sacrifice to God.' Summon Jesse [to join] in the sacrificial meal, and I will tell you what to do. You will anoint for Me the one I designate."[6]

The Baal Shem Tov asked an important question on this passage. Why was Samuel worried? God's message had been directed to him alone, and it was to be carried out in private. How could Saul hear? Furthermore, it had long been Samuel's way to travel throughout the land of Israel helping people: what suspicion would this trip have raised? If anything, Samuel should have worried more about returning home, after he had already anointed David, in the event Saul heard.

The answer, according to the Baal Shem Tov, is that since Saul was the heart of the Jewish people, had Samuel traveled to Bethlehem only in order to anoint David, Saul would have immediately sensed what was happening. He would have felt within himself the kingship being torn away from him, just like the heart feels all that happens to the body.

As a result, Saul would immediately have taken action to prevent this from happening. The prophet's main concern therefore was, "How can I go? If Saul hears, he will kill me!" Namely, Saul will understand what is about to happen and kill me before I have the chance to do anything!

However, from the moment that Samuel anointed David, the kingship would be transferred to the new recipient, and Saul would not feel anything because his soul no longer embraced that of his former people. Therefore, in order to give Samuel time to act, God added a second mission that would conceal the impact of the first and thereby prevent Saul from feeling what was happening.[7]

BUILDING OF THE TEMPLE

These concepts help us understand why the building of the Temple occurred under the reign of Solomon rather than that of his father David.

When we speak of God as King, it means that we, His people, receive from Him material and spiritual sustenance. And a king of Israel is also a giver, and his subjects, the receivers. When they surrender to him their minds and hearts, he can draw down Divine sustenance based on the collective power of the nation. The people then receive more Divine energy than any individual could obtain, as the whole is greater than the sum of its parts. This will be the role of the Messiah: that of a giver who will help us become receivers of the King of kings above.

However, a king who derives his power from his lofty position, whose soul does not embrace the hearts and minds of his people, is considered to be a receiver rather than a giver. His subjects fall into the category of children who receive from him their needs for sustenance and protection as a nation without having to give of themselves. It is then impossible for him to draw down spiritual energy.

If we cast a searching look into the reign of King David, we will see that he was only a receiver, for his rule was weakened by the rebellion of his son Absalom as well as by the different power feuds in his time. It is clear from David's psalms that he did not have access to the collective energy of the people that God intended for a king:

> Turn to me and favor me,
> for I am alone and poor.[8]

and also

> A prayer of the poor . . .[9]

The Divinely conceived kingship may be compared to a two-story structure: it is impossible to build the second floor before the first. In addition, there must first be a king who reigns over his subjects in the way of the nations, and only then can there be the second type of king who has the surrender of his people's hearts and minds.

King David is the very foundation of the kingship. Hence, in our daily Amidah prayer, we ask God to restore the Davidic reign on earth by causing his offspring to flourish.[10] Yet, under David's kingship, the people of Israel related to God as children. Consequently, the Temple, which requires Israel's total *bitul*/surrender to God in a bond of Giver and receivers, could not be built.

In contrast to his father, King Solomon had the full commitment of his people, and was consequently able to draw enough Divine energy to build the First Temple.

It is written about King Solomon's reign:

> Then Solomon sat on the throne of the Lord as king ... and all of Israel obeyed him.[11]

and also,

> And all the kings of the earth sought the presence of Solomon, to hear his wisdom, that God had put in his heart.[12]

Strengthened with the collective soul-energy that the Jewish people had surrendered to Solomon, his reign was based upon the proper interaction of giver and receiver, and he was thus able to draw Divine light into the world.

It therefore follows that the commandment of appointing a king precedes that of building the Temple. Only when the Community of Israel has attained the love and *bitul*/surrender to God defined by the king/subject relationship would God allow His Divine Presence to dwell within the people by establishing His Temple on earth.

Making God King also involves two steps, one above the other. The first—the acceptance of the yoke of the kingdom of Heaven—describes a simple awe of God's omnipotence.

Then comes the loftier level in which we surrender our very soul to the Almighty, as it is written:

> My son, give Me your heart and your eyes.[13]

When the majority of the people of Israel attain this second level, God becomes the Giver returning to His subjects the fruit of their investment.

BITUL TODAY

Let us follow the concept of *bitul* from the onset of Israel's relationship to the Creator into our time.

While in Egypt, the Community of Israel were at the initial stages of the first level of accepting the kingdom of Heaven, for they were still steeped in the forty-ninth gate of impurity. The many signs and miracles provided the impulse they needed to fully realize the foundation level, and, realizing that God is the King of the world, they totally accepted His ruling authority. Yet, they did not yet reach the next level of surrendering their *nefesh, ruach,* and *neshamah* souls to Him until the splitting of the sea. Their exclamation, "God shall reign for all eternity,"[14] points to their eternal commitment to maintain the Divine kingship in the higher level of surrender where His will became theirs.

Like our ancestors in Egypt, we also aim to maintain it, but we know that in fact it is impossible to stay always on the same level of intensity. Therefore, after the fast of the ninth of Av, we will prepare for the forty days that will begin in the coming Elul by reflecting upon what this total surrender of our intellect and emotions means to each one of us. Then we actively plan to translate our intention into deed by adopting new measures of surrender that we feel *we are ready* to keep. Our service in these forty days will be sealed in the last Ten Days of Repentance.

Since, as we will see, *bitul* manifests itself in a highly individual manner, consulting our source of Torah guidance might help us to focus on the priorities of our personal *bitul*. Furthermore, a rabbi generally recognized as a *posek* (having the authority to pronounce in disputes of Jewish legal questions), who knows us personally, will see—better than we do—which measures we are ready to adopt without breaking. A gradual ascent diminishes the risk of falling, which is always present when one takes upon oneself a higher concentration of holiness than one is ready to receive.

A woman may be tempted to buy a dress that fits her like a second skin and rationalize her desire by telling herself that this garment covers all her body parts. When someone points out to her that rabbinic authority forbids women to wear tight clothes, she may claim that this is the age of interpretation and that her understanding of the law does not coincide with theirs. If this woman reconsiders the situation and decides to abstain in surrender to the ruling authority of the Oral Torah that continues to this day, she is using her *nefesh* to serve the Almighty.

An extreme example of male *bitul* of the *nefesh* is that of a man who spent his time studying Torah, and was generally stringent with himself in his effort to observe the commandments at a very high level. Yet, this man was "addicted" to sex and would find himself unable to keep away from his wife during the "seven pure days" required after the completion of her menses. When the man asked his friend to consult a rabbinic authority on his behalf, too embarrassed to do so himself, the rabbi suggested that the man move out of his home during the time of separation from his wife. Since his economic situation did not permit for him to go to a hotel, for one week of every month, the man would sleep in the benches of the *yeshivah* where he studied.

One of his intimate friends, who was aware of the situation, once told him that it was absurd that he undergo such agony of discomfort on a regular basis. "You should leave your house only at the times in which you feel the temptation threatening you," the friend suggested. The man replied, "Once I feel the temptation, it is too late; I no longer have free will. It is as though some unknown factor were forcing me to give in."

On another level, a person might choose to abandon a promising career in order to devote his mind to the study of Torah. He is using his *neshamah,* the part of the soul that dwells in his mind, to serve his Creator.

Rabbi Aryeh Kaplan is an example of such a *bitul*. Although he was one of the most prominent young physicists of his time, he decided to devote himself to the study of Torah. When it came time for him to present his doctoral defense, he did not even appear before the board; he feared that if he received the title, he would become lost in academia.

However, Rabbi Kaplan soon realized that his newly acquired relationship with

God could not provide the sustenance that his family needed. One day, out of despair, he visited a local cemetery. He hoped he might find someone visiting a grave who would pay him to recite a *hashcabah*/prayer for the dead. But, as he told it, "When I arrived, just my luck, it began to rain!"

Wandering about, he found himself at the foot of his mother's grave. He poured out his heart to the Creator, begging for help. The next day, Rabbi Kaplan received a phone call from Rabbi Pinchas Stolper, then head of the Orthodox Union. He had read one of Rabbi Kaplan's articles and was impressed by his uncanny ability to explain difficult concepts with beautiful simplicity. He asked Rabbi Kaplan to write a booklet on the subject of *tefillin*. Thus began Rabbi Kaplan's short but intense career as a writer. As we mentioned, for Israel to relate to God as His Companions of the soul—totally surrendering to Him in a bond of Giver and receivers—they have to give everything they have before receiving.

Then there is the story of a young man whose family had completely severed their connection with Judaism.[15] He had fallen in love with a non-Jewish girl, who was studying Judaism with the intention to convert. As she enthusiastically taught him what she was learning, the holy sparks in his Jewish soul gradually were awakened. Soon after she converted, he too became observant.

On the day of their engagement, following an old tradition, the couple visited the grave of the bridegroom's ancestors. To their dismay, there was an emblem engraved upon the tombstone that indicated that the groom's family were *cohanim*/priests. But if the bridegroom was a *cohen,* he was forbidden to marry a convert. The engagement had to be broken off.

Since the young man's desire to come back to Judaism was sincere and not a result of his love for his bride, he had no choice. In the same way, since the young woman's relationship with God preceded her involvement with her groom, she accepted God's will and understood that the real purpose of their engagement was to bring back the young man to his Creator. In this case, both of them did an act of submission with their *ruach* soul.

FROM ROSH HASHANAH TO YOM KIPPUR

The Ten Days of Repentance from Rosh Hashanah through Yom Kippur are the very last days Moses spent on Mount Sinai. On Rosh Hashanah, we submit our *neshamah* to the Almighty by intellectually accepting Him as our King. During the days of repentance, we submit our *ruach* to Him by our heartfelt regret over past sins. On Yom Kippur itself, we surrender our *nefesh* to God by depriving our bodies of food and drink.

Yom Kippur marks the end of the time of separation during which the Creator, exercising His function of Judge, allows the powers of strict justice and the angels of the nations of the world to come forward and present their claims against Israel.

The Ari questions how can Yom Kippur be the holiest day of the year since the spiritual growth Israel is to achieve over the three weeks of the High Holidays from Rosh Hashanah through Sukkot is not completed by Yom Kippur, and there is no soul-union at this time. Thus, how is Yom Kippur holier than Shemini Atseret with the total union that occurs then?

The answer is that on Yom Kippur the people of Israel unconditionally accept God's kingship over themselves and, as His people, stand before Him "face-to-face," drawing in His response—a time of unprecedented Divine favor. Even though the passionate attachment is not yet complete and there is no union, Israel's total surrender on Yom Kippur demolishes all barriers, creating a quality of bond that does not recur on Shemini Atseret.

Any deep relationship between man and God must involve *bitul* at some level. Thus, only on Yom Kippur, when we submit all to the Beloved, can the love relationship be fully established. Through our total surrender we make God our King and can renew the intimate communion that we long to share with Him. In this sense, every year we receive the Second Tablets that make us the "Community of Israel, His Companion of the soul."

22

"Return to Me out of Love"

CONFESSION AND REPENTANCE

> You will . . . return to God your Lord.[1]

YOM KIPPUR IS THE DAY OF ATONEMENT. The essence of this holy day is for us to repent of our misdeeds throughout the year, which distanced us from our Maker and made us forget our true purpose in life. And yet, the mitsvah of *teshuvah* is not just limited to one occasion a year: it is applicable constantly. Thus the verses say:

> There shall come a time when you shall experience all the words of blessing and curse that I have presented to you. There, among the nations where God will have banished you, you will reflect on the situation. You will then return to God your Lord.[2]

Furthermore, in the daily prayers, we recite the passages of *viduy*–the verbal confession. In a quiet voice, we confess to God all the things we have done wrong, and beg His forgiveness, attempting to convey to Him our intention not to fail Him again.

For those who yearn for the closest of bonds, the mitsvah of *teshuvah* applies not only every day but even every moment. Rabbi Alexander Ziskind wrote that whenever he felt he might have transgressed, even in the slightest way, he would immediately confess his error to God, for he did not want to wait until the next prayer lest he forget his mistake.[3] How, then, is the special mitsvah to repent on Yom Kippur different from our obligation all year round?

Of Yom Kippur, the Bible says:

> On this day [Yom Kippur] you shall have all your sins atoned, so that you will be purified. Before God, purify yourselves of all your sins.[4]

Whereas the basic message of this verse does not add anything to the daily injunction to "return to God," the path to this goal appears to be different in Yom Kippur, for on this day, we stand "before God."

We are faced with a problem: How can we be commanded to do *teshuvah*? We can be told to abstain from eating pork; we can be asked to fast on Yom Kippur and to go to synagogue; and we may even do these things out of a sense of duty. But in order to feel real repentance over past misdeeds, one must strike sensitive chords, feelings that are not always accessible, even when we seek them!

The sages teach that every day, a heavenly voice calls out from Mount Sinai: "Return, rebellious children!" The Baal Shem Tov asks, "What is the use of a heavenly voice if no one can hear it?"

The answer is that most of us do hear it—within our hearts. This "heavenly voice" is a special energy directed upon us from above in order to arouse us to repent. It manifests itself within us as thoughts of regrets and inspires us to be more active in our effort to come close to God. As long as we retain within us a spark of our connection with God, this spark can burst into a flame when we reflect on the special bond we have with our Maker:

Like the loin-cloth clings to man, so did I make you attached to Me, House of Israel.[5]

If we can meditate on this heavenly voice, our hearts will begin to ache at the thought that we may have broken our bonds with the living King for the sake of transient pleasures.

The problem is that most often we do not listen to this voice, and for many of us, such a meditation would not be very moving. Sometimes our lives have led us to situations in which we are very far from hearing the call of God. Our transgressions may have become so commonplace that we don't even feel the damage they cause.

It is as though a shell of insensitivity surrounds us throughout the year. However, on Yom Kippur, God shines on us His light of *da'at/* intimate knowledge that temporarily disintegrates this shell. Suddenly, we perceive that the root of our soul is bound to Him and that we are standing "before God." Seeing the truth with the light of *da'at*, we become filled with deep regret at having distanced ourselves from Him. Thus there can be an injunction to repent on Yom Kippur because: "Before God purify yourselves." The awareness that we are standing before God will help us purify ourselves.

During the year, we fulfill God's will out of a sense of duty. Hence, the repentance available to us is inspired mainly by the fear of God, and by the awareness that straying from the Divine will may bring some form of retribution. Since such a repentance is not complete, the Torah does not command us to do something we are unable to achieve.

On Yom Kippur, however, we acquire the ability to grasp that the prohibitions are an expression of God's love and that retribution serves only to save us the keener suffering that the separation due to transgression brings.

This deeper insight of the inner connection binding us to the Creator is a product of the influence of the light of *da'at*. "Before God" we are asked to purify ourselves by repenting, since it is now within our power to reach the depth of feelings that the total repentance out of love demands.

In the days of the Temple, the climax of the Yom Kippur service came when the High Priest went into the Holy of Holies and burned incense before the Ark of the Covenant. There he saw the cherubs locked in an embrace. As he stood there "before God," he drew onto Israel the light of *da'at*. This enabled them to meditate on their intimate bond with the Creator and become aware that their sins had created a barrier causing them to be expelled from the palace of the King. Torn between the anguish of past errors and the passionate yearning to be reunited with the Beloved, the Jewish people then repented out of love.

Although the Temple is no longer standing, and we have no High Priest to draw the light of *da'at* upon us, God Himself shines this realization upon us on Yom Kippur, allowing us to repent out of love.

This form of repentance is so great in God's eyes, says the Talmud, that God then regards our sins as merits. Not all repentance has this effect. In general, a person who sins must regret the past, make a positive resolve for the future, and then rectify the damage his sins have caused both above and below. In contrast, repentance out of love causes our very sins to become merits; the transgressions themselves become tools for approaching God.

A MATTER OF INTENTION

According to the sages, when a person observes a commandment, his intention and motivation are as important as the deed itself. For example, one should not eat kosher food or circumcise his son for health reasons, but rather out of a desire to observe God's will.

Commandments related to feelings, however, are different. Then, the *intention* to fulfill God's will could actually be an obstacle. For instance, if you love God because you have been commanded to, is that love considered sincere? Can it be said that you love Him with all your heart, when you do so out of duty? When you feel an awe of God, are you doing it to observe the commandment, or does the awareness of His Presence fill you with an internal fear that causes you to forget about your personal needs?

And what about the person who does not feel this love and fear? How can he fulfill these injunctions? Is the Torah asking of man a state of mind beyond his reach?

The answer is that the Torah does not command these feelings themselves, but rather the steps one takes to acquire them. For instance, a person can fulfill the injunction to love the Creator by contemplating the marvels of Creation. If as a result of this contemplation his love or awe of God is aroused, these feelings will not be motivated by the injunction to produce them. The commandment prompts us to take the necessary measures to arouse the feelings for which we are aiming.

The same holds true of repentance. As the medieval Torah sage Rabbenu Yonah expounds in his *Gates of Repentance*, the commandment to repent does not refer to the actual repentance, for if that were the case the person might be repenting in order to observe the commandment, rather than because he regretted his sin.[6]

The Talmud says that a man sins only because a spirit of folly has overtaken him. Let us look into the nature of this spirit and determine how it holds sway over man.

The Workings of Sin

When we do something wrong and later reflect on the incident without the source of temptation to blind us, we often think, "What got hold of me?" The sages take this feeling literally and refer to it as a "spirit of folly" that grabs hold of a person and leads him to transgress.

This spirit of folly stems from our perception that material reality exists independently of the heavenly realm. One who does not realize that all Creation is actually Divine light hidden by ever dense layers of concealment will find it easier to sin for he feels far from God.[7]

As we saw, sincere contemplation helps arouse feelings of repentance within us. This is particularly true on Yom Kippur, because of the illumination of *da'at*. Yet, as Rabbenu Yonah teaches, even throughout the year, when we do not have the light of *da'at* to protect us from sin, contemplating on our inner connection with the Creator can remove the spirit of folly and bring us to regret.

If you have even a glimpse of what a relationship with the Divine could mean to you, its absence would make your heart sink. You will be filled with poignant regrets that will lead you to wonder how could you have distanced yourself from the Light of Life. You will then passionately yearn for such intimate attachment.

The kabbalists teach that the way to acquire the *da'at* knowledge of God and thereby realize the immanence of His Presence is by actually studying the intricate workings of nature. Kabbalah views nature as an earthly reflection of a higher dimension, although only the essence of the spiritual world is reflected down below, for there is no matter on high. Just as physicists today recognize a system of logic different from the classical one, a person whose consciousness can ascend to a transcendental world unlimited by time and space is free from the prevailing logic of this dimension: he realizes that all Creation is Divine light in concealment.[8]

Since nature is like a garment for the Infinite Light of Creation, as soon as you have the resolve to believe, you begin to perceive the truth.

When you realize that you did something that God disapproves of, and resolve never to do it again, you have repented out of awe. But when you repent out of love, you suddenly understand the reason for your sin—that you did not have the clear faith that all Creation is God's light. Instead of revealing His light, you added to its concealment.

If you reach that level of understanding, your sins are counted as merits. For precisely by contemplating the reason that you sinned, you acquire this radiant faith. Had you not sinned in the first place, you would never have come to the realization that all Creation is Divine light in concealment.

Target: The Transgression or Its Cause?

If you allow the spirit of folly to creep into your consciousness, rather than pause to identify it under its guise, it will get hold of you. We are reminded of Esau, returning home hungry from his hunting activities: when faced with Jacob's lentil stew, he felt an insatiable urge to partake of it, even though he was aware that through such action he would lose his most precious possession.[9] Similarly, once you expose yourself to the grip of the spirit of folly it is unlikely that you will be able to hold your ground, for it is an infinitely powerful opponent.

However, it is possible to take the necessary steps *before* a transgression occurs in order to avoid its trap. It is your responsibility to take whatever steps necessary to avoid situations that could lead to your downfall. Every time that you pull back from an involvement that could lead to a violation you build up your resistance against the spirit of folly.

Hence, the sage Rabbi Chayim David Azulay, known as the Chida, notes that in the world to come, a person will not be held accountable for the actual transgressions he committed as much as for failing to entreat the Holy One's help against the evil inclination in the first place.[10]

The aim is to remain aware that our understanding of reality is based on a "spirit of folly," an element of deception. When we reach this level of understanding, teaches Maimonides, God will guarantee that we will never sin in this area again, for if you know that everything around you is actually Divine light, how can you act against His will?

From Transgressions to Positive Commandments

As we have seen, the 613 mitsvot are divided into 365 negative commandments and 248 positive ones. Abstaining from transgression helps us maintain our spiritual level by diminishing our attachment to the physical world and sensitizing us to the damage caused by sin.

On the other hand, the 248 positive commandments imbue our souls with holiness. It is this holiness that can save us from the "spirit of folly." For, unless we first pursue good by observing commandments and thereby distance ourselves from sin, it is not possible to avoid evil. This basic principle is hinted at in a teaching of Maimonides:

> For these reasons, it is customary for all of Israel to give profusely to charity, perform many good deeds, and be occupied with mitsvot from Rosh Hashanah until Yom Kippur to a greater extent than during the remainder of the year.[11]

This statement challenges our understanding. Unless we are either perfectly righteous or evil beyond redemption, on Rosh Hashanah God suspends our sentence: we will only be inscribed in the Book of Life if we attain repentance during the next ten days. Since the essence of repentance is regretting the sin and resolving not to repeat it in the future,[12] how is observing more mitsvot going to help us repent for errors already committed? It is no longer a question of accumulating merits, for the only thing that will affect the impending judgment is our repentance.

We may answer that the repentance of each individual depends on the extent to which he is able to uproot his own proclivity to err. A good way to begin this process is to multiply our acts of kindness and observance of mitsvot during these ten days. The trace of holiness these acts leave behind will readily remove our tendency to go astray and give us the impulse to ascend yet higher in our service of God. This, essentially, is what repentance is all about.

FORGIVENESS, ATONEMENT, AND PURITY

We can now understand the unique form of repentance available to us on Yom Kippur as opposed to the rest of the year.

The Mishnah alludes to two steps in the purification process:

> Praiseworthy are you, O Israel! Before Whom do you cleanse yourselves? Who cleanses you? Your Father in Heaven! As it is written: "And I will sprinkle pure water upon you and you shall be cleansed."[13] And it is also written: "Hashem is Israel's *mikveh*."[14] Just as a *mikveh* purifies, so does the Holy One, Blessed is He, purify Israel.[15]

"Before Whom do you cleanse yourselves?" We are to start the process from below; and then "Who cleanses you?" God completes the process.

Sometimes, when a person is very far away from God, the Holy One Himself starts the process of purification: He "sprinkles water" upon him, causing him to suddenly feel how distant he is, so that he begins to long for closeness. To receive this "sprinkled water," all he has to do is not run away, not block out the feelings of yearning that come to him.

To use a *mikveh*, however, the repentant has to actively lower himself into the water. Similarly, in *teshuvah*, to act on those feelings of longing that come to him, he has to lower himself by regretting his past rebellion. Only then will God act as his *mikveh* and complete the purification of his soul in a way that can only be done from above.

As Rabbenu Yonah explained, we were told to purify ourselves through repentance and were given a special day in which we could achieve it in order to free the part of our soul directly connected to the Divine of the weight of serious transgressions that prevent the desired attachment to God.

In the Yom Kippur prayers, we confess "the sins that we have sinned before You." The expression "before You" implies: "We are now aware that we committed the sin in Your Presence. We realize that we can only sin because we forgot that we were before God." On Yom Kippur, our eyes are illuminated by the light of *da'at*, and we become keenly aware of being before God.

God tells us not to return to Him moved by the desire to repair the damage caused to our soul, for even the intention to rectify the evil we have done to ourselves has a slight self-orientation. Rather, we should answer His call that came to us through the prophet Malachi:

Return to Me, and I will return to you.[16]

God is asking us to return in love, brokenhearted at the thought that we may have severed the bond between us. Our sins cause Him to hide His Presence above, intensifying the concealment here below, which is the root of all earthly misfortune. God calls on us to purify ourselves in order to remove the barrier that prevents us from experiencing Him.

Throughout the year, we first repair the damage that we inadvertently caused through our sins that intensified the concealment of the Divine. Only then does God heal the damage to our souls.

On Yom Kippur, the order is reversed. God initiates the process and purifies us with the light of *da'at*. Then we continue and purify ourselves through repentance. Finally, God completes our purification from above; even the grave transgressions flawing the higher levels of our soul, which we cannot repair during the year, are rectified in Yom Kippur through the "pure waters" of the Divine.

In the *Ne'ilah* prayer at the end of Yom Kippur, we quote God's words, "I have forgiven according to your request."[17] From the onset of Yom Kippur, God had already begun to pour on us the light of *da'at* which begins the process of forgiveness. During the rest of the day, it is up to us to become stronger and stronger in our desire to return to Him.

23

Eternal Joy

WE HAVE SEEN THAT AT THE BEGINNING of the year, our relationship with the Creator is in a dormant state. God separates Himself from the Community of Israel in order to judge them as their King.[1] The resulting concealment of the Divine light arouses in the Children of Israel a deep yearning for union with the Creator.

Yet, Israel does not attain the sought for "face-to-face" relationship until Yom Kippur, after ten days, during which they long to perceive the Presence of the living King. At this point, Israel undergoes another ten days of yearning, this time to cleave to the Beloved in the soul-union of Shemini Atseret. This second waiting period begins with the days between Yom Kippur and Sukkot, in which they are already, as it were, "face-to-face" with their Creator, and the proximity ever intensifies their desire to become One with the Beloved.

Then comes the festival of Sukkot, in which Israel thinks with joy, "With His right hand, He embraces me."[2] But this is not yet the soul-union. Their desire for closeness becomes even keener. The difference between *ahavah*/love and *cheshek*/desire is that you can love many different people, but you can feel an overwhelming desire for only one.[3] In this sense, the month of Tishri stands out in relation to the other months of the year, for the service we accomplish during this month is to be one of total longing and desire.

The effect of this longing in our Divine service during this month is to help us reach the initial thoughts that led to the transgressions in our repentance, thus uprooting the very source of our sins. The sages teach that the desire to sin preceding the actual sin causes much damage to your spiritual structure, even if in the end you do not commit the transgression in question. In fact, the Talmud teaches that the thought of sinning is worse than the sin itself, because your desire to transgress is keener while you think of the forbidden pleasure than when the source of the temptation is in front of you and you actually transgress.

Since this rectification of our thought processes is the pinnacle of the spiritual structure we are to build within these twenty-one days, the waiting period for the "face-to-face" return, as well as the moment of the greatest soul-union of the year, are both delayed. The purpose of these two waiting periods, each ten days long, is that within each soul of Israel the desire for passionate attachment has the chance to grow to the point of becoming unbearable, thus perfecting the repentance begun in the month of Elul.

Sukkot brings us a new factor to help our desire to rise until it climaxes in Shemini Atseret: joy. In the Sukkot morning service we say: "You have given us the festival of Sukkot, this time of our rejoicing." This implies that joy is an intrinsic part of this festival, further and beyond the joy associated with the other festivals—fine food and fine clothes. Indeed, the Torah tells us,

> You shall rejoice on your festival [of Sukkot] . . . so that you will only be happy.[4]

The Torah gives a second injunction to rejoice on Sukkot, in connection with the ritual of "the four species."

> On the first day, you must take for yourself an *etrog* fruit of the citron tree, a *lulav*/palm branch, *hadasim*/myrtle branches, and *aravah*/willows [that grow near] the brook. During these seven days each year, you shall celebrate to God.[5]

This ritual is known as *netilat lulav*, taking the *lulav*, and is done every morning of the festival (except for Shabbat), just as it was observed in the time of the Temple.

Maimonides links the joy of the festival to the water-drawing ceremony that took place in the Temple courtyard.[6] During the intermediary nights of Sukkot, the Jewish People would go to the outer court of the Temple to rejoice with dance and music before drawing water for the libation-offering that followed. They sounded the shofar in order to arouse happiness and joy, in fulfillment of the verse, "And you shall draw water with joy."[7]

Thus the Mishnah teaches:

> Whoever did not see the rejoicing of *Beit haSho'evah*/"the Place of Drawing" never saw rejoicing in his lifetime.[8]

The ritual was referred to as "Water Drawing," because due to the great joy of the occasion, the people *drew* upon themselves extraordinary levels of *Ruach haKodesh*/Divine Inspiration, infusing them with a boundless joy.

REJOICE WITH TREMBLING[9]

What is so special about this festival that we have so many commandments to rejoice on it, in addition to the general injunction to rejoice on the festivals?

Furthermore, how does it apply to us today since we can no longer perform the water-drawing ceremony?

Maimonides discusses the need to observe *mitsvot* with a joy born out of the love of God. He infers this philosophy from Moses' warning to Israel to serve God "with happiness and a glad heart."[10] The verse says, "Serve God with gladness; come before Him with joyous song."[11] Maimonides adds that, in particular, a person who does not rejoice on Sukkot is missing the essence of the festival.

On the other hand, the Mishnah says that we must always pray with reverence, with tremendous awe of the Almighty, as did the pious men of old, who would meditate on the Divine Presence for an hour before beginning the Amidah prayer. Thus it is written, "Serve God with fear, and rejoice with trembling."[12]

How can you do the two things at once? At the moment we stand in reverence and fear before the great King, how can we feel the joy that stems from love?

We have seen that in order to be His Companion of the soul, we must live in the tension between love and fear. What Maimonides adds is that it is specifically through this internal fear that we can reach the level of the "Community of Israel, God's Companion of the soul."

According to the eighteenth-century Hasidic leader Rabbi Dov Baer, the Maggid of Mezrich, it is our fear of God, expressed through our observance of the commandments, that arouses God's desire for passionate attachment with Israel.

The Maggid elaborates as he comments on the verse,

Your God shall rejoice over you as the bridegroom rejoices over his bride.[13]

Here, the joy of the bridegroom is mentioned above that of the bride, for her joy is mixed with nervousness and apprehension, whereas the joy of the bridegroom is strong and sure. The same concept can be applied to Israel's Divine service during the festival of Sukkot. Israel, the bride, is filled with an internal fear of the Beloved, but at the same time they rejoice that He, as it were, delights in an intimate bond with His Companion of the soul.

According to the *Zohar*, it is *precisely* this internal fear that produces the supernal pleasure. Consequently, it is written, "serve God with joy," meaning "feel delight at the thought that you are giving joy to your Beloved." The Ari wrote that all the profound knowledge that he acquired in his life came in the merit of his rejoicing in the Divine joy. When he aroused in himself the fear of God, he could then rejoice in the supernal joy. Thus, he automatically drew upon himself the Divine bounty in the form of the hidden knowledge of the Torah.

Maimonides speaks of the Divine delight during Sukkot, as it were, in anticipation of the soul-union with His chosen people at the close of the festival, on Shemini Atseret. The joy that we derive from pleasing the Beloved can help us understand how to serve Him with fear and joy. We serve Him with fear by meditating on His power and majesty in order to arouse a simple fear, which turns into a profound awe of His greatness.

At the same time, we are elated at the joy God derives, if it can be said, from the love of Israel, as they adorn themselves with His commandments.

Maimonides concludes that serving God with joy on Sukkot involves standing before Him with awe while feeling the inner exultation of the Divine pleasure brought about by our internal fear.

Sukkot, then, as Maimonides explains, marks the beginning of the supernal joy, born of God's intimate relationship with His people. Therefore, we are commanded to rejoice before God in the Temple to show that we are celebrating His delight in His House, as His Companion of the soul.

This explains why the sages referred to the ceremony of the water libation in the Temple as "the rejoicing of the 'place of drawing.'" Those able to feel the joy of being God's Companion of the soul—more intense in the days of the Temple than it could ever be nowadays—drew upon themselves the Divine Inspiration, a joy that defies description.

The water-drawing ceremony is no longer possible, but the mitsvah of dwelling in sukkah booths brings about the contact with the Divine Presence, since it enables us to draw levels of *da'at*, the intimate knowledge of God. The energy we derive from the sukkah, as well as from the *lulav* and its species, was given to us only in order that we use it to bind all our strengths—the special gifts we are born with—to serve God with love, awe, joy, passionate attachment, and desire.

FROM FAITH TO JOY[14]

We have, then, two different types of rejoicing associated with the festival of Sukkot: the joy of the festival itself, and the joy ascribed to the mitsvah of the *lulav*. This is surprising, because as a general principle, the Torah never combines different causes for rejoicing. In this case, however, it seems that one completes the other. We can only wonder, also, how these two mitsvot differ from all the others about which the Torah does not ask us to rejoice.

We mentioned that on Rosh Hashanah, God judges us, and that at the close of Yom Kippur, He pronounces the verdict. Yet, the verdict is only sealed on the last day of Sukkot, on Hoshanah Rabbah. The *Zohar* uses a parable to explain the process of the judgment in the month of Tishri.

One can hope to change the written order of a king as long as he has not signed it. Even if it is signed, however, one can still hope that the king will rewrite it, although it is much more difficult. Yet, when the king stamps the order with his royal seal it is automatically dispatched and thus irrevocable. On Rosh Hashanah, the judgment is written; on Yom Kippur the document is signed. Yet, God does not seal it until Hoshanah Rabbah, after we have experienced the festival of Sukkot.

Why is this time of rejoicing both preceded and followed by judgment rather than starting with judgment and ending with joy? Can we have joy as we wait for judgment?

One might say that the joy comes to temper the apprehension we feel over the sealing of the judgment with the realization that it can still be changed. Yet, there is a deeper reason behind this order of events: although God forgives us on Yom Kippur, sins are addictive. Each transgression leaves behind an impression that makes it difficult for one to maintain a firm front against the lure of temptation. The joy of Sukkot helps erase the trace of former sins so that we may present ourselves to a judgment that is to be irrevocable.

In *Klach Pitchei Chochmah* (Principles of Wisdom), Rabbi Moshe Chayim Luzzato, known as Ramchal, mentions three purposes in God's creation of the world:

1. In order to bring God's attributes from potential to actual, through the revelation of God's Names that are derived from them.[15]
2. To bestow His goodness upon His creatures by making Himself known to them.
3. Above all, the desire to reveal His Oneness, that it should be known that "there is none besides Him"[16] and that nothing in the world—whether good or evil—has any independent existence without the Godly light that gives it vitality.[17]

One who knows this third purpose in his heart cannot be harmed by any curse; on the contrary, it will turn into a blessing, and anything evil in his life will revert to good, explains the Ramchal.

The completion of these three purposes will only be achieved in the ultimate future, however. Nevertheless, there are times during the year when the light of the three purposes shines brightly. In the month of Tishri, and more specifically, (1) in our Divine service of the Days of Awe, including Rosh Hashanah and Yom Kippur; (2) in our fulfillment of the mitsvah of *sukkah,* and (3) in our fulfillment of the mitsvah of *lulav* and its species.

During the Days of Awe, the time during which the world was originally created, we can fulfill the first purpose, that of revealing God's Names and attributes. For example, God's holy four-letter Name, the Tetragrammaton, the Name *Elohim*, and the Name *Adonai* represent the three traits—lovingkindness, judgment, and compassion—with which the world was created. As it is written, "You built a world which manifests Your lovingkindness."[18]

This verse refers to the holy Tetragrammaton, which reveals that God is eternal, beyond time. God judges the world with these three Names and their implications.

On Yom Kippur, God forgives our sins through His attributes of mercy and compassion. Thus, at this time, the full array of His attributes is revealed.

On Sukkot, the Divine Presence is like a mother protecting her children. During these days, God spreads over us the shelter of His peace, and we have a taste of the constant loving care that He has in store for us in the world to come. The essence of the sukkah is to reveal God's second purpose of creating the world: to bestow His goodness upon His creatures.

The *lulav* and its species reveal God's third purpose, the desire to reveal His oneness, that "there is none besides Him." This single mitsvah binds the *etrog*, which has taste and fragrance, together with the *aravah*, which has neither. The symbolic representation is that the righteous man, whose Torah and good deeds are like the *etrog*'s taste and fragrance, as well as the man who does not observe the Torah and is as plain as a willow branch, are both God's creations, expressions of His life force. The difference is that one wears garments of light, whereas the other has a cover of darkness, a product of God's concealment in a world that appears to be evil.[19] By uniting the *aravah* and the *etrog,* we show that both the righteous man and the man who is not share the Divine life force within them. This teaches us that even in its most corporeal form, the force of evil is only from God, and has a unique reason for existence.

Thus, the days between Rosh Hashanah and Yom Kippur, during which God reveals to us the purpose of His Names and attributes, are called "Days of Awe." For we are apprehensive lest God find us unworthy of entering into an intimate relationship with Him.

On the festival of Sukkot, however, God fulfills His desire to bestow His goodness upon His creatures by making Himself known to them. It is a time of joy, which increases in intensity through the perception of God's oneness brought about by the *lulav* and *etrog.*

The joy of the sukkah is the pleasure that comes from feeling God's Presence and goodness, as well as the satisfaction God derives from bestowing them upon us. However, the joy that comes from a perception of God's oneness is much higher; it stems from the realization that there is no such thing as evil. Anything negative that happens in the world is actually sustained by a Divine life force, including man's very desire to sin. When a person understands that all need and darkness merely cover the Divine effulgence, and that all evil is an expression of His goodness under a garment of concealment, his joy knows no limits.[20]

This third purpose of Creation provides an answer to the existential dilemma of the twentieth century. The true pain of our generation is the feeling of loneliness and abandonment in the world. God must reveal His oneness in order to counteract the pervasive feeling of loneliness. When, in the midst of our suffering, we suddenly feel God's light in everything that happens to us, that He is with us even in our darkest moments, and that all that we ever experienced came only from Him, even though we don't understand it, it brings us an awesome joy.

The experience of truly perceiving that "there is none besides Him," like that of receiving Divine Inspiration, is really a different state of consciousness. It is a joy that pervades the entire being.

There is a prayer said before the rite of *netilat lulav,* which cites the verse "they were afraid to come close to him,"[21] referring to the Israelites when Moses came down from Mount Sinai, his face radiant with light after being forty days in God's Presence. Used here, the verse alludes to the forces of evil, which fear the powerful revelation of the *lulav* and its species.

The righteous man—symbolized by the *etrog*–who performs the rite of *netilat lulav* with the intent to absorb its energy, namely, the clear knowledge that evil is only a function of God's will and in itself has no independent existence, renders the forces of evil powerless against him. It is easier for these forces to cling to the people with a lower consciousness, symbolized by the *aravah.* Yet, when the latter do the *netilat lulav* with that same intent, the inner awareness that "there is none besides Him" is also available to them, with the consequent imperviousness to the forces of evil.

We can now understand why the judgment of Hoshanah Rabbah comes after the joy of Sukkot. When we pray on Rosh Hashanah that all creatures recognize God's sovereignty, we are asking that the hidden forces of holiness that give life and existence to Creation be revealed, to show that there is nothing other than God Himself.

On Rosh Hashanah we are only coming toward that level. Even on Yom Kippur it is not complete. Experiencing God's love, as we do in the sukkah, reveals to us beyond a doubt that there is nothing in the world without a Divine force in it. Only after we become God's Companion of the soul, with the ensuing tension of love and fear, can we aspire to the revelation of His Oneness, in which we can perceive that even in the greatest concealment God's kingship exists.

We recite daily in the Shema prayer, "God is our Lord, God is one." During the Days of Awe, we are still on the level of "God is our Lord," whereas by Hoshanah Rabbah, the level of "God is one" is revealed. On this day we cry out, "*Hosha'na*/Save us, please!" as we hold the *aravah* branches by themselves, without the *lulav* and *etrog*, to emphasize that even when the willow is on its own, devoid of taste or fragrance, it still receives its life force from God.

The ultimate purpose of the festival of Sukkot is to bring us to the realization that there is none other than God, and to understand that man should not only avoid sinning in his thoughts, but beyond that, recognize the godliness that is concealed in them and replace them with a longing of such intensity that it completes the healing of his soul.

This is the ultimate repentance, to realize that nothing exists on its own. Then, one can accept everything God sends him throughout the year with love, even the pain, for it is a spark of Divinity wrapped in a cloak of darkness.

The Ari explains that the inner purpose of the water-libation ceremony was to arouse the Divine desire for the soul-union that occurred on Shemini Atseret. In the same manner, explains Rabbenu Bechaye, the effect caused in the heavenly realms by the rite of *netilat lulav* is, just as the water-drawing ceremony, the arousal of the Divine *da'at*–God's yearning, as it were, for passionate attachment with His Companion of the soul.

The effect caused on earth by both these rites is the joy of the intimate knowledge of the Beloved as the Source of all good and all evil. Only this can lead us into the intoxicating closeness we experience when we are invited into the King's private chambers on Shemini Atseret, when God tells His people, "Come, let us rejoice together I and you."*

*This chapter is dedicated to the memory of Estrella, daughter of Mesodi, a true "woman of valor," who passed away in Hoshanah Rabbah. May the inner joy that guided her life be an inspiration to all.

24

Rejoicing with God

God said, "Let there be light."' And there was light. . . . And there was evening and there was morning, day one.

—Genesis 1:3, 5

THE LIGHT THAT CAME INTO EXISTENCE on the first day was not the light of the sun or the moon, for they were formed on the fourth day. The Kabbalah teaches that the light came from God Himself. This Infinite Light filled the universe. Yet, after the first week of Creation, God concealed it in order to avoid its misuse. Some of this luminous energy remains, however, and after passing through myriad layers of concealment, reaches man as physical light.

Yet, God also allowed man to experience His Divine light on a different level.

The Ari taught that the radiant light of Creation was really the illumination of the soul-union between the Almighty and the heavenly roots of the souls of Israel. At an extremely high level, this soul-union between God and His Companion of the soul is constant, as will be revealed in the ultimate future. At a lower level, God conceals this union to prevent its misuse. However, God also gave His people Shabbat, for by ceasing work on this holy day, we can reach a higher state.

Just as the soul-union of Shabbat completes one week of Divine service, so the close bond of Shemini Atseret climaxes a whole year of festivals and Divine service.

Shemini Atseret represents the ultimate crown of the intimate relationship between the Almighty and His chosen people. It is the completion of structure that was started on the first day of Elul. Only after the culmination of our love relationship at the close of Yom Kippur, followed by the inner exultation of Sukkot, are we ready to experience the unique state of consciousness that Shemini Atseret brings.

On this day, the soul-union that was supposed to occur at the Giving of the Torah finally takes place, and God allows us to experience His hidden light of Creation in the most intense outpouring of luminous energy of the year.

Shemini Atseret, teaches the *Tikuney Zohar*, is "a festival unto itself" during which we can absorb the wellsprings of God's Torah. In the Land of Israel, where each holiday is only one day rather than two,[1] Shemini Atseret and Simchat Torah—the Rejoicing of the Torah—are always on the same day.

THE HIGHEST LEVEL

The Torah discusses openly three levels of relation with God: awe, love, and passionate attachment. This third and highest level is the ultimate goal of the commandments, which the *Zohar* calls 613 instructions on how to become passionately attached to the Divine.[2]

The Midrash, however, implies that there is a level of closeness beyond that of passionate attachment. In this world, we are to be passionately attached to God, says the Midrash, citing the verse: "You, who remained attached to God your Lord, are all alive today."[3] In the ultimate future, however, the Jewish people will be compared to God Himself. Just as God is like a consuming fire,[4] so Israel will be a fire: "And the light of Israel shall become fire, and his holy one shall become a flame."[5]

A verse from the Song of Songs helps us understand this Midrash:

> I am sleeping but my heart is awake
> A sound! My Beloved knocks!
> Open to Me, *Achoti*/My sister, *Ra'yati*/My love,
> *Yonati*/ My dove, *Tamati*/My perfect one.[6]

This verse expresses God's love for Israel in the four degrees of intensity revealed from the onset of Elul until Shemini Atseret.

In comparison to the quality of repentance that we reach in Elul, during the rest of the year, "I am sleeping but my heart is awake." "A sound! My Beloved knocks!" The idea of knocking portrays the service God wants from us in Elul, hinted to in the Hebrew letters of the word *Elul*, an acronym of *Ani leDodi veDodi li*/"I am my Beloved's, and my Beloved is mine."[7] It is now Elul and "My Beloved knocks," urging me to aim for the highest level of repentance so that I may become "the Community of Israel, His Companion of the soul."

The call of the shofar resounds throughout the month of Elul, when Israel awakens with the dawn to recite *selichot*, the special prayers of entreaty expressing Israel's yearning for intimacy with the Beloved. The powerful sound of the shofar pierces the heart; I feel my Beloved attempting to arouse me, asking me not to make Him leave me ever again.

On Rosh Hashanah, my accusers are aroused to participate in the Divine judgment. As my King, my Beloved keeps a certain distance while He deals with my detractors. At this time, God dons the attribute of "Brother," and calls me *"Achoti,"* My sister, with an unconditional love precluding separation. I begin to relate to Him with a profound internal fear. I cry out to Him with the speechless sound of the shofar. This is the kiss of the Song of Songs, given through the breath of the mouth.

> If only You could be like a brother nurtured at the bosom of my mother! When I
> would find You in the street I would kiss You.[8]

This brotherly love manifests itself in the week between Rosh Hashanah and Yom Kippur. Then the commandment of the day is speech, the confession that is crucial to repentance. On Yom Kippur I give myself to Him. During the *Ne'ilah* prayer that closes the service, I no longer have to fear the accusers. My past behind me, I am "face-to-face" with Him. The time of separation is over, and the light of His love toward Israel begins to shine. I become God's beloved (*Ra'yati*). He reveals His "great love" for me, the fiery love of Companions of the soul that demands constant care and attention.

On Sukkot, I enter the dimension of "His right hand embraces me."[9] He now calls me "*Yonati*/My dove." A dove is always faithful to her mate and she will never exchange him for another. So God expresses His trust in His beloved. My faith in Him no longer needs testing. I reveal this faith by taking shelter in the sukkah, a structure physically weak but spiritually strong. Internalizing the knowledge that "there is none besides Him" fills me with joy for the entire year.

On Sukkot we are elevated to the level of *devekut*, and we can feel this passionate attachment with all our heart. This is as the verse says: "Just as the loin cloth clings to a man, so I have caused the entire House of Israel to be attached to Me."[10] Only by being attached to the Source of light are we truly alive: "Only you, the ones who remained attached to God your Lord, are all alive today."

Yet the level of passionate attachment that we feel on Sukkot is still like the cleaving of two separate entities. Higher still is the bonding of Shemini Atseret. At this time, God joins His Companion of the soul in a perfect soul-union. The Almighty now relates to Israel as *Tamati*/My perfect one. This is the level of closeness to God of *Ishi*, beyond the intimacy of passionate attachment, to which the Midrash was alluding. A soul-union like that of Shemini Atseret occurs only once a year, and for but a fragment of time. It is like the merging of two flames.

The revelation of Shemini Atseret is only a spark of the intimate union that we will know in the ultimate future. Then, the light of Israel "shall become fire," similar to God's. There will no longer be two separate entities cleaving together, but One.

COMING DOWN TO EARTH

How can we experience this state of oneness? It is only through the gift He gave us for that purpose: His Torah. The Torah is the link between Israel and God, the object of God's delight and Israel's.

There is no greater passionate attachment than learning to know God through the Torah. The *Zohar* says, "The Torah, the Holy One, and Israel are One," for the soul-union between God and Israel is actualized through the Torah.

On Shemini Atseret, God tells His Companion of the soul, "Let us rejoice, I and you, together," through the Torah that brings joy and delight to us both. Consequently, on Simchat Torah we complete the yearly cycle of Torah reading with the final words of Deuteronomy, "before the eyes of all Israel," and continue with the opening line of Genesis, "In the beginning. . . ." By immediately starting the Torah anew, we seek to give pleasure to God by immersing ourselves in our common object of delight. According to the sages, God Himself studies Torah; we study the revealed aspects, and God studies its hidden dimension.

The Torah is hinted to in the first verse of Genesis. "In the beginning, God created heaven and earth." "Beginning" refers to the Torah, which is the beginning of wisdom;[11] "heaven" alludes to its hidden teachings, while "earth" hints at the revealed teachings.

The sages teach that the First Tablets of the Covenant contained a Torah that was completely spiritual, whereas the Torah of the Second Tablets was enclosed in matter. Before the sin of the Golden Calf, the Israelites learned from the Torah to know their Creator with a direct, mystical knowledge. After the Golden Calf, the teachings of the Torah were divided into two parts, the hidden teachings of the Kabbalah and the revealed part of the Written and Oral Torah. Now we must first learn the revealed teachings before going on to study its hidden knowledge.

Moses realized that as a consequence of the Golden Calf, Israel could no longer absorb the hidden teachings of the Torah; on the other hand, without Torah the nation might cease to exist. He therefore broke the First Tablets. God then had to give him the Second, whose contents were applicable to Israel in their fallen state. Thus, the last words of the Torah, "before the eyes of all Israel," indicate that this Torah is for all of Israel, not just for the perfectly righteous.

When we continue from the last words of the Torah to the beginning, we immediately read: "In the beginning God created heaven and earth. The earth was without form and empty, with darkness on the face of the depths."[12] This darkness alludes to the material garment that now enclothes the Torah, the same type of garments that enclothe man and prevent him from grasping its mysteries. If a person were freed of physicality and its drives, the Torah would also be open to him.

But when God said "Let there be light," He granted man the ability to understand the Torah's revealed portion, which leads him to grasp the hidden teachings as well. Therefore, at the close of the holiday cycle, God says to Israel, "Let us rejoice, I and you, together." This Torah with its hidden and revealed teachings will be our intimate bond.

Consequently, not only the scholars who devote their lives to the study of Torah can feel the soul-union. Anybody who studies Torah seriously on a regular basis and dances on Simchat Torah receives an indelible impression of a total intimacy with God. It is as if his body were electrified with a Divine vitality compelling him to dance. This day is to him the crown of an entire year of struggle in Torah study, from biblical commentaries to Talmud. This very struggle is what enables him to absorb the energy of the day.

Those who are fortunate enough to find a master and study under his direction *know* why the Torah is referred to as an object of delight. Whether they study with the master an entire day or an hour in the evening after a harrowing day's work, on Simchat Torah they will be dancing with a fire within that is distinguishable even to the onlooker.

The numerical value of the initial letters of the four types of relationship with the Divine—A*choti*/My sister, **R**a'*ayti*/My beloved, **Y**o*nati*/My dove, and **T**a*mati*/My perfect one—is 611, identical to that of the letters of the Hebrew word *Torah*.

From the beginning of Elul through Shemini Atseret, there is a special addition to the prayer service: Psalm 27, "The Lord is my light [on Rosh Hashanah] and my salvation [on Yom Kippur]. . . . He will hide me in His *sukkah*." In this psalm we cry out in yearning for the completion of all four levels of relationship with the Divine:

> One thing I asked of God,
> That I shall seek:
> That I dwell in the House of God
> All the days of my life.[13]

We yearn for the day in which God will make true His promise, which we only know for an instant on Shemini Atseret, when we become totally attached to His essence through the joy of the Torah:

> You will no longer need the sun for daylight or the moon to give light at night. God will always be your light, and your God will be your glory.[14]

PART FOUR

DEALING WITH CONCEALMENT

25

Days of Affliction: Darkness before Dawn

THE TORAH PORTION THAT CLOSES the Book of Numbers—*Massey*/Journeys—is always read during the Days of Affliction—the three weeks between the seventeenth of Tammuz and the ninth of Av. *Massey* begins:

> These are the journeys of the Israelites, who had left Egypt in organized groups under the leadership of Moses and Aaron. Moses recorded their stops along the way at God's command. These were their stops along the way:[1]

The next forty-three verses list the names of all the places where the people of Israel camped in the desert on their way to the Holy Land. What makes these forty-two stops important enough to record them in Torah?

According to the Midrash, each stop constituted another step toward holiness, a path very dear to the Creator. As such, they were recorded as precious mementos for generations to come.

The Ari teaches that with each rung we ascend in the spiritual ladder we do not add to the preceding structure, but begin to build a completely new project. The Maharal of Prague[2] illustrates this pattern of progression by reminding us that Israel's future redeemer is to be born on the fateful ninth of Av.

The Maharal explains that the light of the Messiah does not continue that of the Temple; rather it is a new form of Divine energy that God will direct on us. Hence, this new illumination could not come into being as long as the Temple was on its premises: the light of the Messiah could begin to shine only after the previous one was extinguished. Similarly, one who has an old building is unable to erect a royal palace in its place until the previous structure has been cleared from the site.

Hence, Israel is compared to the moon. When the light of the moon reaches its peak, it gradually has to wane until it disappears before receiving the renewed light of the next month. Of a similar nature is the Divine service that Israel must fulfill. On the path to redemption, our task is to build a succession of structures on the same site.

Hence, each of our structures must be destroyed before a new one can be started. Yet each structure surpasses the previous one in complexity and beauty.

Each one of the forty-two stops in Israel's long journey to the Holy Land marked a step of ascent to a higher level of closeness to God: consequently a renewed effort had to be provided for each and every rung. At the successful completion of each journey, the people experienced an appreciable loss of Divine awareness. This allowed a renewed Divine light to flood the darkness. Some of the incidents that occurred as a result of the concealment of the Divine Presence are recorded or hinted at in the list of stops:

> [They] camped in Rephidim, where there was no water for the people to drink. . . .
> They left the Sinai Desert and camped in Graves-of-Craving. . . . Aaron climbed the
> Hor Mountain at God's command and he died there.[3]

The Torah is presenting a pattern for all Jews, for all time. Each member of Israel has to successfully complete forty-two such trials through the physical world. From the moment of his birth, until he returns his soul to his Maker, a Jew experiences a series of ascents and descents of varying intensity—illumination followed by darkness—each one offering a unique form of growth that could be reached by proceeding from a point of concealment.

At each stop, one rises to the next level. Yet, before the actual ascent we go through trial. By showing our full trust in God during this "desert stretch," we show that we are worthy of ascending.

In the Book of Psalms, King David sang of his own spiritual journey. It was while stranded in the Judean desert, fleeing from his enemies and with a low state of Divine awareness, that he composed one of his most poignant psalms:

> A Song of David,
> when he was in the wilderness of Judah.
> O God—You are My God,
> I seek You, My soul thirsts for You,
>   my flesh longs for You;
> in a land barren,
> and weary with no water.
> Thus I have beheld You in the Sanctuary;
> to see Your might and Your glory.[4]

Before we ascend to a new level, the light that helped us climb to the previous one is obscured. Yet, although we feel that we are once again building anew, in truth we are really adding to the structure we have been building since the time of our creation. The more we grow, the greater is expected from us, and patterns of behavior that would have been praiseworthy at a lower structure could incur Divine displeasure.

We may now understand why we have to go through the Days of Affliction before receiving a new light on each succeeding Tishri. The tragedies that have befallen Israel during the Days of Affliction have given these three weeks a quality of wilderness, evoking the journeys of the Israelites in the Desert.[5] Our efforts to maintain a radiant faith during these difficult weeks form the foundations for the goals we set for ourselves in Elul. A look at our past shows that this time of affliction is meant to help Israel soar to new heights.

During the era of the First Temple, Israel had not yet fully accepted the Oral Torah. It was only after the Temple's destruction, on the ninth of Av, that they took willingly this new yoke upon themselves. The study of the Oral Torah flourished during the time of the Second Temple. But in order for the light of the future redemption to begin to shine, the light presently shining upon Israel had to be extinguished. Hence, it is on the very day on which we mourn the destruction of the Second Temple that the Messiah is to be born.

The sages therefore decreed that the Torah portion *Massey* be read during these difficult weeks to remind us that we only advance "at God's command."[6] Our awareness of God's constant guidance can draw down a renewed light to illuminate each of our steps.

Another example of this pattern of growth is the twenty-one Days of Affliction, closely followed by the twenty-one days from Rosh Hashanah to Hoshanah Rabbah, in which we receive our final judgment for the coming year.[7] Together, these two sets of days add up to forty-two, the number of stops on Israel's journey to the Holy Land, thus showing that the essence of the days of darkness is identical to that of the days of light.

The forty-two days link the past year with the year ahead. They conclude on Shemini Atseret, when we join the Beloved in the most intense soul-union of the year. Twenty-one is the numerical value of *Ehyeh*, the Divine Name hinting at the Light of the Crown, and the renewed light imbued upon the coming year. It is also the numerical value of the Hebrew word *ach*/surely, which begins the Psalm: "*Ach*/Surely, God is good to Israel,"[8] a further indication that both sets of twenty-one days are of equal benefit to Israel.

IN THE DARKNESS OF A SHELL

The Days of Affliction open the way for the upcoming year, just as a constriction of light allows for a renewed influx to shine. According to the Midrash, in the ultimate future, these days will be seen to contain only goodness for Israel. These twenty-one days are the beginning of the spiritual structure that we build during the twenty-one days of the month of Tishri, for one can only recognize light in contrast to darkness. It is written,

> God saw that the light was good, and God divided between the light and the darkness.

As we can see, the light was called good even before its division into light and darkness. This implies that there is good in the darkness, since prior to the division, it was included in the "light." Moreover, it is easier to detect the goodness of the light when it is closely preceded by darkness.

The concept of light and darkness fused into a single entity is behind this statement of the sages:

Were it not for the shells that conceal them we would not be able to find pearls in the depths of the ocean.

In this example, the sages convey that the oyster shells enclosing pearls are not obstructive but helpful; they enable us to find the treasures they protect. Likewise, each one of our character traits is a complete entity: when seen from outside it appears like a shell, conveying bad qualities, but upon peeking inside, one beholds the pearl that was waiting to be revealed.

Polishing one's character traits is more difficult than observing the entire Torah, say the sages. However, it is the effort that we make that is precious in God's eyes. The Gaon of Vilna teaches that the entire world was created only for man to perfect his traits.

The process of rectification from shell into pearl first involves the awareness of the shell. Only when the shell is identified can we shine light onto its contents and discover the pearl.

This is not possible when heavenly light is directed at a person, illuminating his Torah study or Divine service. Then the person's bad character traits are subdued, for he is totally absorbed by the vibrant Divine energy that he feels.[9] As the chasidic master Rabbi Abraham of Slonim, author of *Beit Abraham*, notes:

As soon as I feel illuminated by the Divine energy of the spirit, anything related to matter becomes darkness in my eyes and does not even tempt me.

One can only discern one's negative traits when the heavenly light directed at us is constricted. Things then begin to go wrong: no major catastrophes, just annoying incidents that weaken the feeling of being connected to God. For instance, one morning, after an uplifting prayer, you have to mail an important document at the post office. Yet, because of different impediments, by the time you actually get there, it is almost too late. The shell or unrefined aspect of your personality will likely surface. At this time, you may either retort sharply to the clerk, the person before you on line, or the parking attendant, or you may stand back and analyze the scene objectively. Then you will see that impatience is one of the negative traits of your character that needs your improvement.

The paragon of patience is Moses, called "the humblest man on earth." Rashi explains that his humility denoted mildness and patience.[10] Impatience is the desire for things to happen precisely when one wants them. But within this shell is the realization that things occur only "at God's command." One who has this knowledge deeply rooted within him is humbled by the constant surrender of his own will in submission to the Divine will. And the pearl is when God's will becomes his will.

An example of an incident that causes doubt could be as follows. Let us say that you are travelling to Israel to enroll in a yeshiva. In your hand luggage are your most important possessions: your prayer book, books on Torah, a set of *tefillin*, and so forth.

You suddenly realize your hand luggage has disappeared. What might surface now are deep doubts. Surely, you might think, if God believed in the importance of my trip, He would have protected me from losing these very items that brought me close to Him. Furthermore, even if my project were not as important as I see it, He could nevertheless have spared me from this loss, if only because He cared for my closeness to Him!

If you could just stand back at this moment and examine the situation, you would have little difficulty in detecting the shell of doubt and, by prying it open, you would cast light on the awareness that God's motives are not to be questioned, even when they defy human logic. Your very acceptance is the final effort you needed in order to find the pearl: the radiant faith that allows you to "see" that God Himself is responsible for the disappearance that brought turmoil in your life. Just as your motive behind this trip was to come close to the Creator, so did He send you this frustrating incident to teach you that there is an imperceptible veil that distances you from Him—the trait that needs polishing—and that you must begin to rip it open, even if He helps you complete the job.

There are times in life when, despite the fact that everything seems lost, you still have to be able to enter a space beyond reason and logic, a space filled to capacity with your innate trust in God. When in this space, you instinctively know that God wants the initiation of the relationship to come from below, from you.

When we catch but a glimpse of our personal shells—whatever their nature—we may begin to rectify them. Without the absence of light, the pearls within us would ever remain enclosed in hard shells, and we would be unable to find the spiritual treasures that are within our reach. Hence the beneficial aspect of darkness.

The shells in our depths reveal themselves in two stages; during the time in which God constricts His light, the coarser aspects of our character traits are most easily aroused. If at this stage we apply our efforts to subdue them, we then reach the second stage; when these traits surface once again, we have a further opportunity to work on the aspects of the traits that are harder to detect.

For instance, a person might have a proclivity to anger. In the first stage, he makes an effort to control it, and succeeds in avoiding his usual outbursts. In the second stage, he no longer lashes out at the people around him when things go wrong, but rather reproves them in a quiet tone. Yet, he knows that deep down, the anger is still there, and the person he is addressing is able to feel it as well. This is his chance to polish the subtler aspect of his negative trait, in order to complete its refinement.

To that end, we were given two sets of twenty-one days in which strict judgment prevails. In the Days of Affliction the luminous Divine energy that was directed on us throughout the entire year is concealed; at this time the roots of our character traits emerge. It is now possible to perceive each trait with all its shades. Our efforts of self-improvement during these three weeks prepare us for the coming Elul.

In the twenty-one days of Tishri, there is no concealment. God is close to us, but it is still a time of strict judgment, for He adopts His function of Judge.

The twenty-one Days of Affliction are a time for contemplation. In our efforts to become sensitive to the needs of our soul, we try to recognize our coarser patterns of behavior. When the shells reveal themselves, we may catch a glimpse of the spiritual treasure in store for us when we attain the inner, perfected aspect of each trait. In Elul comes a strenuous effort of eliminating the shells we have detected. We refer to the work of Elul as "fleeing from evil," as the verse says, "flee from evil and do good."[11]

The New Year dawns. In Tishri the pearls within our character traits are finally exposed, devoid of shells, and emit their harmonious glow. Hence, although in the second set of twenty-one days we also undergo a time of strict judgment, we now have attained the second stage of refinement, that of "doing good." Then, on the awaited Shemini Atseret, all our pearls radiate around the crown of the King in the most intense soul-union of the year.

The verse says, "but towards evening there will be light,"[12] for it is from darkness that light emerges. It is the darkness behind us that allows us to peek into the light ahead of us. As the verse says,

Even in the darkness a light shines for the upright.[13]*

---

* To Samuel Aryeh, with love.

26

Tisha B'Av:
Call from the Divine

TISHA B'AV, THE NINTH OF THE JEWISH MONTH of Av, is the date of the destruction of the First and Second Temples. It is the day of mourning over our estrangement from God, and over the many tragedies that have befallen our people throughout the long centuries of exile. Yet, though God's call has grown fainter, it has followed us through history, and is still identifiable today.

As we discussed above, although God allows the power of evil to exist in the world, He also desired that there be one place where His Presence could dwell undisturbed, a place where evil could not enter. This was the Tabernacle in the desert and the holy Temple in Jerusalem.

According to the tradition, it was on the site of the Temple that Jacob dreamt of "a ladder set upon the earth, its head reaching to the heavens."[1] For this is the essence of the Temple, to bridge heaven and earth, the physical and the spiritual. In the dream, God communicated to Jacob His desire for a physical setting to hold His revelation.

When Jacob left, fleeing from Esau, "he came to a familiar place and spent the night there because the sun had already set."[2] A careful reading of the Hebrew shows that the sun had set suddenly, before the proper time.[3] Jacob received his vision in the still of the night, for the time of revelation had not yet arrived. God was showing him a vision of the future, when the Divine revelation would be bright as day. This happened centuries later, when God told Moses, "Make Me a sanctuary, and I will dwell within them."[4] This was the *Mishkan*, the desert Tabernacle and precursor to the Holy Temple. Note that the verse does not say "I will dwell within *it*," but rather, "within *them*"—within the vessels,[5] or spiritual organs, of every Jew, for this was the role of the Temple, to create a soul-union between man and Creator.

TABERNACLE AND TEMPLES

After leaving Egypt and receiving the Torah, the Israelites were to have entered the land of Canaan. There they were commanded to fulfill three *mitsvot*, in the following order:

1. Appoint a king
2. Exterminate Amalek, the prototype of evil[6]
3. Build the Temple

And yet, immediately after the sin of the Golden Calf, God changed the order of these commandments and instructed the Israelites to erect a Tabernacle. They were to furnish it with different spiritual objects that could draw down a Divine light and raise the spiritual consciousness of the people.

In addition, the Divine Presence was visibly manifest in the Tabernacle. A pillar of cloud stood near it by day and a column of fire by night. Even when the Israelites sinned, the Divine Presence did not leave the Tabernacle.

There were other signs of God's love. The cherubs above the Ark of the Covenant were locked in an embrace (representing the union of God and Israel), a fire descended from Heaven to consume the sacrifices, and the center candle of the *Menorah* remained permanently lit as testimony that the Divine Presence dwelt among the Jewish people.

But the question still remains: Why did God change the order of His commandments? What is the connection between the Golden Calf and the Sanctuary?

THE BELOVED PENITENT

"In the place where the penitent stands, even the perfectly righteous cannot stand," says the Talmud. That is, one who has never sinned in his life cannot attain the closeness to God of a person who has sinned and done *teshuvah* (repented).

> A repentant should not consider himself distant from the level of the righteous because of the sins and transgressions that he has committed. This is not true. He is beloved and desirable before the Creator as if he never sinned.[7]

Such expressions of endearment are found in Scripture only in regards to a penitent. Because the penitent is brokenhearted over his sins, because he fears that he has blemished himself and the heavenly realms, there is danger that he might sink too far. He might think God holds him in contempt; or, in his despair, he might return to his old ways. God knows that depression is one of the major weapons of the evil inclination, and so He shines His light and love on the penitent at all times. On the other hand, a person who has always been righteous receives no special revelation. The Divine light reaches him in exact proportion to the quality of his worship.

In Egypt, the Israelites had sunk to the lowest possible level of impurity. When they left, they were on the level of penitents to whom God reveals His lovingkindness. God went in front of them in a pillar of cloud by day and camped with them in a pillar of fire by night to demonstrate to them His love. The revelation of the Divine Presence at the foot of Mount Sinai was a similar testimony of God's love for His people.

However, forty days after Moses went up the mountain to receive the Tablets, the people feared that he would not return. They were seized by confusion and panic, and as a result, stopped feeling God's Presence within them.

They gathered around Aaron and declared, "We have no idea what happened to Moses, the man who brought us out of Egypt."[8] They believed that the only reason they had enjoyed the Divine light until then was in the merit of Moses; they felt themselves unworthy of it on their own. Now that Moses was gone, they thought, there was no one able to draw down the Infinite Light. In a desperate attempt to find an intermediary between them and the Divine, they made a Golden Calf. "This, Israel, is your god, who brought you out of Egypt," they declared.[9]

However, Moses did return, and the people repented of their sin. To reassure them that His love for them was unconditional, that it did not depend on their worthiness, God asked them to build the Tabernacle. This dwelling space of the *Shechina/ Divine Presence*, Who did not leave the premises even when they sinned, was the tangible proof that the flame of love binding them to the Holy One was infinite and eternal, unextinguishable by the many waters of sin.

SETTLED IN THE LAND

The generation of the desert needed visible miracles in order to feel close to the Infinite Light and to sense the Divine Presence among them with infinite love, despite their waywardness. Yet, when members of the generation entered the Land of Israel and built the Temple, the situation changed. There was no pillar of cloud by day, nor fire by night. As for those signs that did remain, the embrace of the cherubs, the permanent glow of the center branch of the Menorah, they were no longer unconditional. They occurred only when Israel was doing the Divine will.

At this point in Jewish history, the people were no longer considered penitents. The many miracles they had witnessed in the Tabernacle—the iridescence of the clouds of glory, the embrace of the cherubs, the constant glow of the Menorah's center light, and the fire descending from Heaven—had impressed upon them God's love forever. They only needed visions of the Divine Presence in accordance with the level of their devotion.

Therefore, in the First Temple, God revealed Himself only in relation to how much they reciprocated His love. When they fulfilled His will, they merited to see the cherubs locked in an intimate embrace, the center light of the Menorah glowing, and a fire on the altar shaped like a lion. When they did not fulfill His will, the cherubs did not face each other, the center light of the Menorah died out, and the fire on the altar took the shape of a dog.

THE SECOND TEMPLE

All this changed when, as a result of Israel's sins, Nebuchadnezzar, king of Babylon, destroyed Jerusalem and exiled the Jewish people. The First Temple was set aflame on Tisha B'Av, and the Jews were exiled to Babylon for seventy years. Afterward, part of the nation returned to the Holy Land and built the Second Temple in Jerusalem.

In the Second Temple five major elements were missing: (1) the Ark of the

Covenant; (2-3) the two cherubs; and (4-5) the *Urim* and *Tumim* of the High Priest's breastplate—the prophetic device that allowed him to receive God's will.[10] The essence of holiness—the source of Israel's invulnerability to evil—was concentrated in these five elements. Without them, Israel's defenses were greatly weakened. Furthermore, the flame in the altar was always low, and no fire fell from Heaven to burn the offerings. The only remaining sign of the Divine Presence was the center flame of the Menorah, which remained aglow when the High Priest was righteous.

The two Temples showed the power of *teshuvah* to the people of Israel by allowing them to see the changes in the Temple at the times they were not fulfilling the Divine will. The two Temples were like a heavenly voice calling, "Return to Me, rebellious children!" Their role was to show Israel how beloved penitents are to God.

The First Temple actually showed Israel which flaws they had to mend. The Second Temple only showed them that they had sinned. Yet, even this perception was lost with its destruction. The single tangible sign of the Divine Presence remnant in the Second Temple helped them to see how the heavenly voice was to diminish in intensity in generations to come, making it more challenging to repent with the passing of time. We await the Third Temple era, when God will reveal Himself more fully than ever before.

After the painful loss of the symbols of God's love, intimacy with the Divine became possible only through the light of Torah study. Just before the Temple was destroyed, Rabbi Yochanan ben Zakkai obtained permission from the Roman general besieging Jerusalem to found the Academy of Yavneh. Yavneh provided the fertile ground where the Tannaic sages (c. 10-220 C.E.) developed the parameters of the new relationship for the long exile. This was the Mishnah, the basis of the oral tradition. Their teachings were later expanded by the Amoraic sages of Palestine and Babylon (c. 220-489 C.E.) to form the Talmud, the main body of knowledge that has guided the life of Jews until today.

In the time of the Tannaim, when the sages learned Torah and fulfilled God's commandments with love, they received luminous Torah insights. If a sage would commit a sin, he was immediately aware of it, for he lost his clear understanding of the Torah.

Over the centuries, however, the light of the Torah slowly diminished. By the time of the Baal Shem Tov and the Gaon Rabbi Eliyahu of Vilna, the light was revealed only to a chosen few. For the most part, this means of communing with God was lost.

Now that the mysteries of the Torah were seldom revealed, the heavenly voice through which God called His people back to Him moved from the mind to the heart, from the light of the Torah illuminating the mind, to the feelings of love, awe, and passionate attachment arousing the heart.

Those who observed the commandments felt enthusiasm and passionate attachment to their Creator, in fear of the slightest transgression that might separate them from the Beloved, felt in their hearts the powerful love described in Song of Songs: "Love sparks are fiery coals, a flame of the Divine." Yet, as soon as a person sinned, his heart was blocked and he was unable to feel anything in his Divine service and his observance of the mitsvot.

As time passed and people sinned, we were deprived even of the inspiration to do mitsvot. We no longer felt ecstasy in our Divine service. The heavenly voice of the heart was dying out.

In our times, we are suffering from what Kabbalah calls "the birth-pangs of the Messiah," namely, the period of darkness that precedes the coming of the Redeemer, and the heavenly voice has become very faint. To use Rabbi Kaplan's example, it is as if God is sending us a message on a very weak radio station with a lot of static. The Divine call is like a feeble voice reverberating inside the heart of every Jew, calling him to return to the relationship he was created to enjoy.

In Rabbi Tsadok haCohen's words, "God's way of calling out to man is to implant in his mind every day thoughts expressing man's yearning for God."[11] As we find in Proverbs:

> Because I have called, and you refused; I have stretched out My hand, and no one paid heed.[12]

A person must be ever alert to hear these inner thoughts. As soon as he feels within himself a thought of repentance, he must quickly seize it and act upon it, as we learn from the Song of Songs:

> I held on to Him, determined that my deeds would never again cause me to lose hold of Him.[13]

The understanding that his longing for God is a mere reflection of God's calling out to man, "like water mirrors a loving look," is the more powerful indication that, as we make our way back, our struggle will be upheld by the most effective help of all.[14]

God did leave us one heavenly echo that remains clear and vibrant: Shabbat. If we feel elated by the sweetness of Shabbat, if our heart and mind respond to it, we know that God takes pleasure in our deeds. If we do not feel the joy of Shabbat, it is a sign that we need to examine our conduct. As the hasidic Shabbat song proclaims:

> Those who love God and long for the rebuilding of the Temple, exult and rejoice on Shabbat as if they received the rebuilding of the Temple.[15]

The call that was once heard through the Temple and then through the Torah is now heard through Shabbat.

27

"My Eyes, My Eyes, Are Flowing with Tears!"

THE TWO MONTHS OF TAMMUZ AND AV are like Israel's eyes, which weep uncontrollably over their loss. On the seventeenth of Tammuz the enemy made a breach in the wall surrounding Jerusalem: thus ended our ability to experience consciously the soul-union between the Holy One and the Community of Israel, with the group energy of a unified nation. On the ninth of Av, the day in which the destruction of the Temple began, we mourn,

My eyes, my eyes, are flowing with tears![1]

The image of eyes lends to the destruction of the Temple its usual connotation of da'at/intimate knowledge of God and devekut characterized by God's bond with the generation of the desert:

You, God, have revealed yourself to them face-to-face [literally, "eye to eye"].[2]

As we will illustrate, the image of the eyes runs throughout the theme of the destruction. In his final address, Moses tells the assembled nation:

Three times each year, all your males shall be seen in the presence of God your Lord in the place that He will choose: on the festival of Matzahs, on the festival of Shavuot, and on the festival of Sukkot. [In those times] you shall not appear (be seen) before God empty-handed.[3]

This repetition of the expression "to be seen" gave rise to a peculiar comment of the sages:

One who is blind in one eye is exempt from seeing, for it is taught "just as you come to see with two eyes, you come to be seen by two eyes."

Rashi explains,

Just like man would go to the Temple for God to see him with His "two eyes," man came to see God with his own two eyes.

154

How can this be? Is it not written, "For man will not see Me and live"?[4] And how do Rashi's comments explain the idea of exempting a blind man from seeing?

A third question: What about women? How did this "seeing" and "being seen" affect them?

PILGRIM FESTIVALS

Pesach, Shavuot, and Sukkot were designated as the three pilgrim festivals in which the Israelites traveled to Jerusalem to appear before God. In the pilgrim festivals, the *cohanim*/priests would lift the cloth partition and allow the Israelites to look at the cherubs.

Since the cherubs were the physical image-model of the special relationship between the Community of Israel and the Creator, the cherub representing the Almighty was formed in the figure of a boy, and the one portraying the people of Israel was formed as a girl. The Talmud teaches that although the cherubs were made as solid gold figures, they miraculously intertwined in an embrace when the majority of the people of Israel was acting in accordance to the Divine will. In contrast, when the people of Israel were in a state of sin, the cherubs would look away from each other, revealing the curtailing of intimacy resulting from the people's obliviousness to the Divine will.

Since the same word, *impurity,* is used to describe the effect of sin as well as that of menstruation, it is important to understand that the comparison refers to the effect of any source of impurity, but not the cause. The impurity of evil from sin affects the spirit, clouding the mind's sharpness and deadening the feelings, whereas the impurity of menstruation regards the physical body, clinging to the woman temporarily until her process of purification is completed. The only person affected by the impurity of the menses is the husband, in that he is forbidden to have any physical contact with his wife.

The reason the sages compare the physical estrangement of the cherubs when Israel was in a state of sin to that of the menstrual period is to stress that the feelings during the time of estrangement were similar to those of a couple who long for each other when deprived of physical contact.

The Israelites were not allowed free access to the Holy of Holies; only the High Priest himself entered the chamber once a year, on Yom Kippur. On the festivals, however, the priests lifted the curtain and revealed the embrace that shook the men to the deep recesses of their being, similar to a person feeling aroused upon seeing desire in the eyes of his beloved. The onlookers were experiencing physically the earthly soul-union with God.

The statement of the sages that when the people of Israel were not fulfilling God's will the cherubs looked away from each other really means that during those times of estrangement there was no soul-union with Israel below. When, on the festivals, the priests showed Israel the cherubs intertwined and declared, "See how great is your love before God!" they were alluding to the soul-union known as *Jerusalem Below,* within the souls of the people of Israel.

The purpose of the men making a pilgrimage to Jerusalem on the three festivals was twofold. One, each was to appear before God not only for his Creator to see him, but secondly, for him to "see" his Creator, or, in other words, to experience the *shefa/* Divine luminous energy of the Shechina. Essentially, then, the commandment of the pilgrimage is based on the concept of God looking at Israel and Israel, as it were, "looking" at God.

"Looking" at God

If we follow the concept of "looking" throughout the Torah, we are reminded of God's request that the Israelites be taught that at the moment of the *Kedushah* prayer in the Amidah,

> They should lift their eyes to Heaven and be carried aloft at this time, for I have no greater pleasure in the world than the moment that they lift their eyes to Mine while My eyes are on theirs. At this time, . . . I hasten their redemption.[5]

We have also seen the verse of the Song of Songs:

> Turn your eyes away from Me, for they overwhelm Me.[6]

Rashi observes that the image of the eyes intensifies the love between God and Israel.

We shall now try to understand how the concept of "seeing eyes" is related to Divine service. Also, just what does the commandment of seeing and being seen in the Temple involve?

Three times a year, in the additional service of the pilgrim festivals, we exclaim longingly, "we cannot ascend to appear and prostrate ourselves before You!" We are praying that God give us, once again, the opportunity of observing this commandment, the time in which Isaiah's prophecy will be fulfilled:

> For eye to eye they shall see when the Lord returns to Zion.[7]

All Jewish males have the commandment to "be seen in the Presence of God" three times a year. In His infinite kindness, the Almighty gave Israel three festivals in which they had the opportunity to rid themselves instantly of the impurity caused by sin. As the men entered the Temple Court, a holy place where "evil does not sojourn," the evil forces clinging to them were compelled to loosen their grip and part from them. Moved to tears by the haunting beauty of the Levites' songs, they would bitterly regret the deeds and thoughts which, as they now realized, had so effectively insensitized them to the call of the Divine.

The effect of their repentance was galvanizing: the men were roused from their stupor. Suddenly, they felt ablaze with a deep longing for union with the Holy One. And just as they came "to see," they came to "be seen," as God's longing for Israel was aroused in response.

The men were then shown the cherubs, whose embrace revealed to them the love of fiery coals, a flame of the Divine. This flame always burned on Shabbat and festivals, acquiring on these occasions a quality of unconditional love. This explains why the cherubs were always in a state of embrace for the pilgrims to see, irrespective of the state of observance of the nation at the time of a festival.[8]

In addition to the moving sight of the cherubs, what each individual saw and experienced was personal, depending on his level of readiness. The ecstatic merging of spirits with the Beloved shook them from the deep recesses of their souls to their very bodies, filling the basic need of union they had grown oblivious to. The men walked away with a surplus of spiritual energy that would enable them to draw upon this pining for the Beloved that consumed them, until the following festival.

Hence, the essential goal of the commandment of travelling to the Temple on the festivals was using the eyes to feel an arousal that could only be satiated by union with the Source of desire.

As for women, God created them with the inborn ability to arouse themselves to the same burning desire for union without the need of visual stimulation. The pilgrimage was therefore for men only, but the women could also experience the ecstasy of the contact with the Divine energy according to the effort each woman expended toward self-improvement.

The Torah's attitude to women's spiritual attainments is reflected in the deaths of Miriam, Aaron, and Moses. Whereas all three of them left this world with a kiss of God, in Miriam's case the Bible merely notes that she died and was buried. Rashi explains that although she, too, died with a Divine kiss, the expression "by the mouth of God" is not stated in her case out of respect for the Holy One.

Each individual woman has her own ladder of ascent to the Source of Light. The main difference is that, according to the Divine will, unlike the ascent of a man, her own elevation may not be done in public. Hence, she is not asked to go the Temple in the pilgrim festivals, nor even to pray in a synagogue with a minimum group of ten men, nor to don *tefillin*,[9] wrap herself in a *tallit*, or wave the four species in Sukkot.

Before Creation each woman is entrusted with a number of missions to accomplish during her stay on earth. Although some of these are clearly revealed to her, others are hidden for her to find. These concealed missions are engraved in the deepest recesses of her soul; the more layers of self that each woman is able to surrender to the Higher Will through her involvement in her revealed path, the clearer her personal ladder becomes to her. And when she reaches the top of the ladder, the meeting point, and fuses into His light, she is together with all the souls of the people of Israel, men and women alike.

Since the stimulation of desire that brought about the soul-union—for a man as for a woman—depended on and was measured by the cleansing effect of repentance, those covered by such a dense layer of sins that they were desensitized were referred to as "blind," in the sense that they could not "see." The sages note that it is impossible for such a person to arouse himself to feel Divine longing, and he is therefore considered dead in the sense that he is simply unable and thus exempt from receiving the visual impact of the pilgrimage.

Thus, the main prayer that echoes during the three festivals is an anguished cry: "We can no longer ascend and appear before You!"

And yet, although bereft of the Temple, and subsequently of the highest level of refinement known to stir the embers of feeling, we nevertheless pray that our regrets for past sins may have a purifying effect on us, and leave us ablaze with the desire to cleave to Him as we felt on Sinai.

While in a prophetic trance, the evil Balaam realized that:

> [God] does not look at wrongdoing in Jacob, and He sees no vice in Israel. God their Lord is with them, and the Divine Presence of their King does not leave their midst.[10]

As Rashi understands it, the simple explanation of this verse is that even when Israel provokes God with their sins, He does not move from their midst despite the fact that there is justice and a Judge to mete it out.

The kabbalistic insight is that at the moment in which the people of Israel lift up their eyes to Heaven, trembling with the intensity of their yearning to attach themselves to the Beloved, "their eyes into His," they noticeably sense how they are striking the chord of the Divine feelings. Then, like waters mirroring a loving look, their sins no longer form a barrier preventing the soul-union from taking place. Hence, the end of the verse, "the Divine Presence does not leave their midst."

This is the sorrow that invades us anew, year after year, on *Tisha B'av*, the time of the destruction of the two holy Temples: Israel's ability to "look into the eyes" of the Beloved and, in return, to feel the blazing fire of Divine emotion with the collective energy of a unified nation, is now blocked.

> A voice is heard wailing on High, the voice of lamentation from the illustrious city of Zion. Please, merciful Father, return to Zion, so that we may see eye to eye the rebuilding of Your Sanctuary, and this [third] house will be supreme. Then those redeemed will shout for joy.[11]

28

The Symbolism of Garments

O N THE MERRY HOLIDAY OF PURIM, men, women, and children pour into the synagogue for the public reading of the Megillah (Book of Esther). They hear how the Jews under the rule of the Persian king Ahasuerus were saved from extermination by a remarkable series of "coincidences." The Name of God is never mentioned in the text, for the Megillah is a book of concealment. Yet, behind the scenes, the hand of God is clearly manipulating events according to His plan. Let us look behind the text to see some of the hints concealed in the Megillah.

GARMENTS IN THE MEGILLAH

The text of the Megillah places an unusual emphasis on garments. The story begins with the opulent 180-day feast held by King Ahasuerus. At the feast, Ahasuerus "displayed the honor of his splendrous majesty."[1] Our sages explain that he wore the garments of the High Priest, which he inherited from Nebuchadnezzar, who destroyed the holy Temple.[2]

When Ahasuerus' heart was drunk with wine, he ordered Queen Vashti, granddaughter of King Nebuchadnezzar of Babylon, to appear "[adorned] with the royal crown, to show off to the people and the officials her beauty."[3] Our sages say that she was to appear *only* in her royal crown—and nothing else. This was poetic justice, they add, because she had forced her enslaved Jewish girls to work for her in the nude on Shabbat.

Vashti refused to come and was executed. Ahasuerus declared a nationwide search for a new queen, and Esther, a Jewish girl, was forcibly brought to the palace. She hid her Jewish identity, and was chosen, above all other candidates, to be crowned as the new queen. Afterward, the king promoted the wicked Haman as his new viceroy.

Nine years later, Haman began a personal vendetta against Mordechai and convinced Ahasuerus to issue a decree of annihilation against the entire Jewish people. When the Jewish sage Mordechai heard of it, "he tore his clothes and donned sack-cloth with ashes"[4] as a sign of mourning. "He went out into the midst of the city, and cried a loud and bitter cry. He came to the front of the king's gate but did not enter, as it was forbidden to enter the king's gate in a garment of sackcloth."[5]

Deeply distressed, Queen Esther "sent garments to clothe Mordechai and to remove his sackcloth, but he would not accept [them]."[6] He sent a reply that she was to go before the king and plead for the lives of her people. This meant risking her life, for the king had made a law that whoever came before the throne unbidden would be put to death—unless the king extended his golden scepter.

Although, as we will see, Esther was at first reluctant, she nevertheless undertook the mission. Her only request was that her people fast together with her for three days. "On the third day, Esther donned royalty"[7] and went to the king. The *Zohar* explains that Esther donned the ethereal garb of the spirit.

Ahasuerus extended his golden scepter. "What is your request?" he asked. Esther did not reply immediately but invited the king and Haman to a private banquet that same evening. At the banquet, Esther promised to reveal her request at another banquet the following evening.

That night, Ahasuerus could not asleep. His book of chronicles was read to him, and he was thereby reminded that Mordechai had once saved his life. In the meantime, Haman came to the palace, and Ahasuerus asked him, "What shall be done with a man whom the king desires to honor?" Haman answered, "Let the royal apparel be brought which the king has worn . . . and a royal crown for the head . . . that they may array the man whom the king delights to honor."

Ahasuerus liked Haman's suggestion and told him to do so to Mordechai. And so,

> Mordechai left the king's presence clad in royal apparel of turquoise and white with a large gold crown and a robe of linen and purple; then the city of Shushan was cheerful and glad.
>
> —Esther 8:15

Here again, the *Zohar* explains that Mordechai wore the ethereal clothes of the spirit.

GARMENTS OF LIGHT

Let us take a deeper look at the symbolism of garments in the teaching of Kabbalah. Before the sin in the Garden of Eden, Adam and Eve were not corporeal beings as man is today. They wore "garments of light" (*ohr* spelled with an *aleph*). However, after the sin, they fell into the physical state and were clothed in "garments of skin" (*ohr* spelled with an *ayin*). Our mission in this world is to remove these garments of skin by turning away from evil, and then enclothe ourselves in garments of light by following the path of the Torah.

The sixteenth-century kabbalist Rabbi Moses Cordovero of Sefad explains that these garments of light enable the soul to serve the Almighty. "It was forbidden to enter the king's gate in a garment of sackcloth."[8] The only way the soul can acquire these garments is by enclosing herself in a body and acting according to the Divine will despite the pull of the physical.

Why does the soul need special garments to stand before the king?

PASSIONATE ATTACHMENT

God created the universe so that the souls of Israel would be able to attach themselves passionately to Him through their own efforts. "Is it possible to bind oneself to the Living God? Isn't God like a consuming fire?" the sages ask. They answer, "Yes, by attaching oneself to His attributes. Just as He is compassionate, so should you be compassionate." By emulating His attributes, which we recognize through His actions, we attach ourselves to the Divine.

The blind kabbalist Rabbi Isaac de Acco explains that corporeal beings cannot grasp the infinite God for He is beyond our perception and understanding. To allow us to experience Him, God constricts His light by "clothing" it in attributes. "The King's garments," as the Kabbalah calls the attributes, attenuate His light in a way that both conceals and reveals Him, just as clothing both conceals and reveals the wearer. Cleaving to God means attaching ourselves to the revelation that we experience when He enclothes His Infinite Light in a certain attribute.

Just as God dons the "garments" of attributes so that Israel can know Him and cleave to Him, so the people of Israel must don the precious garments of light, the ethereal clothes of the spirit, in order to attach themselves passionately to God. Our yearning for God is a reflection of God's beckoning to us. "As water reflects a face back to a face, so one's heart is reflected back to him by another."[9] Like water mirroring a loving look, man's attempt to draw closer to God will be reflected in God's drawing closer to him.

The Ari explains that each *mitsvah* we perform, each prayer we utter has the power to draw down the Infinite Light. We can direct every prayer and every *mitsvah* we do to bring about the soul-union we long for.

PRAYER

In the love song between God and Israel, God asks: "Let Me hear your voice."[10] Whereas the Children of Israel say, "Better is Your kindness than life."[11] For more than the thing they pray for, it is the very relationship with God achieved by the prayer that they want.

The ultimate curse would be not having to pray, not being in a relationship with God. The punishment of the serpent who tempted Adam and Eve was "dust shall you eat." Its food would always be available without Divine influence. God would never have to hear its voice in prayer. This is indeed a curse.

The Bible calls the serpent *arum*, "guileful."[12] But *arum* also means naked. The serpent lacked the garments that bind God and man in *devekut*.

The aim of our daily prayers is therefore to connect us with God's own garment of Infinite Light. In contrast, the observation of mitsvot provides us with the ethereal garments of light through which we can find grace in God's eyes and be invited to enter His Palace in the Amidah prayer. In the Amidah, we experience His own garments of light as we become passionately attached to Him in a total state of *devekut*.

Loss of the Garments

Unfortunately, there are sins that can sully man's garments of light and cover him in garments of skin, of pure physicality. Only through repentance can he free himself from this state.

There are even more serious transgressions that cause God to divest Himself of His own garments, so that He becomes completely inaccessible. The Midrash says that at the time of the destruction of the Temple, God wrapped Himself in sackcloth, as it were, and His Divine Influence disappeared from the world. Our sages teach that each generation in which the Temple is not rebuilt has committed transgressions that drove the *Shechina*/Divine Presence away. For such transgressions, a higher form of repentance is needed, powerful enough to bring God back into His holy attributes and back down to the world.

At Sinai, the people of Israel were healed of the serpent's poison that had infected man; the rectification of their past was completed, and they were now on the level of angels. "We wish to see our King!" they exclaimed. God came down on Mount Sinai "dressed" in His attributes, and the Community of Israel was indeed able to see God: "Your eyes will see the King in His beauty."[13] Upon receiving the Tablets of the Law, they were wrapped in the precious garments of light with which they were to reach the soul-union. But immediately afterward, they damaged their relationship with God by making the Golden Calf. "Now take off your jewels,"[14] Moses told the people; "remove the ephemeral garments of light that you had worn."

To return the garments of light, God commanded the Children of Israel to build the Tabernacle, in which their sins would be atoned. The highest level of service in the Tabernacle, and later in the Temple, was performed by the High Priest, whose function was to bring about the passionate attachment between God and His people through the principle that "Love covers all transgressions."[15] The High Priest wore special garments that restored Israel's own garments of light so they could attach themselves to God.

The High Priest had two sets of garments: in the Temple throughout the year he wore the golden garments "for honor and for splendor." These consisted of eight pieces, including a blue coat trimmed with bells and pomegranates, and the breastplate of twelve precious stones set in gold. On Yom Kippur, the holiest day of the year, the High Priest dressed in special plain white garments—"garments of salvation."[16] Only with these white garments could he enter the otherwise inaccessible Holy of Holies, where the golden cherubs above the Ark turned toward or away from each other, reflecting the relationship between Israel and God. During the course of this unique day, the High Priest changed four times between the golden garments and the white ones.

The white garments symbolized the essence of unshaded Divine light that he was able to draw on this day. The shades of color in the second set of garments represented the access to the Divine luminous energy through the garment of his intellect, namely, by entering a state of focused consciousness with which he could perceive the inner dimension of the light and direct it onto the people.

BACK TO THE MEGILLAH

According to the Talmud, in the beginning of the Babylonian exile, the Jews had bowed down to an idol that Nebuchadnezzar had made. Furthermore, seventy years later, the Jews of the generation of King Ahasuerus bowed down to an idol that Haman wore. Hence, just as they had lost their garments of light when they worshiped the Golden Calf, so too did they lose them again at that sin. Mirroring their actions, God, as it were, divested Himself of His royal garments, thereby hiding Himself on high. With the First Temple destroyed and the Second Temple not yet built, Israel could not attempt to regain a close relationship with their Father in Heaven by bringing an offering.

When Nebuchadnezzar's granddaughter, Queen Vashti, forced Jewish girls to serve her in the nude on Shabbat, she was showing that the Jewish souls were naked of their spiritual garments. Consequently she was ordered to appear in public wearing only her royal crown, a symbolic reminder that the King on high had divested Himself of the attributes that permitted the people below to relate to His royal crown; the King and His Divine Presence had receded from us.

Ahasuerus, too, wore the garments of the High Priest, whose function was to bring about the passionate attachment between God and His people. By wearing these garments, Ahasuerus showed that Israel no longer had any garments of light. On hearing of the decree, Mordechai tore his clothes in mourning and donned sackcloth and ashes. This alluded to the very cause of the decree of annihilation: the disappearance of the two-way garments creating our passionate relationship with God. With the garments of holiness gone, the relationship was severed.

AMALEK

The decree of annihilation was engineered by Haman, a descendant of Israel's archenemy, Amalek, who had attacked the newborn nation soon after it left Egypt. When Israel wandered in the desert, "the clothing you wore did not become tattered"[17] for they were robed in garments of light, represented by the clouds of glory. Amalek had no power over those who were within the clouds, but those who had damaged themselves spiritually and were denied the protection of the clouds were left without garments of light and were overpowered by Amalek. Haman, too, attacked Israel precisely when they were stripped of their garments of light and therefore vulnerable to attack.

RETURN OF THE ETHEREAL GARMENTS
THROUGH THE ORAL TORAH

Mordechai did not accept the clothes Esther sent him, for he saw that the damage of the garments had not yet been rectified. As the leading Torah sage of his time, Mordechai did not look at the threat of annihilation of the Jews as a product of the whims of a capricious ruler, but rather, as a Divine reaction to their behavior. On Mount Sinai, the Israelites had accepted the Torah with their simultaneous response "We will do and we will hear!" The Talmud, however, reports that their enthusiastic response related exclusively to the Written Torah. The Oral Torah, in contrast, they had accepted only under coersion, for it is a highly demanding study, requiring much intellectual effort to understand it. They had no objection to the practical study of the Oral Torah relating to the observance of the 613 commandments of the Pentateuch, for they knew that without the Oral Torah, it would be impossible to interpret God's will as it appears in the Written Torah. What they feared, however, was the physical strain needed to engross oneself in the deep analysis of the subtleties hidden in the Torah.

Due to this superficial acceptance of the Oral Torah, the Jews did not have the faith in the sages that essentially defines it. Hence, when in the incident that precipitated this chain of events, King Ahasuerus organized a feast and invited the entire Jewish community, the people felt no qualms about accepting. There is no intrinsic prohibition in accepting the king's invitation, they claimed, unable to understand Mordechai's reasoning that once they would be immersed in the atmosphere of the banquet, consuming a wine that was forbidden to them, their resistance to the lures of transgression would considerably diminish.

Yet, the gracious invitation had been a trap extended to them with the intention of making them sin. This was Ahasuerus's added measure of precaution to ensure that the rebuilding of the Temple and consequent Divine protection remained beyond the reach of his subjects. The Israelites enjoyed the king's regal hospitality, unaware that they were also playing into his game.

Their refusal to accept the teaching authority of the sages also resulted in their becoming involved in affairs with the gentiles, thus misusing sexual energy and desecrating the covenant of the circumcision. The misuse of sexual energy, referred to as *Pegam HaBrit*/Flaw of the Covenant, is, as we will see, the main obstacle to the love bond with the Creator.[18]

Mordechai was fully aware that Haman had been able to incite King Ahasuerus against the Jews as a consequence of these two transgressions. His warning to the Jews not to go to the feast illustrates the difficulties Israel experienced in accepting the rabbinic enactments of the Oral Torah insofar as it curtailed their freedom. When the decree of annihilation became public, their initial reaction was quite natural: even though they were aware that their actions had put them in this terrible situation, somehow, they found a way to justify themselves and put the blame on Mordechai. Hadn't he brought this calamity upon their heads by refusing to bow in front of the powerful Haman?

At first, Esther herself disagreed with Mordechai when he told her that the salvation of the Jewish people depended on her following his bidding that she endanger herself by going to the king.

Mordechai's uncompromising rebuke of Queen Esther's attitude is clear and to the point:

> Do not imagine in your soul that you will be able to escape in the king's palace any more than the rest of the Jews. For if you persist in keeping silent at a time like this, relief and deliverance will come to the Jews from another place, while you and your father's house will perish. And who knows whether it was just for such a time as this that you attained the royal position![19]

Mordechai understood that the present estrangement of the Jewish people was such that they needed to reach the level of repentance where the "Knower of all secrets" could testify that they would never go back to the sins that had brought about the present situation. They had to find the strength to make the irrevocable decision that never, never again would they commit actions that would inevitably entail their separation from the Source of light. Each and every one of them had to show the honesty of his or her decision and enlist the active support of the sages by their total acceptance of the Oral Torah.

Esther soon realized that the situation was a direct consequence of the people's loss of faith in the teaching authority of the sages. God's Providence had led her to the throne; it was therefore her duty as queen to be the role model, showing the people that *she* was ready to risk her own life, if that was what the leading sage of their time required of her.

She then enlisted the people's cooperation, so that the attempt to arouse the Divine compassion in that month of Adar should have the collective power of the entire nation in exile. When the people saw what she was ready to do, they followed suit and repented, fasting for three days, together with their queen. On the third day, Esther dressed in her royal apparel in a desperate attempt to draw the holy garments of light down upon Israel.

Through their repentance, not only were they able to receive the precious garments of the spirit, but God once again clothed Himself in His attributes. The Jews of Shushan rejoiced when Mordechai went forth from the presence of the king in royal apparel, for his appearance showed symbolically that the love relationship between God and His people was restored at the highest level.

When the people realized how they escaped destruction by following Mordechai's leadership, they understood what the Oral Torah was about, and then accepted it willingly.[20]

Why, in fact, did they accept it? To all appearances, the reasons for their reticence at Sinai were still in force! It could not have been out of gratitude for the miracle, since the numerous supernatural occurrences they had witnessed, such as the Exodus from Egypt, the conquering of the land of Israel, and the miracles that took place daily in the First Temple, had not caused them to feel the moral duty to accept it.

This time, however, Mordechai had shown them that the direct Divine protection they had prayed for required a full commitment on their part. Accepting the Oral Torah, and with it the teaching authority of the sages, would be the only way to protect themselves in the future from threats such as the one they had just escaped.

History tells that, in fact, the Israelites built the Second Temple immediately after the cancellation of the decree, thus showing that its completion was indeed dependent upon their commitment to the Oral Torah. They now understood what Mordechai was trying to tell them: over and beyond its aspect as a challenging intellectual discipline, the Oral Torah is the basis of the covenant binding the People of Israel to their Creator in an eternal passionate union.

Reflecting back on how they had narrowly escaped, the Israelites saw that with a flick of the wrist Haman had been able to sign an order that would annihilate their entire nation in one day, women and children alike. They then realized that God was showing them that as long as they had not accepted the covenant sealing their union, He was not willing to have the abode of His Presence among them. The Jews saw that they had to do everything in their power to bring about the completion of the Second Temple, for without it they would be at the mercy of any ruler obsessed with the desire to destroy them. This danger would continue to exist in every succeeding generation until they took it upon themselves to do something about it.

They now realized that their hearts had to be totally aligned with their minds in their decision to become close to God with the closeness of a Companion of the soul, no matter what effort or risk it would involve. The only thing that could bring about this level of intimacy would be the willing acceptance of the Oral Torah.

THE PURIM FEAST

Purim's joy is an expression of the crystallization of Israel's intimate relationship to the Almighty as "the Community of Israel, His Companion of the soul." Although we have seen that there are other festivals in which we reach the level of Companion of the soul, still, the only one in which to attain this level in completion by reenacting our acceptance of the Oral Torah is Purim.

As a result, our joy overflows as it does in no festival other than Sukkot. The joy of Sukkot is illustrated in the water-drawing ceremony at the time of the Temple. This ritual derived its name from the unusual levels of Divine inspiration that the judges of the *Sanhedrin*/Supreme Court and Torah sages were able to *draw* upon themselves out of their boundless joy.

In Purim, however, our joy stems from God's relating to each and every one of us as a member of the Community of Israel, His Companion of the soul. Such a high degree of intimacy with the Holy One could paralyze us with inhibition, however.

Hence, in order to express freely our exultation without being overwhelmed by a dread of the Divine majesty, we consume intoxicating spirits until we lose our self-awareness. As the story of Esther climaxes, it is written that the Jews experienced "light and joy (*orah vesimchah*)."[21] The word *orah*/light, with its unusual feminine ending, alludes to Oral Torah that the Jews had accepted.

The story of Esther is a book of concealment: there is no explicit Divine Name mentioned throughout the text. The kabbalists teach, however, that Esther's Megillah contains allusions to all forty-one Divine Names and to the entire Torah, and as a result has a powerful effect upon our intellect.

When we listen to the reading of the story of Esther in the Megillah, it is up to us to draw the light of the Torah onto ourselves. During the reading of the Megillah, with conscious thought and willful desire we can accept upon ourselves the yoke of the Oral Torah anew. The effort will enable us to imbibe light at the level of our soul-root.

This is the special heavenly light that shines for us exclusively during the time of Purim, the holiday that will ultimately overshadow all others. This light without garments will leave an indelible imprint within us so that we can summon it throughout the ensuing year and continuously expand our insights into the Oral Torah.

29

Ateret HaYesod/
The Foundation Coronet

FOUR EXILES

AT THE BASIS OF THE CREATION of the world is a system of opposites, as the verse says, "God has set the one over against the other."[1] Thus we have day and night, good and evil, exile and redemption. By allowing both elements to exist, God establishes a system in which man has free will to choose between deeds that bring light or those that cause darkness.

However, God does not empower the side of evil arbitrarily; it is we who give it strength through our deeds. A careful look at Jewish history reveals that whenever Israel has had to bear the yoke of a foreign dominion, it was because the love bond with the Creator had been broken.

Historically, four powers rose to subjugate the Jewish people and the land of Israel.[2] These were Babylon, Persia, Greece, and Edom. Which power Edom represents is the subject of a rabbinic controversy beyond our scope. Briefly, the prevailing opinion is that Edom refers to the Holy Roman Empire and its legacy, namely, Christianity. The commentator Ibn Ezra claims that Edom is also meant to include the Islamic powers, descendants of Abraham's son Ishmael, based on the fact that the influence of Rome in the formation of Arab and Turkish empires allows one to consider them outgrowths of the Roman empire.[3]

Maimonides taught that the tribulations the Jews would suffer at the hands of Islam would progressively increase until they would be finally terminated with the coming of the Messiah. These periods of exile were not only a Divine retribution for our deeds. On a deeper level, they are part of God's plan for bringing the Messiah, and revealing God's glory in the world.

In the second verse of Genesis the sages found an allusion to these four exiles:

Now the earth was without form and empty, with darkness on the face of the depths, but God's spirit moved on the water's surface.

"Without form" refers to the Babylonian exile, as Jeremiah prophesied at the time, "I saw the earth, and behold, it was without form."[4] *Bohu*/empty refers to the exile of Persia, based on the verse from the story of Esther "*Veyabhilu*/and they hastened to bring Haman."[5] "Darkness" refers to Greece, for the Greeks darkened the eyes of Israel with their decrees against the light of the Torah. "On the face of the depths" hints to Edom, for no one can fathom the depth of their cruelty.

Nevertheless, the verses continue: "But God's spirit moved on the water's surface." This alludes to the Messiah, for "the spirit of the Lord shall rest upon him."[6]

THE GREEK EXILE

The Greek domination is compared to darkness. There was an intense hellenization of the Jews at the time, and they were becoming increasingly distanced from their Father in Heaven. Secularization was rampant, and religious Jews even had to flee Jerusalem. The sages have compared a blind person to one dead, and the people of Israel, whose vision of Torah had been darkened, were as if spiritually dead.

The character of the Greek dominion was different from the others. The Babylonians, the Persians, the Romans, all sought to kill or exile us and to destroy the Temple. In contrast, under Greek rule, the Jews were allowed to remain in the land, and the Temple stood on its premises.

Yet the sages of the generation who saw the miracle of Chanukah enacted that whenever Jews entered the rededicated Temple, they had to prostrate themselves thirteen times to thank God for saving Israel from the Greek dominion. Thirteen correspond to the thirteen cracks that the Greeks made in the Temple.

> In front [of the women's court] was a partition measuring ten handbreadths, and it was marked with thirteen cracks that the Greek rulers made on it.[7]

This partition was the dividing point between different Temple courtyards; no gentile or uncircumcised person could go beyond that point. The cracks were an expression of the Greeks' resentment of this barrier. The edict to bow down at this point applied not only in the Second Temple; it will also apply in the Third Temple, when it will be rebuilt. No such edict was ever made in remembrance of the Babylonian, Persian, or Roman exiles.

The Greeks issued decrees prohibiting the Jews from sanctifying the new moon, performing circumcisions, and keeping Shabbat. They told the Jews, "Carve on the horn of the ox that you are not connected to the God of Israel."

What were the Greeks trying to prove with this statement? Why did they claim that Israel was not connected with their God? And how is this decree related to their attempts to prevent Israel from observing the other mitsvot mentioned above?

NESIRAH/SEPARATION

Kabbalah teaches that Creation took place in five general stages, referred to as "heavenly universes." At each level, there was greater contraction of God's light, culminating in the physical world and the near total concealment of the Divine Presence.

According to the Ari, when the creation of the world began, the souls of Israel were already made, attached to the Foundation from where all Divine energy stems. However, in order to give these souls free will, God had to disconnect Himself from them.

There are also five levels of the soul. Three reside within the body:[8] the *nefesh, ruach,* and *neshamah.* Two exist beyond the body: *chayah*/Living Essence, in which our life force is still within the realm of the Divine, not yet separated from God; and *yechidah*/Unique Essence, where our level of existence is still contained in God's innermost will.

The five levels of the soul are the inner dimension of the five stages of Creation, and in this sense they constitute the steps of the ladder leading to the sought-after "face-to-face" bond with God.

Hence, whereas the soul-roots remain attached to their Maker, on the physical level God had to conceal His Presence to allow man to accomplish his task. Without freedom of choice, man could not convert evil into good through his own effort.

The essence of Israel's task is to reconnect themselves consciously with their soul-roots while living in this world, thus infusing the world with holiness, while they themselves cleave to their Maker in the "face-to-face" relationship which their soul longs for.

The Greeks believed that God created the world, and selected as His nation the people of Israel.[9] Yet they denied that there was any special bond that united God to Israel, as opposed to the other nations. Whereas God brought about the *nesirah*/separation as a means to an end—to create an even stronger union—the Greeks regarded the separation as an end in itself. According to their view, God created the souls and allowed them a totally independent existence, determined only by the fixed cause-and-effect laws of nature. This was manifest in the Greeks' love of mathematics, and in their adulation of beauty as an end in itself.

NEW MONTH, CIRCUMCISION, SHABBAT

The Greeks forbade the Jews from observing three commandments—Shabbat, circumcision, and sanctification of the new moon. In order to understand the significance of these particular commandments let us briefly review the kabbalistic principles of Creation. As we have said, this world is characterized by a near complete concealment of God's Presence; it seems totally disconnected from the Divine. Yet, despite appearances, the world is attached to its Maker through an inner dimension called the Foundation Coronet (*Ateret HaYesod*)—the Divine source of all blessings and sustenance. The *Ateret HaYesod* is the meeting point where the soul-union between the Creator and Israel's soul-roots takes place.

The same principle applies to the Community of Israel, as it is written,

> "Just as a loincloth clings to a man's hips," says God, "so did I make the entire House of Israel . . . cling to Me."[10]

Due to this inner connection, Israel has no independent existence; they are like branches of a tree that would wither and die without the constant flow of sustenance from the roots.

The backbone of our connection to the Foundation Coronet is represented by the three commandments the Greeks attempted to forbid.

On Shabbat, the heavenly worlds return to their source, and the Divine concealment is lifted. The root of the Hebrew word *shabbat* is *shivah*/return. On Shabbat, we receive sustenance and energy for all the days of the week, showing that nothing is separated from God, for the blessings of the entire week stem from Shabbat. By preventing Israel from observing Shabbat, the Greeks would in effect be preventing the soul-union at *Ateret HaYesod* from taking place, for this union is the object of Shabbat observance.

This concept is physically represented by the act of circumcision. The male organ, the tool which makes man God's partner in the creation of a soul, is covered at birth by a thin membrane. This represents the occluding power of the physical and the potential to distance ourselves from God through sin.

The first step, therefore, involves the excision of the entire foreskin so that the entire glans, including the corona, is visible. In addition, in order to mark a perpetual reminder of our acceptance of God's kingship over every aspect of our lives, whatever skin remains is folded back so that it exposes the glans and remains behind the corona.[11]

We can now understand why the circumcision must be done according to rabbinic tradition. When the foreskin is surgically removed as a measure of hygiene, as is commonly done today, the circumcision precludes the second step—forming the crown—which underlies the essence of the commandment.

The sixth day of the week represents the removal of the foreskin that sensitizes us to spiritual perception, whereas the seventh day brings the revelation of the Foundation Coronet. In the Shabbat experience, God makes Himself perceivable and responds to the ardent longing of the soul to attach herself to her Source.

How the mitsvah of circumcision can affect Israel—what the Greeks wanted to avoid—may be understood by analyzing the first time that this commandment was observed: by the Patriarch Abraham.

After Abraham circumcised himself, it is written that he was sitting at the entrance of his tent when God appeared to him.[12] Rashi explains that God came to visit the sick, and in fact, this revelation was not prophecy for there was no message transmitted. The kabbalists understand that as a reward for his perfect observance of the commandment of circumcision, Abraham received a revelation of his bond to the Creator at the Foundation Coronet.

We may infer the *devekut* that this vision gave rise to, for two verses farther on we find the Divine Name *Adonai*. Although in a simple reading of the text the Name seems to apply to three angels who came to visit, the Talmud teaches that the Name hinted at the Divine Presence. The reason behind the choice of this particular Divine Name rather than the omniscient Tetragrammaton is that at this point, Abraham and His Maker were One.

The mitsvah of sanctifying the new moon was especially important for establishing the dates of the festivals, each of which manifests a special form of Divine union with Israel. This union enables Israel to absorb Divine energy at its Source. The basis of this energy is the quality of Divine Providence of the particular festival that God makes available to us every year on the date of the festival.

The main objection of the Greeks was Sukkot, in which we come "face-to-face" with the Beloved.

When we wave the four species on Sukkot, three are bound together, while the *etrog* is held separately. The *etrog* represents this world, which is separate from the heavenly realms. Yet, the *etrog* also has a small crown at its end which, although fragile, is all-important because the commandment of waving the four species can be performed only when it is intact. This crown represents this world's attachment to the Source of all blessings, while the *etrog*'s independence from the other species shows Israel's disassociation from God while in our daily state of awareness.

Like Sukkot, the festival of Chanukah is eight days long. This implies that the light that shines during Sukkot when we wave the four species also illuminates us on Chanukah, for the miracle of the oil parallels the joy of coming "face-to-face" with God during the eight days of Sukkot. Yet, although both festivals reveal our inseparable link to the Foundation Coronet, the revelation of this bond as we commemorate it on Chanukah is stronger than that of Sukkot. The reason is that in the rebellion against the Greeks, the Jews went to war, ready to risk their lives to regain the connection they had lost.

The Greeks were hoping to destroy the bond that made Israel part of God's essence by forcing the Jews to carve in the horn of the ox that they had no portion in the God of Israel, thus denying their bond. The ox is the prototype of power, and the strength of an ox is manifested through his horns. Moreover, the horn of the ox is evocative of the ram's horn that we blow on Rosh Hashanah, and by the same token related to the *nesirah*/separation God reenacts at this time in order to bring about the "face-to-face" reunion in Yom Kippur.

Hence, in their desire to quell the Jews' spiritual power, the Greeks kept saying to the Jews, "At the time you blow the *shofar*/ram's horn on Rosh Hashanah which you believe marks the separation, be aware that what you are doing is a meaningless ritual. There will never be a reunion, because, as you inscribed, you are not connected with the God of Israel at the Foundation Coronet. The original separation enacted at Creation was complete and irrevocable."

The Greeks and Nature

It was the Greeks' denial of Israel's intimate relationship with the Creator that brought them the appellation of "darkness." They sought to undermine Israel's pure and simple faith in God and their direct bond to the Source of light. And although they allowed the Jewish people physical freedom, they enslaved them in a spiritual sense.

The Almighty created the world and rules over it, they affirmed. They even admitted that God originally selected the people of Israel to be His nation. What they sought to prevent was the intimate connection between the Creator and His people. They were aware that this bond was made possible by the existence of the Temple and by the terms of the covenant. If they could coerce Israel to break their half of the covenant, then logically their personal relationship with God would end.

The sages explain that of all the nations who overpowered Israel, Greece was the closest to holiness and the hardest to oppose because they accepted a part of the truth, namely, that God's bond with Israel dated since the creation of the world. The Greeks did not seek to convert or destroy Israel; they allowed them to teach and study—but only as a cultural phenomenon rather than as a way of life. In this new way of relating to mitsvot, Shabbat and festivals would become days of leisure, relics of their past, rather than opportunities to draw closer to the Source.

In the case of other exiles, when the physical oppression ceased, so did the underlying spiritual forces. However, the Greek exile was different. Even when their political control of Israel ended, their spiritual influence remained. Today it has wormed its way into modern Israeli society. The new generation in Israel is being taught that the study of Torah is just like the study of history: it does not require them to adopt ancient customs, and rites such as circumcision and bar-mitsvah should be considered obsolete![13]

Thus, when the Temple is rebuilt, we will bow down thirteen times to thank the Almighty for having annihilated the Greek "way of life." We will not be thanking Him for something no longer relevant. On the contrary, we will know that it was very close to home!

The significance of the miraculous oil was not only that it enabled them to light the Menorah. More importantly, it showed that the Divine Presence was still in their midst, bringing holiness down to this world. This was the purpose of the Temple, the foot of Jacob's ladder: to draw the spiritual emanations of holiness into our lives until we become filled with a Divine energy that makes us impervious to evil.

Although Israel physically overcame the Greeks, their victory was not complete, for the objective of the Greeks had been spiritual, not physical. Greece wanted Israel to conform to their way of thinking, which excluded the concept of holiness. If, in the Temple, the priests had not found any pure oil, they still could have lit the Menorah, for the Temple service takes precedence over the prohibition of sullied oil. However, in this case, purity was the point in question. During the entire time of the Greek dominion, Israel had lived without the holiness and purity that underlay their relationship with God. Total liberation from Greece called for lighting the Menorah with an oil that had never been touched by impure hands.

The revolt of the Jews showed that this love bond was more important to them than their very lives. God therefore responded with His love, by showing them that He had jealously hidden one flask from the eyes of the enemy, waiting many years for the time His beloved people would make the first step to overthrow darkness from their midst.

THE CENTER FLAME OF THE MENORAH

The Greeks were intent on disproving Israel's claim to a unique bond with the Creator. Why didn't they destroy the Temple, since this was the very source of Israel's strength, the place on earth were their souls below were infused with Divine energy?

The Greeks believed that God had asked the Jews to build a Temple as a site of holiness, fit for His Presence to dwell on earth, from where He would direct His blessings toward the Children of Israel.

The Greeks therefore wanted the Temple to continue to stand and to draw Divine sustenance down to earth. Their object was to draw down to themselves the Divine sustenance that now stemmed from the Temple directly to Israel, and through Israel to the rest of the world.

The only way they could achieve their objective was by preventing the soul-union between the Holy One and the Community of Israel.

The heavenly soul-union was instrumental in directing the Divine luminous energy exclusively to Israel, as expressed in the words of the verse: "Only you have I known (*yada'ti*), among all the nations of the world."[14] From the moment that *da'at* is involved, the thought of any other nation is impossible, as suggested in the verse "from my flesh I will see God."[15] This aspect of *da'at* is called *devekut* in the sense that as soon as *da'at* begins to glow, there is no room for any other thought.

In order to attain their goal, the Greeks used their power in two ways. One was directed against Israel themselves, as their captors forced them to transgress the terms of the Covenant.[16] The other aimed at tarnishing the purity of the Temple vessels, each one of which had a spiritual "light," or energy, of its own.

Among the vessels was the golden Menorah. Each evening, the priest would kindle all the lights in the candelabrum. He would pour an equal amount of oil into all the golden bulbs. When he entered the Sanctuary on the following morning, the lights would all have burnt out, except that of the center branch. He would then rekindle the lights, and by evening he would find once again that the center branch was the only one that continued to burn. The center flame of the Menorah was the unshakable proof of the union between Israel and their Maker, and affirmed that God's separation from the souls of Israel was only in appearance, but that the inner connection remained intact. In the priest's daily lighting of the candelabrum, he drew down the heavenly soul-union that took place above. His goal was that the union should not occur just in Heaven at the lofty level of our soul-roots, but also within each one of us, in the soul-union known as *Jerusalem Below*.[17]

It is written,

The nations shall know that I am God, the Holy One, within Israel.[18]

And indeed, the Greeks knew: though the curtain of the Holy of Holies hid the soul-union from the eyes of the world, the Menorah was placed outside. Only the priests were allowed in the altar where the candelabrum stood, but the doors of the altar were kept open so that onlookers could perceive the lights glow from a distance. Consequently, everyone could see the miraculous eternal glow of the center branch of the

Menorah, revealing the close bond between Israel's soul-roots and the Holy One. Thus the Greeks were well aware that as long as this center lamp kept burning, they would be unable to harm Israel.[19] Hence, they took to breaking the intimate bond by defiling all the oil. They sought to extinguish the center lamp of the Menorah which provided the evidence that Israel's soul-roots were in direct contact with the Divine source of energy.

We have seen that to help us experience Him, God constricts His Infinite Light by "clothing" it with His Thirteen Attributes.[20] On the twenty-fifth of Kislev, after the military conquest, Israel began to divest themselves of their former impurity, and as the days of Chanukah went by, the Almighty enclosed Himself in succeeding attributes. Seven days elapsed for Israel to cross the bridge from impurity to purity.

When God enclosed His Infinite Light in the last attribute—*Venake*/One who purifies—on the eighth day of Chanukah, Israel became permeated by purity. The relationship could now revert to the spiritual union of Companions of the soul. On this day the Children of Israel cleave to their Maker in a total soul-union, whose intensity is similar to that of Shemini Atseret.

Maimonides teaches that one who is so poor that he cannot afford the oil needed to kindle the Chanukah lamps should sell his coat and make his purchase. The light of the center branch of the Menorah was the proof of the heavenly soul-union *Jerusalem Above*, whose illumination at the *sim shalom*/establish peace blessing is double in the morning Amidah prayer throughout Chanukah.

On Chanukah, when we commemorate the lighting of the candelabrum by kindling our own lamps, we are in effect drawing down the heavenly union so that its luminous energy infuses our souls. In fact, the optimum time to kindle the Chanukah lights is twilight, the time when God showed Jacob the foot of the ladder, the soul-union of *Jerusalem Below*.[21] Also, the optimum place for kindling the Chanukah lights is no higher than ten handbreadths above the ground, to sensitize us to the soul-union that we are to experience in the Amidah prayer of the following morning.

Candle-lighting time is infused with Divine favor. We stare at the soft glow of the Chanukah lamps, as Jews have done through the centuries, renewing the face-to-face bond with the Beloved. This is a moment of special intimacy in which all prayers are propitious, in particular the cries for God's powerful help to bring us close to Him.

Throughout Chanukah we attain the level of *devekut* that we know in the Amidah prayer of Shabbat afternoon, when we become part of God's essence. In fact, it is on Shabbat within Chanukah that we read in the prophetic portion,

Sing and rejoice, people of Zion, for I am coming. I will dwell within you, declares God.[22]

30

Shovavim/
Rebellious Children

B EFORE LEAVING THE FESTIVAL OF CHANUKAH, I would like to discuss a violation of the Torah. I must remind the reader that as I stated in the preface, this book is not a book of Jewish law, nor of the customs associated with each festival. Several good works are available in English on the subject, and I felt that a discussion of those laws would distract the reader from the main focus of this book, which is to lift the veil leading to an intimate perception of God.

My decision not to discuss commandments and transgressions made the faithful rendition of Rabbi Luria's work easier: since his teachings are addressed to a readership equipped with an extensive knowledge of Talmud and Kabbalah, he hardly needs to dwell on the nature of commandments. Yet, toward the end of his book on Chanukah, Rabbi Luria devotes several chapters to a transgression he refers to as *shovavim/* rebellious children.

It is interesting that this transgression is not one of the 613 commandments, nor one of the seven enactments decreed by the sages, and yet the standard code of Jewish law refers to it as "the gravest violation of the Torah."[1] I greatly hesitated to address this topic, for even the English books on Jewish law designed for the Orthodox public carefully avoid it. The subject is related to man's greatest physical pleasure: sex.

On the one hand, this single chapter puts the entire book in jeopardy. Yet, on the other, the purpose of this book is to help the modern reader attain an altered state of consciousness in which he or she is in intimate contact with the Creator. Is it fair to omit the discussion of the greatest stumbling block preventing the access to the Infinite Light? In the end, I decided that it was not for me to make decisions on behalf of the reader. The permission to divulge, for the first time in translation, the secret teachings of the Torah about the ultimate love bond one may reach necessarily involves the description of its main obstacle.

The "Rebellious Children" in History

The Ari teaches that God gave man the ability to use his sperm in order to create a holy soul.[2] Thus, whenever a man has sexual contact with his wife at the time that she is ritually clean, whether the union engenders a child or not, he is creating a soul of holiness. If the union is not to produce a child, this soul then joins others in what Kabbalah calls the "Palace of Souls." When it is this man's time to die, these souls come out to meet him and speak on his behalf: they are referred to as his children. These souls join the powers of holiness, thus doing their share to fulfill the ultimate purpose of Creation.

However, when a man misuses his sexual energy by using his sperm for anything other than intimate contact with the woman who is rightfully his wife under the holy bonds of matrimony, whether he is a Jew or a gentile, intentionally or accidentally, he also creates a soul, but she—the soul—joins the powers of evil. These souls are referred to as a man's "rebellious children."

In addition to their physical possessions, we inherit many of our parent's tendencies and mistakes. The misuse of sexual energy comes to us from the people in the time of Noach, known as the Generation of the Flood. The men of Noach's generation fell prey to the transgression of "rebellious children" by voluntarily engaging in sexual aberration. This led to the destruction of that entire generation through the waters of the flood.

The next "heir" to this weakness was the generation of the Tower of Babel.[3] In addition to sexual corruption they rebelled against God and thus scattered across the earth. The misuse of sexual energy then found its way into the generation of Sodom and Gomorrah.[4] Once again, God destroyed the entire generation. All of this has been recorded by the sages of the Talmud and Kabbalah.

The first time this transgression is openly mentioned in the Torah is in the episode of Judah's sons, Er and Onan, whose behavior is described as "evil in God's eyes."[5] Yet, it was not just these two, but all of Jacob's grandchildren who fell prey to this sin. In fact, the primary reason for the Egyptian exile was to rectify their sin.

Inner Light, Surrounding Light

According to the *Zohar*, any willful misuse of sperm is worse than murder,[6] for "a murderer kills another man's children, but this person kills his own and he spills much blood."[7]

The Ari explains that, whereas murder involves destroying a person's body, the soul is nevertheless free to enter the heavenly realms. On the other hand, engendering a soul and enclosing her in garments of evil after a momentary sexual weakness means condemning her to live an existence of evil.

Since the soul engendered was never attached to a human body, she is unable to enter the realms of holiness. Thus she suffers the most intense estrangement from

God, and rectifying this is very difficult—not until the very man who cast the soul down retrieves her from the evil where he placed her.

In his discussion of Israel's descent into Egypt, the Ari explains that every man has a soul enclosed within his body—his Inner Light—and there is another soul surrounding him, whose glow reflects the radiance above.[8] Some people purify their physicality to such an extent that their Surrounding Light can actually be perceived. The paradigm of this was Moses, whose face shone with light when he came down from Mount Sinai.[9]

The Surrounding Light sensitizes a person to the spiritual light or energy around him. In fact, as the *Nefesh HaChayim* points out, a high level of Surrounding Light endows the person with a superior intelligence to perceive the internal logic hidden in the Torah, as well as a sharp memory.[10]

When man sins, however, his inner soul begins to descend. If he continues to sin, she falls entirely into the realm of evil. At this point the soul that previously surrounded him is drawn inside. Although he still has the use of the Divine energy of his surrounding soul, his inner soul is now referred to as "dead," in the sense that he can no longer perceive the light.

If a man continues to sin, there comes a point where his second soul is compelled to descend to the realm of evil, thus losing all contact with the spiritual world above. This almost total separation from the collectivity of souls of the Community of Israel is referred to as *caret*/excision. Nevertheless, as long as a breath of life remains in the person, he can retrieve his soul from the depths of impurity

The consequences of such actions are not just that part of a person's spirit dwells in the realm of evil, but that the temptation to indulge in forbidden behavior slowly increases its power over him until it overwhelms him totally.

The Ari writes that the Surrounding Light serves as a powerful agent to strengthen the Inner Light, for the latter is weakened by human physicality. Each day, the Surrounding Light is renewed with Divine energy. It in turn reinforces man's Inner Light. The only way to overcome evil temptations is with the influence of the Surrounding Light, for man's attraction to physical pleasures is stronger than the powers of the spirit within him.

Therefore, when a person's Surrounding Light is engulfed within the physical forces of his body, he loses in two ways. First, the light connecting him to holiness from without is now much weaker and he no longer has the strength to overcome his physical impulse. Secondly, the inner soul that constitutes his essence is now in the depths of evil and pulls him down, inciting him to indulge in acts that can sever his bond with the Creator.

We have seen that God created the universe to bestow His goodness upon His creatures by making Himself known and revealing His oneness to them. God also created the forces of evil, whose goal is to tempt man and prevent the Divine purpose to be completed. Thus, as Ramchal—Rabbi Moshe Chayim Luzzato—points out, man finds himself in a raging battle between good and evil. Just as his heavenly soul, connected to the Source of good, infuses him with holiness, so will his soul, if steeped in impurity, constantly arouse his lust for physical pleasures.

It follows then, that just as man's seed is endowed with the Divine power to engender a complete holy soul with all its aspects, in the same way, when used for any purpose other than the correct one, it can draw down a complete soul, compelling it to become a disembodied evil spirit. Since this negative force is intimately connected with the person's soul that gave it existence, it has the innate ability to pull down man's entire spiritual structure.

Man's power to bring down a soul, whether to engender a physical child after sexual union with his wife, or to become a disembodied spirit by misusing his sperm, stems from the heavenly root of his soul. Therefore, the sins that the physical children commit damage the father's connection to the Divine. Hence, referring to the violence of his sons Simeon and Levi, Jacob exclaimed:

Let my soul not enter their plot; let my spirit not unite with their meeting.[11]

These children, however, have bodies of their own; they are only connected to their father in the sense that they descend from his root. Nevertheless, the other children, who do not have separate bodies, attach themselves to man's entire spiritual structure and damage every aspect of it. Lacking physical bodies, they remain an integral part of man's essence, condemned to remain in the realm of evil until man succeeds in rectifying them through repentance. As long as they are not rectified, their essence remains that of the man who created them. By misusing his sexual energy, man is then immersing his own Divine essence in the impurity of evil.

Since God does not dwell among impurity, this transgression drives the Divine Presence from the world. Furthermore, a man will be constantly attracted to the negative forces that cling to him; these will form a dense cover around him until he is unable to attach himself to God.

We can now understand the Ari's statement that this sin is more damaging than any other, for when a man commits any other transgression, only a part of his heavenly soul is drawn down into evil. Since the greater part of his outer Surrounding Light remains connected to the Divine, it continues to draw down upon him powers of holiness that arouse him to repent. However, regarding the "rebellious children," it is not only his own soul that is drawn down, but another complete soul as well. In this case, the negative forces become immensely more powerful than the forces of holiness. The resulting spiritual insensitivity makes it very difficult to arouse in oneself enough yearning to repent.

Nevertheless, as we mentioned, as long as a man lives, a link, frail though it may be, always remains, connecting a man with his Maker. A desire to renew the love bond with his Creator enables man to draw down the radiant light of the Higher Forces of Creation, the only force able to overpower the negative attraction to evil. Then, he can repent over misusing the Divine power entrusted to him. Repentance is now possible, for contact with the Divine light annihilates the powers of evil, and he can now elevate the souls that he caused to fall.

LILY OF THE VALLEYS

The same phenomenon occurs with the collective souls of the people of Israel, for in the root of their souls, they are like one person. The souls of the righteous infuse Israel with holiness, whereas the souls of transgressors arouse their illicit desires.

The Midrash notes that when Jacob died, the eyes and hearts of the Israelites became blinded to how they were gradually being enslaved. As long as Jacob lived, he drew down to them the Infinite Light, and the power of his personal holiness was able to overcome the influence of the evil side. After his death, however, his sons no longer had access to that lofty source of holiness. Consequently, evil began to take hold of the people. At this point, however, their forces of holiness were still strong enough to overcome its influence.

However, after Jacob's sons died, the soul of the nation that dwelt in evil was gradually able to take over, pulling the nation down into impurity: they were overcome by an irresistible attraction to the idolatrous practices of the Egyptians.

And yet, we know that during the exile from Egypt, and at the crossing of the Red Sea, the Israelites reached an amazing level of closeness to God. How could a generation that had sunk to the forty-ninth gate of impurity—one before the last—be worthy, immediately after redemption, of experiencing Divine revelation?

We have seen that as soon as man's Inner Light joins the forces of evil, the Surrounding Light penetrates his body. After man repents and regains the powers of his inner soul that were lost, his outer, heavenly soul still does not depart.

In His desire to be united once again in a love bond with this man, God restores his Surrounding Light to its former radiance without removing the powers of holiness that had previously taken the place of the redeemed Inner Light. Consequently, the spiritual power of the repentant is doubled in comparison to the amount of Inner Light he had before.

After the redemption of the people's Inner Light, the added power of the Surrounding outer Light remaining in place, they became infused with a Divine energy of tremendous intensity. This is the meaning of the talmudic statement, "a repentant reaches a higher level of closeness than the perfectly righteous."

Israel exclaims in the Song of Songs:

I am a rose of Sharon, an ever fresh lily of the valley.[12]

The Midrash explains:

I was sunk into the darkness of Egypt, but in a short time I rose to the light of freedom, moist with good deeds like a rose.

As a bud, the rose of Sharon is overshadowed by its petals; only later does it blossom to its full radiance. Similarly, the Israelites in Egypt were enclosed by the forces of darkness until the time that they were redeemed and brought into the light of the Divine.

RESCUING THE CHILDREN

History teaches us that God executed a two-way plan to help His people rescue "their children." First, He had them suffer the poverty experienced in exile and bondage. The sages explain that, essentially, the notion of affliction refers to the restriction of God's *shefa*/luminous energy from the man who engendered a soul, whether by involvement with a woman or not, and caused this soul to be taken over by the forces of evil. The restriction will also affect, although to a lesser extent, any woman who, as a willing partner, lent herself to reinforce the powers of darkness through her behavior. Man is thus deprived of God's light and sustenance until the only thing remaining available to him is his own life essence to draw on, and as a result, the forces of evil clinging to him are unable to derive their nourishment from him.

The second facet of God's plan was to draw onto the root of man's soul His holiest light, whose power would surround man as a shield from which evil cannot get any nourishment.

The question is, How does this Divine plan of rescue apply to us today?

The spiritual constraint of Divine energy results in a physical constraint of man's freedom. Hence, the equivalent of the binding effect of slavery in today's time might be, for instance, poverty. Just as evil limits the freedom of man's spirit, God limits the freedom of man's body in the knowledge that only the physical subjugation of his body will rid him of these negative forces.

The sages teach that the constraint of Divine sustenance forming the first facet of God's plan can be brought about by subduing man's physical matter through fasting. Comparable to the afflictions of slavery or poverty, the deprivation of physical nourishment lowers man's energy so that the part of his soul dwelling in evil is no longer able to overwhelm him by infecting him with uncontrollable lust. This is an essential part of the plan, for as long as man's eyes and heart are attracted to evil nothing will help to get him out of it.

Fasting, however, is not practical today. In fact, contemporary enacters of Jewish law advise the public against it because depletion of energy easily leads to impatience, shortness of temper, and anger, which are likened to idolatry. Nevertheless, since the people of Israel are considered a collectivity of souls forming one single spiritual structure, some kabbalists of each generation undergo a series of long fasts with total deprivation of food and drink, in order to bring about the redemption of these lost souls. These fasts are referred to as "days of *shovavim*/rebellious children."

Independent of these fasts, however, each individual must further his own cause by constraining his physical matter in a way that enables him to function efficiently throughout the day. Delaying breakfast for half an hour, not finishing a tasty morsel on one's plate, or depriving oneself of a tempting food item are techniques that help bring about the first facet of God's plan as long as they are accompanied with the resolution to restrict the use of one's sexual energy to its designed purpose.

THE INFINITE LIGHT

God constricts His Infinite Light to help us experience Him, and encloses it into attributes. When we attempt with all our might to emulate a Divine attribute, we draw down to ourselves a Divine energy that boosts our own efforts to acquire this particular attribute.

When man gives free reign to a certain sexual propensity to the extent that it becomes habitual and part of his very nature, there comes a time when, even if he feels the desire to put an end to this practice, no prayer or expert counseling seems to help.

At this point, the only thing that man can do is to summon the highest of God's attributes: will. Man's unshakable decision never to indulge in this sexual transgression again, to the point that the "Knower of all secrets" could testify for him as to the sincerity of his intention, is ultimately the only thing that will enable him to put an end to his proclivity. The reason for this is that by exercising his own will he is drawing down to himself the Divine attribute of will, thus strengthening his will with the iron determination he requires for the titanic task he has undertaken.

When man succeeds in his resolution to remain on the path of sexual purity, God directs the beam of the Infinite Light of His Forces of Creation on the holy souls man caused to come down, thus redeeming them from evil.

This is what happened with the Community of Israel in Egypt: even though they had sunk to the forty-ninth level of impurity through their involvement with idolatry, the bondage and backbreaking labor helped them gain an upper hand over their subjection to evil desires. Only then, through the revelation of the Divine Presence on the night of Exodus, the Israelites left Egypt. The fact that their souls had a very high origin, boosted by the double intensity of Inner Light, helped them gradually to purify themselves from the evil they left behind until they reached the point where they were worthy of receiving the Torah.

Our history illustrates the two ways in which God helps man rescue the parts of his soul lost to evil: filtering the Divine light and sustenance so that the forces of evil clinging to man cannot derive their existence from it, and reinforcing man's soul power with the Infinite Light of His Forces of Creation, against which evil is powerless.

Nevertheless, God always begins by helping a man through an increase of light. It is only when man remains insensitive that God takes the step to diminish the radiance of His light that reaches the man. The reason is that, through His infinite wisdom, God knows that this man will be unable to overcome temptations on his own because a great proportion of his soul power is already sunk in evil.

Hence, the talmudic sages teach:

> If your evil drive is getting the better of you, conquer it with our source of Good. If this does not suffice, reading the Shema prayer before retiring for the night will help you conquer it. If it still does not suffice, remind yourself of the day of your death.

Aware of the irresistible pull of physical lust, the sages are telling the man who sees temptation getting the better of him the way to enlist God's help. A less cryptic wording of their advice could be as follows:

What you have to aim for is to draw onto yourself the power of God's light. With Divine light the powers of evil exercising their influence on you will not be able to derive their sustenance by absorbing the share that was coming to you. You can achieve this by studying Torah, which is referred to as "light." If this does not help, then you recite the Shema prayer, "Hear Israel, the Lord is our God; the Lord is One," before going to sleep, having in mind the conscious intention to draw to yourself the illumination of faith. This will infuse you with the Infinite Light of the Forces of Creation, for the appellation "the Lord our God" is the root of the souls of Israel. If this still is not enough, remind yourself of the Divine judgment after your death. Death is the extreme constraint of God's light.

We can see here both facets of the Divine plan of rescue—constraint and profusion of God's light—but in this case, the increase of Divine light is mentioned first. The sages are advising man not to be passive and wait for the Divine intervention to help him redeem his lost soul power, for that may involve the more painful constraint of God's light, which entails the curtailing of his freedom. Since *both* facets of the Divine plan are necessary to help man overcome his temptations, he should bring about the constraint of luminous energy in a way that would bring an increase of light at the same time.

He can do this by studying Torah, which is known to weaken the flesh, in the sense that its study captivates man to the extent that he will diminish his time of sleep and food intake in order to make his study more quantitative and intense. Yet, at the same time, this challenging study is accompanied by a profusion of rarefied light to which the forces of evil cannot attach themselves.

Furthermore, the sages specified that the mental concentration required for the study of Jewish law weakens man's physical strength to the extent that he is considered a spiritual light unshielded by the physical barriers of the body. At this point he can draw onto himself the luminous energy of his soul-root.[13]

The second choice in the sage's advice concerned the nightly Shema prayer, our basic declaration of faith. Rabbi Kaplan discusses its unique ability to dispel the forces of evil.

The Shema is said in bed, just before one goes to sleep at night. According to the Talmud, night is the time when the forces of evil are strongest, and the Shema has the power to protect us against them.

The reason for this should be obvious: evil has power only when it is seen as disconnected from God. If one thinks that there can be a force of evil apart from God, then one can be harmed by it. However, if a person recognizes that even evil is a creation of God, then it no longer has any power over him. God Himself said through His prophet, "I form light and create darkness, I make peace and create evil; I am God, I do all these things" [Isaiah 45:7].[14]

Later commentators wondered why the talmudic sages did not begin by evoking the day of death in order to shock man, coercing him with the fear of punishment to help him get hold of himself. They answered that this is not the way of the Torah. God's wish is not to restrain His luminous energy in order to vent His wrath against those who turn their back to Him. On the contrary, God wants to shower a transgressor with the outpouring of His love so that it acts as an irresistible magnet drawing the repentant back to Him. It is only when man is so steeped in evil that he is insensitive and unable to be aware of the pull of the magnet that the only way to help him is through constriction.

Propitious Time

As part of His plan of rescue involving the weakening of physical energy through Torah study and the nightly recitation of the Shema prayer, God imbued a particular time of the year with a special property to succeed in the arduous task of redeeming the souls of one's "rebellious children."

Someone who wants to detach himself from the influence of the negative forces will receive heavenly help as long as he still has some resisting power left within him, for the Divine prerequisite for helping man redeem his lost soul power is for man to begin an effort to gain mastery over the lure of lust. Yet, it is undeniable that time affects the way in which the forces of Divine Providence relate to us.

The most favorable time for working on deep-rooted transgressions such as that of the "rebellious children," for which repentance is difficult to achieve, are the months Tevet and Shevat, which immediately follow Kislev, the month of Chanukah. Let us examine why these months are better than any other time of the year.

We have seen that the main reason that the Chanukah lights should be kindled outside the door of one's house is to publicize the miracle that took place. Yet, to the sages, the Chanukah lights were to remind man that he could begin rectifying his soul in the coming weeks by kindling a spiritual light in the darkness he created by sinning, and so redeem his "rebellious children," "who sit in the darkness and the shadow of death, shackled in affliction and iron."[15] The sages instituted the reading of the weekly Torah portion regarding the end of Jacob's life and the bondage of the tribes in Egypt during Tevet and Shevat because they knew that, on the one hand, the forces of evil have an increased power at this time of the year. On the other, these months are imbued with a Divine energy designed to help man rescue the souls that he caused to fall.

The task that Jacob, following in the footsteps of his father and grandfather, accomplished in his lifetime was to make the nations aware of God's Providence in the world. Hence, the act of reading about Jacob draws down the illumination of faith that dispels the forces of evil. Furthermore, Kabbalah teaches that the verse "Your faithfulness surrounds You,"[16] alludes to the Surrounding Light which belief in God revitalizes. Faith is a light that man does not comprehend with his intellect: he merely knows that there is something that lies beyond the power of his brain. In this sense, man's belief draws down the Divine light that surrounds him, shielding him from evil.

Halfway through the month of Tevet we begin the Book of Exodus. The act of reading how the afflictions that our forefathers suffered in Egypt served to overcome their subjection to evil makes available to us a special energy to conquer our own evil impulses. Hence, at the beginning of Exodus, we find:

The more [the Egyptians] oppressed them, the more [the Israelites] proliferated and spread.[17]

The Hebrew word for "spread," *yifrots,* stems from the root *parats*, meaning to break through. Ramchal teaches that the hidden meaning of this verse is that the more they were oppressed, the more they demolished the barriers that separated them from their Father in Heaven.

Beyond the fact that the word *shovavim* literally means "rebellious children," the acrostic of this Hebrew word hints to the first six weekly Torah portions of the Book of Exodus: **S**hemot, **V**aera, **B**o, **B**eshalach, **Y**itro, **M**ishpatim. In these six weeks we read about the development of the Community of Israel in Egypt, how they guarded the holiness that was available to them, how they were redeemed to become a nation and receive the Torah, and how they took on the commandments that enabled them to preserve their holiness.

As man absorbs the energy available throughout the six weeks in which the Torah narrates how our ancestors delivered their inner soul power from the hands of evil, man reinforces himself for the arduous task of restoring his own Inner Light.

CHILDREN OF GOD

Let us attempt to grasp the soul power of our ancestors after they left Egypt.

We mentioned that the son is an integral part of his father's *neshamah* soul. Hence, it is only because part of his father's soul is enclosed within his own body that he exists as an independent being. In contrast, a "child" who is the fruit of misused sexual energy and does not have a body of his own remains attached to his father's *neshamah* soul.

How then shall we understand the biblical expression that we are children of God?

The souls of Israel have a direct link to God on high. Just as in a human relationship, they become "children of God" when they are enclosed in material bodies. According to this system of relationships, as soon as man refines his physical lusts, his existence is considered a spiritual light. His body no longer has any power to corrupt the essence of his *neshamah* soul. This man's *neshamah* is then "a part of God in Heaven," as it were.

Such was the level of closeness of the Israelites to God after leaving Egypt. The profusion of Inner Light they acquired through the refinement of their bodies enabled them to receive the Torah, to hear the voice of the Divine Presence, and behold Its radiance.

The talmudic sage Rabbi Meir claimed that whether we fulfill God's will or not we are still His children. If this is the case, in what way are we closer to God by observing His wishes?

If children are seen as part of the father enclosed in a body of their own, it is clear that although they stem from the same source, their very body separates them from their father. The same is true of God and His children. The only difference is that when a person observes God's will, his body reaches such a high degree of refinement that it no longer represents a barrier between him and his Creator. In a sense, he becomes part of God's essence. The paradigm of this is Moses, as we can see from the fact that in the fifth book of the Pentateuch, Deuteronomy, Moses delivers all God's messages by speaking in the first person, as if he were delivering his own discourse rather than God's.

And yet, becoming part of God's essence is not restricted to men of Moses' spiritual stature: all of those who made it out of Egypt reached that level. Thus, the difficulty involved in redeeming "rebellious children" should not discourage man and lead him to think that, like the majority of Israelites in Egypt, he has already sunk to the level where he is helpless against the lure of lust. Rather, if he is undergoing afflictions, he should look at the suffering as a rope ladder of rescue the Divine Providence is offering him, echoing the Divine call, "Return, rebellious children."

Looking at suffering as a Divine invitation to repent brings man to the realization that if he had possessed *da'at*, a true intimate knowledge of God, he would never have transgressed. At this point, the sin he intentionally committed becomes but an error. Although he still has to rectify the sin, as Rabbi Akiba says:

> You are fortunate, Israel: see before Whom you purify yourselves, and Who purifies you—Your Father in Heaven.[18]

Even those who have incurred heavy spiritual debts and are suffering to expiate them are actually benefiting from God's kindness, for the goal of the varying degrees of affliction is only to help man reach the state of purity of the Temple days.

A keen desire to restore his original state of *da'at* will help him rise in consciousness to a transcendental world not limited by time and space, and he will thereby realize that all Creation is Divine light in concealment. His very transgression will have been instrumental in driving home the awareness that the Infinite Light is with him at all times.

When he strives to discern the immediacy of God's Presence, the Creator Himself will lead him to the appropriate source of spiritual guidance where he will learn how to redeem his "rebellious children."

Epilogue:
I Lost My Fire

I

T IS TO THOSE WHO HAVE EXPERIENCED the Divine energy of Shabbat and
festivals, and then lose their newly acquired sensitivity and find themselves in a
stagnant wasteland of religious routine, that we dedicate this chapter. We will now
examine the original bond that made the Community of Israel part of God's essence,
to discern the underlying pattern behind all the rises and "falls" of the Jewish people
throughout history, and in each individual's life. God first inspires a person by giving
him a small taste of the Divine energy, and then withdraws this energy in order to
allow the individual room for personal growth, until he returns to the level of soul-
union. The knowledge that this is a never-ending process, continually repeated
throughout a person's life, will help us regain and surpass the original level of fulfillment that we experienced before the fall.

TAKING AWAY TO GIVE MORE

According to the kabbalists, in the beginning, God's Infinite Light filled the universe.
To make room for His Creation, God withdrew the light, creating a void or vacated
space within the Infinite Light. He then drew a simple, concentrated ray from the
Infinite Light into the vacated space. It was through this ray that God directed His creative power into this space.[1] We may recognize the three stages: expansion, withdrawal, and once again, expansion.

The same process is illustrated in Creation. The Ari explains that when the creation of the world began, the souls of Israel already existed, and were attached to the
Foundation from where all Divine energy stems. God took from His simple unified
light to form His Companion of the soul, using the light's coarser aspect for the body
parts that were to become vessels to contain His light within this "collective person."
The purer essence of the light He reserved to fashion the person's soul.

This "person" is the Shechina, also known as "the Community of Israel," for She

187

is the collective souls of the people of Israel. The Ari further explains that God condensed the part of His light intended to fill His creation's vessels, taking the surplus to add it to His own light above. The Ari concludes that the reason the Community of Israel pines for union with her Beloved is that, essentially, She feels a lack, an emptiness within, a basic need for something that was initially Hers but now lies within Him, and hence only He can fill. She instinctively yearns to be passionately attached to Him so that He illuminates Her with the part of Her He kept within.

The sun and the moon provide us with a metaphor of this relationship. Originally, the *Zohar* points out, the two luminaries were identical, their light equal in intensity. The Creator then asked from the moon that she make herself smaller, bearing no light of her own. Her illumination would therefore depend on the sun, who held the light that had once been hers. Consequently, the moon is depicted yearning to merge with the sun, which holds the light she is now lacking.

Like the moon, to whom the Community of Israel is traditionally compared, we yearn for union with our Source of Light, with a basic need to recover what was intended to be ours. The Creator's own yearning, as it were, blazes stronger in intensity, either because we are part of His essence, or because He holds within Himself a part of us.

In contrast, the gentile is likened to the sun, in that at Creation he is given a measure of Divine light that is not subsequently taken away from him. No limits are placed on his ability to elevate himself and get closer to his Creator, but it is often the case that his search is not as keen, for he has never experienced what it means to have holiness and then be suddenly deprived of it.

As we have seen, it is Israel's choice to relate to God as servant, child, or Companion of the soul. If we liken the individual's relationship with God to the various human bonds, it is easier to understand.

The question is: How is marriage to a partner from whom one may divorce a closer relationship than the relationship between parent and child, which is permanent? Kabbalah answers by saying that just as Adam and Eve were originally created as one being,[2] each married couple was created as one being, and a person's soul mate is part of his very essence. However, a child is a descendant of his father in much the same way that a seed from a tree will in turn produce a tree of his own. A wife, in contrast, is like a branch of this tree and is attached, as a spouse, from the root. If the couple eventually divorces, or if one of them dies, it means cutting a branch from the tree, but the roots of the relationship—a host of emotions and experiences once shared—remain.

Hence, when the Children of Israel choose to relate to their Creator as "His Companion of the soul," and lead their lives accordingly, they become part of His very essence, thus verifying the kabbalistic principle that "a being emanated—separated from its source of creation—always seeks the reattachment to its original source."

The eternal pining for union between Giver and receiver emerging from this order of Creation is hinted at in the prophet's injunction that those who are thirsty search for water.[3] Said the commentators, "there is no water other than the Torah," and the only way one can receive the light of the Torah is by thirsting for it. In turn, only a lack of something that initially belonged is strong enough to give rise to such a lasting thirst.

This process is behind the image of the sages of the fetus in its mother's womb, a lit candle on its head, with whose light an angel teaches it the entire Torah. Before birth, the angel taps the fetus lightly on the mouth to make it forget what it has learned. The candle represents the Divine light, while the angel illuminates the fetus with the light of the Torah, so that, at creation, the Jewish child carries within himself the light of the Torah and the essence of the Divine service to be done in this world.

In the early stages, the child is not consciously aware of his lack, but as he grows, so does his longing for the Torah and passionate attachment to God, for these are an integral part of him. Eventually, this very yearning will drive him to cleave to his Creator. Had the Jew not initially been the recipient of this Divine energy and then had been deprived of it, he would not instinctively search for it throughout his life.

COMPANIONS OF THE SOUL

We can see this pattern manifested in Israel's initial relationship with the Creator. The kabbalists liken the Israelites in Egypt to a fetus in a womb. The years of bondage are the birth pangs, and the Exodus symbolizes birth. It was through the pain of exile that God bonded so closely with His chosen people. As it is written,

I will go to Egypt with you, and I will also bring you back again.[4]

Also, on the day of the Exodus, we find, "all of God's armies left Egypt in broad daylight,"[5] thus implying that just as the people of Israel went down to their Egyptian exile, so did the Almighty go down with them. And the image of the burning bush that He showed Moses implies "I am with them among [the thorns of] their affliction."[6]

The sages stressed that this means not only that God shared their distress, but rather, literally, if it can be said, that He inflicted the Egyptian exile on Himself as well. This sharing of Israel's symbolic gestation period thus created their bond with God as part of His very essence. Through the hardship of bondage, Israel reached the point of *bitul*/surrender and shed all vestiges of their individual egos. They were then empty vessels, ready to become One with their Creator in body and soul. The relationship was fully realized when God Himself—not an angel or an emissary—took the Children of Israel out of slavery in Egypt, brought them to safety by splitting the Red Sea, and gave them instructions for attaining their ultimate goal: how to cleave to the Divine Presence.

Consequently, the foundation of all the commandments of the Torah is built on the Exodus from Egypt. This does not mean that we are to observe the Torah out of mere recognition of the miracles God enacted on our behalf. Rather, we are evoking the degree of closeness to God that the Israelites attained at the Exodus, and the commandments are essentially instructions telling us what to do or to avoid in order to attain the ultimate goal of the Torah: cleaving to the Divine Presence. Such a bond goes beyond love, and is based on ever being passionately attached to Him.

The sages question whether it is at all possible for material man to experience such a closeness to God, Who is described as a "consuming fire." The kabbalistic commentator Nachmanides answers that since the people of Israel became part of God's essence through their bondage in Egypt, their attachment to Him would always be that of the emanated being, ever seeking the reattachment to the Source.[7]

It is no wonder, then, that the first of the Ten Commandments is "I am the Lord, **your** God, who took you out of Egypt." In this cryptic message, which appears to be more a statement than a commandment, God is saying to those who are about to become His people: "Your roots lie within Me. Therefore if I ask you to observe all My commandments, it is not as the Lord to his servant, nor as the Father to his child, for they are really opportunities to cling to Me and return to your Source."

Hence, the Torah asks us to remember the Exodus from Egypt each and every day, for that event enabled us to achieve the level of closeness that is within our reach today.

The Song of Songs, Holy of Holies

Rabbi Akiba's tears as he read the Song of Songs at the onset of Shabbat were an expression of his passionate attachment because he understood between the lines of the song the degree of *devekut* the Israelites attained through the Egyptian experience. His emotion is similar to the tears shed by those while immersed in prayer, thus revealing the longing of the emanated to cleave to the Source.

It is important to note that Rabbi Akiba's weeping happened precisely on Shabbat, in that Shabbat is referred to as a memento of the Exodus from Egypt. And yet, if we consider the teaching of Maimonides' *Guide of the Perplexed* that Shabbat is to remind us of the work of Creation, it is not clear why the seventh day was given to Israel on account of the Exodus.

The explanation of Maimonides' claim is that it is for God, Who created the world and rested on the seventh day, that Shabbat is a reminder of the work of Creation. The day is therefore referred to as the Sabbath, a day of rest. But why does the Community of Israel, who did not create the world, rest on Shabbat? We say in the Amidah prayer of Shabbat afternoon, "Your children will know that from You comes their rest," for the commandment of observing Shabbat does not concern Israel as much as it concerns the Creator, and in this sense, from Him comes our rest. However, from the moment that Israel became part of God's essence by undergoing a gestation period together with Him during the exile in Egypt, it followed that they had to conform to the principle that when the Root rests, the branches must do the same.

The essence of their bondage had been the thirty-nine activities of labor in order to accomplish what the Egyptians demanded of them. Thereafter, the essence of their freedom would be the ability to cleave to God in a soul-union by restraining from doing anything on Shabbat related to these same thirty-nine activities.

The commandment of Shabbat was therefore given to them exclusively as a memento of the Exodus from Egypt, which made possible the union in which Israel must rest on Shabbat in the same way that God Himself rests.

Rabbi Akiba, as he was reading the Song of Songs, understood that on Shabbat Israel's intimate bond with the Creator could no longer be seen as the yearning of two separate entities one for the other. This bond is a union in which the Community of Israel ascends to become part of God. At this realization, Rabbi Akiba achieved a level of *devekut* of such intensity that his tears began to flow as he connected to the Source of his life.

Rabbi Akiba called the Song of Songs "the holy of holies," for the song reveals the same perfected bond as the embrace of the cherubs whose image is carved in the innermost chamber of the holy Temple. And so, as he was reading the Song soon after the Second Temple was destroyed, at a time when God's concealment was painfully felt, Rabbi Akiba was profoundly moved to think that this fiery love bond could still be attained on Shabbat.

THREE LEVELS OF REVELATION

The threefold process by which God relates to us—revelation/separation/soul-union— helps us understand the three historical stages of God's revelation to Israel: the night of the Exodus, the splitting of the sea, and the Giving of the Torah.

When the Jewish people were "born" on the night of the Exodus, their relationship with the Creator was crystallized: they were bound to His essence. They went after Him into the desert, as the verse says, "you followed Me in the wilderness, a land not sown."[8] With a pillar of fire God led the way, while they were like branches pulled toward their root. The Haggadah speaks of the "great awe" that they felt at that moment.

There was no vision involved, for, as long as the Israelites were in Egypt, they could not perceive the spiritual dimension.

The biblical text contains veiled references to Israel's spiritual oblivion during their gestation period in Egypt. First, we have the exclamation of Pharaoh's magicians, awed by the devastation of the plagues, "This is the finger of God!"[9] Then, at the Red Sea, "the Israelites saw the powerful hand that God had unleashed against Egypt."[10]

The fact that while in Egypt, the awareness of Divine justice is referred to as *the finger of God*, whereas after the splitting of the sea, it is seen as *the hand*, is not arbitrary. To the kabbalists, the single finger suggests that as long as they were in bondage, the Israelites were restricted to the lowest level of soul, the *nefesh*, which precludes sensitivity to the spiritual.

In contrast, when juxtaposed to "the finger of God," the five fingers of the hand allude to the five levels of the soul, *nefesh, ruach, neshamah, chayah,* and *yechidah,* which

Israel acquired as they left Egypt. This access to the complete structure of their soul enabled them subsequently to cleave to their Creator in a soul-union, being fully aware of an expanded state of consciousness.

However, the relationship was still in a state of infancy, and in order for it to grow, a separation was necessary. God therefore withheld His Presence from the Israelites during the following seven days, and the awe they experienced changed into a longing to recapture their initial ecstasy.

By the time they reached the Red Sea, the Israelites were in a state of despair. The sea raged before them and the desert surrounded them; behind them, Pharaoh's troops were in hot pursuit. Furthermore, the verse says, "God's angel . . . now moved and went behind them,"[11] suggesting that God and Israel were no longer in a direct "face-to-face" relationship. The people panicked; some cried out to God, others expressed their wish to return to Egypt, and some even gave up hope of redemption.

Initially, it is difficult to understand why God deprived them of the conscious awareness of His Presence at this early stage, allowing the people to fall into a realm of darkness and despair rather than helping them immediately.

In light of the threefold process that we have analyzed, Israel needed the separation in order to be once again face-to-face with their Creator. This brought them to the times of affliction and concealment, experiences that in turn helped them to reach the point at which they could exclaim, "This is my God and I will build Him a Sanctuary," thus indicating that they were actually looking directly at the Shechina.[12]

It was the fiery ecstasy of the revelation, rather than the gratitude for their redemption, that prompted Israel to burst into song. At the time of the Exodus, their spiritual stature was still in the form of a dot—their *nefesh* soul. After enduring the separation, however, their collective soul structure had grown to full size, enabling them to say, "This is my God and (anvehu)/I will build Him a Sanctuary." The consonant letters—n-v-h—of the Hebrew term *anvehu* form the word *neveh*/dwelling space, thus hinting to the *devekut* they could now experience as the Community of Israel, His Companion of the soul, the branch passionately attached to her Root.

At the splitting of the sea, Israel was able to shed some of the paralyzing dread of the revelation that they had experienced seven days before, on the night of the Exodus. This time they fully related to God as the Community of Israel, singing to her Companion of the soul.

The Midrash specifies that at the splitting of the sea, even a simple handmaid saw what the prophet Ezekiel had not seen. In contrast, the midrashic comment on the verse, "God will descend on Mount Sinai in sight of all the people,"[13] in the account of the Giving of the Torah is, "Israel saw what Ezekiel did not see."

We note that the subject of the clause is no longer the "handmaid," but rather a matured "Israel," because whereas at the Red Sea the impurity prevented total attachment, only allowing the return "face-to-face," at the Giving of the Torah there were no barriers. As we have seen, the total numerical value of the Hebrew words describing the five levels of the soul—*nefesh, ruach, neshamah, chayah, yechidah*—is equal to the combined value of the words *anafim*/branches, and *shorashim*/roots. At long last, the branch had joined the root.

LEVELS OF CLOSENESS IN THE AMIDAH PRAYER

Our daily Amidah prayer, particularly that of the morning, also shows the threefold process through which God has related to Israel since the time of Creation. During the first blessing, sensitized to the immensity of God's love for us, our collective soul-roots go up to Him. By the end of the first blessing, we may have a taste of Abraham's bond to his Maker: our own love is infused by His own, with the closeness of a shield.

To help us impress this initial upsurge of love upon our heart, it is at this point of the Amidah that we create a precious vessel to contain it: that of awe. The next blessing, evoking God's might, temporarily breaks the intimate bond; we stand back as we remember God's sobering power of strict justice. Yet, as Kabbalah explains, this withdrawal does not cause us to go back down. On the contrary, our soul-roots continue to grow throughout the main body of the Amidah prayer, as we attempt to draw a profound sense of awe toward the Master of the Universe, the only fitting vessel that may prevent the core of insensitivity from surrounding our hearts.

The newly born Israelite nation was deeply aware of the need to intertwine love and awe from the moment that they began to relate to the Creator as His Companion of the soul. Hence, it is first written:

> The Israelites saw the great power that God had unleashed against Egypt, and the people were in awe of God.[14]

After they broke into song at the Red Sea, Israel's initial awe turned into a passionate attachment that overpowered them to such an extent that Moses had to lead them away.[15]

In the same manner, at the Giving of the Torah, the trembling of terror that overtook them at the thunder and lightning[16] gave way to a trembling of intense *devekut* which led them to implore: "We wish to see our King!" God was voicing His desire that Israel should always have access to the precious vessel of awe to contain His love as He exclaimed: "If only their hearts would always remain this way, where they are in such awe of Me!"[17]

It is for the same reason that in the Amidah prayer of Shabbat afternoon, at the moment of the greatest soul-union of the entire week, we do not feel an outburst of joy, but rather awe, so that we may hold on to the ecstasy of His closeness.[18] Consequently, we try to maintain the perception of reverential awe throughout the separation in the main body of our daily morning Amidah. At the end of the Amidah comes the moment we longed for: "face-to-face" once again, we now experience the soul-union whose intense *shefa*/luminous energy is to last us throughout the day. The soul-union of the evening prayer does not reach the level of our soul-roots, and as a result, it is unable to produce such Divine energy.

These different levels of closeness in morning and evening prayers are alluded to in the slight difference with which we refer to the splitting of the sea at both these times. Immediately prior to the morning Amidah, we say, "the beloved companions You brought across," while before the evening Amidah we have, "Who brought His children through the split parts of the Sea of Reeds." The contrast between the "beloved companions" of the morning and the "children" of the evening hints at the different quality of relationship between morning and evening.

ENEMIES OF ISRAEL

The process of elevation, descent, and higher elevation is an integral part of God's order of Creation. Let us try to understand Israel's despair as they found themselves cornered between an angry Pharaoh and the Red Sea, in light of the threefold process.

How could a people who had witnessed the ten plagues and seen the light of the Shechina on the night of Passover ever sink to total despair, to the point of thinking that slavery was preferable, and wanting to return to Egypt? From the moment they left Egypt, the pillar of fire had lit the darkness of their nights, and the pillar of cloud had shown them the way during the day. Furthermore, the clouds of Glory had surrounded them. How is it possible that they fell so low from their high level of awareness, despite all these tangible proofs of God's loving protection?

The mind-expansion they had attained on Passover eve—a state of consciousness where they were able to see the Shechina—was not the product of their efforts but a Divine gift that lasted only for the duration of the night. On the following day, they were to have drawn this Divine energy on their own, but were unable to do so. As a result, when they saw the Egyptian army in hot pursuit, they thought they were not worthy of another miracle and despaired.

The Ari explains that the withdrawal of this Infinite Light recurs every year. On Passover eve, God initiates the process of our arousal, directing His radiant Divine energy upon us. On the following day, the energy withdraws, but we were given the Torah and commandments as tools to draw the light back to ourselves. In particular, throughout each of the forty-nine days between Passover and Shavuot, when we observe the commandment of counting the Omer, we are drawing down a distinctive part of Divine energy, until it is back in its totality on Shavuot.

As they were leaving Egypt, the Israelites did not have the Torah yet to help them achieve mind-expansion on their own. This being the case, it is difficult to understand why they needed to undergo an elevation and then a fall, followed by another elevation, particularly since it was God who initiated the process of giving them back the light seven weeks later, just as He had done on Passover.

From the time of the Giving of the Torah, the Community of Israel receives each year the gift of mind-expansion from the Creator for the duration of Passover eve. They apply their efforts to retrieve it on their own throughout the ensuing weeks. Hence, when Shavuot arrives, once again they are able to enter a state of consciousness whereby they can experience a soul-union with the Almighty. This time it is no longer a gift; it is the fruit of their personal struggle.

In the case of Israel after the Exodus, however, the mind-expansion was God's gift to them on the day of the Giving of the Torah, just as it had been on Passover eve. Why, then, couldn't God shed His light upon them continuously from the time of Exodus until the Giving of the Torah?

Similarly unclear is Pharaoh's brazen pursuit of the Jews after they left Egypt. Given the severity of the plagues, how could he have a change of heart and decide to go after them, without fearing further afflictions from the God Who was evidently on their side?

Pharaoh's behavior is less puzzling when we look at Haman's in the story of Purim, for the intentions of these two enemies of Israel were identical. Due to his knowledge of the occult, Haman understood the threefold process delineating God's relationship to Israel: a revelation, followed by a separation, leading to a soul-union. He saw that before the Second Temple could be rebuilt there had to be a separation during which God withheld His Presence from them.

It was precisely while Israel's sensitivity to the spiritual was almost nil that Haman thought he should attempt to make the temporary estrangement perpetual, and indeed, as the Ari points out, the Jews were at the time in mortal danger. But God directed on His people a special light of infinite compassion, opening their eyes. Realizing that they had behaved as if the world was led by chance rather than a personalized Divine Providence, they repented and were saved from danger.

In the same way, Pharaoh became aware that after the revelation of the night of the Exodus the light had withdrawn from Israel. He realized that it was now, when the contact was considerably thinner, that a little pressure could lead them to believe that they had been left to their own devices. He understood that this feeling of abandonment would weaken the spiritual contact between God and Israel even more: this was his chance to overcome them. This explains Pharaoh's comment, "the Israelites are lost in the area and trapped in the desert!"[19] And he went after them with more determination than ever.

It was precisely at this point that the angel appointed over Egypt came before the powers of Divine justice in the heavenly realm and accused the Israelites, indignantly questioning whether they were worthy of redemption, given their recent involvement in idolatry.

The fact that the angel did not raise such an objection during the actual Exodus shows that he was fully aware that it was now, while the Jews were temporarily deprived of their invincible Divine protection, that he had a chance to be heard. Also, as long as they were in Egypt, the Bible refers to Israel as God's children. It is only at the crossing of the sea that they are referred to as *yedidim*/beloved, indicating their present state of Companions of the soul. The indulgent forgiveness a man often exhibits toward his child is rarely present when he is relating to his beloved companion. Indeed, this was the auspicious time to accuse Israel.

However, this moment of concealment helped them reach the next state of revelation. Moses cried out for Divine assistance. "Why are you crying out to Me?" God asked.[20] When Israel faces a mortal enemy while standing united as God's Kingship on earth, God does not require their prayers, just as a human king does not wait for his subjects to ask him to mobilize the army in the event of invasion.

Moreover, a prayer is an attempt to arouse Divine mercy, and it is written that "His mercies are on all His creatures."[21] While the Egyptians were drowning at sea, God did not allow the angels to sing Israel's deliverance: "The work of My hands is dying, and you wish to sing!" Hence, Mercy was not the Divine chord Israel needed to touch, but the highest of all, Will. They needed to remind God of His desire to delight in Israel, which the kabbalists call the arousal from above, and consummates solely as a result of the arousal from below.

The wounds that the Creator inflicted on Israel's pursuers at this time were much worse than the ten plagues, for God was finally "face-to-face" with His Companion of the soul, and when the Egyptians tried to harm her, the Almighty responded with consequent furor. As they realized what was happening, the Egyptians exclaimed in fear, "God is fighting for them against Egypt!"[22] The Divine response thus verified what Zechariah would prophesy centuries later with regard to Israel:

Anyone who touches you, touches the pupil of His eye.[23]

The Divine favor with which God related to the Israelites at this time is beyond our grasp, similar to the "face-to-face" return on Yom Kippur. As the Ari explains, the Holy One forgives Israel's sins and silences all accusers. It is no wonder that it was precisely in the Red Sea that Israel sang in unison to their Companion of the soul!

A song implies a separation in that if two people are as one, there is no one to whom to sing! On the night of the Exodus, the Israelites were—if artificially—on the level of the Patriarchs who had a direct perception of God. Hence, when each of the Patriarchs was saved by miraculous Divine intervention, their awareness of the Divine was so immediate that they could not stand back and sing. In a similar note, in the Temple service, the *cohanim*/priests were on a higher level than the Levites, and yet, the task of singing was incumbent upon the Levites.

A song is not only the sign of a separation, but also of the return "face-to-face" that is now taking place. In this sense, a song can be seen as an expression of direct contact with God, which is why music may be so arousing. The present promotion of trance music as conducive to mind-expansion is only a distortion of the effect of songs such as the Song of Songs and the Song at the Sea, namely, the ultimate mind-expansion of union with God.

THE BRANCHES JOIN THE ROOT FOREVER

Let us take a brief look at the injunction to remember the Exodus in the future. Says Jeremiah the prophet:

"Yes, a time is coming," says God, when people will no longer say, "As God lives, Who brought the Israelites out of the land of Egypt," but "As God lives, Who brought the children of the Israelites out of the north land and took them out of all the countries where I had scattered them." They will dwell on their own soil.[24]

Jeremiah is predicting that in the days of the Messiah, the miracles of the Exodus from Egypt will no longer be referred to. By then, those miracles will have been surpassed by those of the messianic era, so much so that there will be no need, and no obligation, to remember the former.

It is important to understand that the miracles we experienced in Egypt concerned not only the redemption from bondage, but also the birth of the bond of Companions of the soul between the Almighty and the Community of Israel. The kabbalists reveal that, just as in a human pregnancy there can be a gestation of seven months and one of nine months, in a symbolic sense, the gestation of the intimate bond that emerged out of the Egyptian exile was one of "seven months." This gave rise to a bond in which Israel became attached to His essence, at the time that the relationship was not fully matured.

In contrast, in the present, the Jewish nation is in what is called its last exile: as long as the Jewish people do not have a government based on the Torah, they are considered to be in a state of exile. In the present exile, Israel is under the threat of the descendants of Abraham's son Ishmael, the father of Islam.

The sages have predicted that the exile of Ishmael would be the last and the hardest of all. Presently, the collective spiritual structure of the people of Israel is once again in the form of a dot, having a minimum level of Divine awareness. Our present situation is comparable to that of the new Israelite nation between the sea and the Egyptian army. We are therefore undergoing the birth pangs of the Messiah, except that this time, the gestation must be full term. It must "give birth" to a completely matured bond where a separation will no longer be needed to fuel the fiery coals of our love. The passionate attachment between the root and its branches will thereafter be permanent, and with Jeremiah, we will praise the Creator for bringing the house of Israel from all the countries where He drove them, and "they will dwell on their own soil."

On the eve of Passover, we dwell on the bitterness and affliction of the Egyptian exile in great detail rather than stressing the aspect of our freedom from bondage. This reminds us that our suffering was that which made us His Companion of the soul and part of His essence. And so, every succeeding Passover, as we eat bitter herbs dipped in symbolic tears, we should realize that in its present suffering, the Jewish nation is growing toward a similar goal . . . but so much greater!

Passover is therefore at the forefront of all the festivals, for on all the other festivals we build onto the original soul-union between the Creator and Israel as His Companion of the soul, which was first set in Egypt.

The sages find an allusion to the bond of Companions of the soul in the vision Israel received at the Giving of the Torah:

> They saw a vision of the God of Israel, and under His feet was something like a sapphire brick, like the essence of the clear [blue] sky.[25]

According to Rashi, this brick indicated the extent to which God had been aware of Israel's forced labor and how close to Him these afflictions had made them. Ever present in the Divine mind, the brick reminded God that Israel had become part of His essence through their slavery, and this memento prompted Him to redeem them to actualize this bond.

Hence, the brick represents both the people of Israel and their Egyptian labor. It was portrayed as under "His feet" for the people of Israel are sometimes referred to as God's "footstool" and, as the kabbalists explain, the beginning of their intimate bond to Him had been like a little dot. This means that throughout the Egyptian gestation period, Israel had access only to the first and most basic level of their soul, that of *nefesh*. This dot was attached to the Foundation Coronet, the meeting point where the soul-union between the Creator and Israel's collective souls occurs. The dot had then undergone a separation during which it had grown to full size, Israel's complete spiritual structure. As the vision showed, however, the souls are still attached to the brick, eternal reminder of the roots of the Community of Israel.

THE FOUR PORTIONS:
DAWN OF THE LIGHT OF REDEMPTION

Four Torah portions that are read on Shabbat during the few weeks preceding Passover carry the identical message of this gestation period. Their aim is to gradually amplify this message, which created the bond of Companions of the soul.

A HALF-*SHEKEL* OF FIRE

The first portion bears the name of silver coins, *Shekalim*, referring to the money that the Israelites were asked to donate in the desert toward the construction of the *Mishkan*/Tabernacle. The sages note that this donation was supposed to expiate the construction of the Golden Calf.

The Midrash portrays Moses as wondering how the Israelites were going to be able to expiate such a terrible sin. God then showed him the image of a coin of fire, half concealed under the Throne of Glory, and said to him, "They will give one like this." Nevertheless, it was still difficult for Moses to understand how half a shekel was going to expiate the sin of idolatry.

Although it was clear that from the moment Moses came down from the mountain, Israel truly regretted what they had done, such a serious infraction still required expiation, particularly since it was committed intentionally.

The half-coin seen under the Throne of Glory was a pictorial representation of the relationship that made the Israelites the essence of God's essence at the Exodus. Even though as human beings, the people of Israel have an exterior, material cover, their root remains attached above, in the Foundation Coronet. The half-shekel of fire under the Throne was therefore a variant of the sapphire brick "under His feet."

By giving half a shekel, each Israelite was stating his deep belief that in the same way that this half-shekel was linked to the other half under the Throne, he saw himself as a half that would only be complete when cleaving to his Source with total passionate attachment, forming One with God. And at this level of union, "love covers all transgressions."

By extension, when we give part of our money—our security, that which enables us to stand up on our own two feet—to a Divine cause, we are reasserting our faith that Divine Providence will sustain us in the way that we personally need. God marks His acceptance of true charity by elevating the giver beyond the point where he flawed his spiritual structure by sinning. In this sense, money can be seen as a ladder of ascent to the Throne of Glory, and accordingly, the numerical value of Hebrew word *mamon*/money is identical to that of the word *sulam*/ladder.

A similar whitewashing of the past is accomplished on Shabbat. As Ramban writes, during the Temple days there was no need to bring a sacrifice on Shabbat, for on this day the Community of Israel is God's Companion of the soul, and perfect peace reigns. On Shabbat Israel is totally engrossed in their relationship with the Creator; this reinforces their faith in the fact that they are part of His essence, and as such there is no need for expiation.

The concept of the half-shekel produces similar results in that the donation reminds Israel that they relate to the Creator as His Companion of the soul. Consequently, any sin they may have committed is thereby expiated. The sages therefore teach that those who observe Shabbat according to its laws are forgiven of all their sins—even idolatry.

The commentators explain that this claim refers to one who regrets the sins he committed but has not expiated them yet. The attention he devotes to reviewing all the intricate Shabbat laws in order that his observance be flawless—and the care with which he practices what he has learned—are his proof that he sees himself as part of God's essence. The trouble he takes to please his Creator with perfect observance of His day arouses Divine feelings toward him, and as a result he is totally forgiven.

Since the first expression of the Shabbat bond "was born" in Egypt, the initial glow of the luminous energy of Passover begins to shine every year at the time the Torah portion of *Shekalim* is read, on the Shabbat preceding the first of Adar. However, the actual giving of the donation occurs on the first of Nisan, to sensitize the congregants to the essence of the coming Passover festival.

God chose the people of Israel at the time that they were still contained within the Patriarch Jacob, as hinted at in the verse "God chose Jacob to be His." He then made "Israel for His treasure," passionately attached to Him.[26]

God's acceptance of Israel's half-shekel thus meant: since we were, if it can be said, together in Egypt, you are necessarily attached to Me. This makes you a part of My very essence, for God "will not abandon His people and His inheritance, He will not forsake."[27] I cannot leave that which is a part of Me. This was God's message to Moses, delivered through the visual model of the half-shekel concealed under the Throne of Glory.

"Now, if You would, please forgive their sin," Moses had implored,[28] asking the Creator to forgive His people for the Golden Calf. The Hebrew word used to render "forgive" is *tisa*/elevate, so that, literally, the message is "if you would forgive them by elevating them to the point in their spiritual structure where they can still expiate."

When Moses' time on earth was coming to an end, he said to God, "After I die, I will no longer be remembered!" God answered him: "Every year, when Israel will read the Torah portion concerning the half-shekel, I will take the census of the Israelites to determine their numbers; each one shall be counted by giving an atonement offering for his life."[29]

As we can gather from the Divine reply, Moses was concerned that no one was going to fill his role as the King's friend, who constantly reminded God that He should forgive the Israelites, if only because while in Egypt, they had become part of His essence. Moses therefore said, "After I die, no one will reach my status of King's friend, having access to the King, and thus be able to defend Israel."

Said God, "Every year, as I hear them read about their donation of a half-shekel, I will remember to be merciful, since they are My Companions of the soul." As the kabbalists point out, the numerical value of the word *nefesh*, the soul that is within the body, is identical to the value of the word *shekel*. This shows that the bond between God and Israel is not restricted only to the spiritual realm, at the lofty level where the soul is part of the Divine, but also exists at the level where the *nefesh* soul is enclosed within the body parts. Below, as above, each of the Children of Israel is still a half who is only complete when attached to his Source on high.

Remember!

On the Shabbat before Purim, we read the Torah portion known as *Zachor*/remember, to remind us of Amalek's attack on Israel in the desert. The subject matter of this reading concerns Passover more than Purim, however: Amalek did not attack Israel immediately after the Exodus, nor after the Giving of the Torah, but between the splitting of the sea and the Giving of the Torah. Amalek had seen how Pharaoh had attempted to take advantage of the Divine concealment after the night of the Exodus. Hence, he realized that after the splitting of the sea there would necessarily be another stage of separation, since, for every ascent, there must be a descent in order to ascend even higher.

The principle of descent after ascent explains Israel's puzzling behavior: after a revelation of the Divine Presence such as they experienced at the splitting of the sea, "the entire Israelite community began to complain," that they had no food.[30] Somewhat later, when they were missing water, "they began demonstrating against Moses,"[31] and Moses exclaimed, "Before long they will stone me!"[32]

As we become familiar with the pattern of Divine behavior of revelation—separation—and return face-to-face, it becomes easier to understand why God did not immediately give them the food and drink He knew they needed. In order to elevate them once again to meet Him face-to-face at the Giving of the Torah, He inflicted upon them the confusion of Divine concealment and the pangs of hunger and thirst before He returned to sustain them.

Similarly, at the Giving of the Torah, the Israelites needed to go through the terrifying experience of the thunder and lightning; in order to be face-to-face with Him once again, they had to undergo the stage of separation and concealment of His Presence. Later, during the moment of the Giving of the Torah, they joined the Creator in a soul-union whose effect is reminiscent of the Song of Songs, "My soul departed as He spoke,"[33] such was the love and passionate attachment that invaded them.

And again, Amalek saw the confusion prevalent among the Israelites, who reacted to the sense of loss that invaded them during the separation stage, as they muttered, "Is God with us or not?"[34] He then understood that the Divine reunion was imminent and he should attack immediately. Amalek's reasoning reflected his goal: preventing the soul-union from taking place.

THE RED COW

The third of the four Torah portions before Passover is known as *Parah*/cow, deriving its name from the Red Cow (*Parah Adumah*) whose ashes purify one from the defilement caused by a corpse. In biblical times, the Red Cow was burned the day after the construction of the Tabernacle, on the second day of the month of Nisan. Its original purpose was to purify the people of Israel after the sin of the Golden Calf, which had occurred after the giving of the First Tablets.

The sin of the Golden Calf caused Israel to have a spiritual fall, and they lost all the Divine consciousness that they had acquired while "face-to-face" in the Red Sea. According to the order that God built into Creation, a sinner opens himself to rampant evil forces. Consequently, the sinner is deprived of his prior ability to enter into an expanded state of consciousness—one in which he can experience direct contact with the Holy One. This occurs in order to prevent the evil forces from gaining access to the Source of purity.

The commentators derive Israel's spiritual decline from God's reaction to their sin:

> God told Moses to say to the Israelites, "You are an unbending people. In just one second I can go among you and utterly destroy you. Now take off your jewelry and I will know what to do with you." From [that time at] Mount Horeb, the people no longer wore their jewelry.[35]

The "jewelry" here is interpreted as their newly acquired awareness of the Divine to which they no longer had access. They were now, as the Kabbalah puts it, "back-to-back," like one who after sinning loses his ability to enter a state of expanded consciousness because of the evil forces that cling to him as a consequence of his sin.

Moses began to plead: "O God, why unleash Your wrath against Your people, whom You brought out of Egypt with great power and a show of force?"[36] reminding God of the exile that had made Israel essence of His essence. And in response, "God refrained from doing the evil that He planned for His people."[37]

THREE LEVELS OF "FACE-TO-FACE" REUNION

Nevertheless, the "face-to-face" relationship this forgiveness brought about was only on the outer level in the sense that it was not an unreserved whitewashing of the past.

Once again, Moses went up to the mountain to plead for the people, asking God to pardon them by elevating them to the level of their spiritual structure where they were still blameless:

> Now, if You would, please forgive their sin. If not, you can blot me out from the book that You have written.[38]

And the Divine reaction: "I will send My angel before you."[39]

Although we can already see a higher level of forgiveness in God's words, we can detect that there was still an inner reservation from the fact that God is sending His angel rather than going Himself. It was then that the Israelites observed the commandment of the red cow with total faith so that its ashes would bring them ultimate cleansing. We read the Torah section of the red cow to remember the third and highest level of "face-to-face" reunion that it brought the people of Israel just before the Passover festival, for purity brings with it the inner level of forgiveness that paves the way for the soul-union.

THE SANCTIFICATION OF THE LUNAR MONTH

The fourth Torah portion before the Passover festival is that of the first of the month of Nisan, where the first issue discussed is the sanctification of the lunar month. The crescent moon reminds us of the kabbalistic teaching that the smaller luminary has no light of her own, since she gave the sun all she had in order to receive in return all she needs from him. The discussion of this subject at the beginning of Nisan reminds us of the Community of Israel, who longs to be reunited with the Beloved, recipient of the Divine energy that was once her own.

The light that the sun directs on the new moon represents the soul-union that comes about after the return "face-to-face" on all three levels.

Hence, the juxtaposition of the sanctification of the new month to the Exodus from Egypt is to show the people of Israel that it was through their exile and gestation that they became like the moon, who surrendered all she had to the sun in order to have a rightful share of his light. Similarly, the soul-union represents those who were emanated finally basking in the light of their Source of Creation.

The first three Torah portions represent the three succeeding levels of forgiveness and ensuing return "face-to-face"; the fourth portion on the new moon points to the soul-union itself.

THOUGHT PRECEDES DEED

The reading of these four Torah portions preceding Passover illustrates the principle that thought precedes deed. These sections of the Torah are not just Jewish biblical history that we read to educate ourselves but, rather, four steps of growth that God wants us to undertake every year until the end of the sixth millennium. At this time, the reunion "face-to-face" will be complete and eternal.

We first have the symbolic birth on Passover eve, in which we become part of His essence. Then comes the seventh night of Passover, in which we experience the initial return "face-to-face." Third are the days of the Omer period between Passover and Shavuot, crowned by the intermediary return "face-to-face" that occurs at the end of the Omer period, in the Giving of the Torah. The Omer period is the time to polish our character traits in order to cleanse ourselves in preparation for the soul-union. Finally, the festival of Shavuot brings the innermost return "face-to-face" in the soul-union that occurs at the Giving of the Torah.

We can trace the development of this four-step process in Divine thoughts as early as the portion of *Shekalim*, while the Giving of the Torah was the thought in the Divine mind that preceded His Creation of the world.

FROM IDOLATRY TO ADULTERY

The Midrash teaches that, in the Ten Commandments, the first five are parallel to the second five, and the second commandment, "Do not have any other gods"[40] parallels the seventh, "Do not commit adultery,"[41] for idolatry may be likened to adultery.

In the first of the Ten Commandments, "I am God your Lord, who brought you out of Egypt," God was telling them, "Since we were [if it can be said] together in Egypt, you are necessarily attached to Me. This makes you a part of Me and I cannot ever leave you."

If we understand the first commandment in this way, namely, "My getting you out of Egypt made you essence of My essence," it follows that having other gods could be seen as equivalent to adultery. Consequently, in the Bible, up to the Exodus the Creator is referred to as:

the Lord God (*Y-H-V-H/Elohim*) Who took you out of Egypt,

whereas, after the Exodus and the Giving of the Torah, He becomes:

the Lord *your* God.

Initially, God and the people were separate, independent one from the other. After the gestation period in Egypt, He became "the Lord *your* God," expressing a personal link based on Israel's emerging from Egypt as essence of the Almighty's essence.

The commentator Ibn Ezra points out that the fact that all the commandments relating to the heart and the emotions begin with "I am the Lord *your* God" indicates that it is a positive commandment for each and every one of us to believe with all his heart that the God who took us out of Egypt is *his* God.

The Exodus from Egypt is the root of all the commandments to help us understand the depth of the soul-union between the Community of Israel and the Holy One, Blessed be He, Who was with us in our sorrow while we were in exile, in order to enable us to become part of His very essence.

It is written that we can only begin to tell the story of the Exodus on Passover eve when a plate of *matzah*/unleavened bread and one of bitter herbs are laid in front of us on the table, and not before. We are also taught that one who does not say "*Pesach*/Pascal lamb, *matzah*/unleavened bread, *umaror*/and bitter herbs" has not fulfilled his duty on this night.

The reason for these injunctions is that, essentially, the main message of the Exodus concerns not only the Exodus itself, but also the gestation period and the exile that took place prior to the Exodus, which led to our becoming part of God's essence. In that sense, the gestation period throughout the exile constitutes the main story. Hence we begin to fulfill our duty as we are looking at the unleavened bread and the bitter herbs, reminiscent of the back-breaking labor and the oppression in the midst of which the Israelites were becoming His Companion of the soul.

THE LAND OF ISRAEL: GIFT OR INHERITANCE?

When God told Abraham about the beautiful land that He wanted to give Abraham and his descendants, Abraham's reaction was: "O Lord, God, . . . How can I really know that it will be mine?"[42]

God said to him:

Bring Me a prime heifer, a prime goat . . . and place one half opposite the other.[43]

Later on in the evening,

The sun set and it became very dark. A smoking furnace and a flaming torch passed between the halves of the animals.[44]

God gave Abraham an answer while the torch was burning by showing him a vision of the Egyptian exile and of the ensuing Exodus, where the Israelites were laden with wealth and riches.

Prior to the vision of the smoking furnace, Abraham had fallen into a trance, and God had shown him all the exiles that would be suffered by his descendants. The Patriarch was then "stricken by a deep, dark dread,"[45] as he feared for his offspring.

What is the meaning of Abraham's request that God give him proof? Was it not enough for him that he had received God's promise earlier? The Creator had not set any conditions before Abraham in return for the land, and Abraham still needed proof? The Ramban answers that, initially, the land of Israel was given to Abraham as a gift:

All the land that you see, I will give to you and to your offspring forever.[46]

Now, in contrast, the message was slightly different:

I am God Who took you out of Ur Casdim to give you this land as an inheritance.[47]

It was when he heard that the land would be given to him and his descendants as an inheritance that Abraham asked for proof: "How can I really know that it will be mine?" And God's answer was that they will inherit the land after going through the

exile in Egypt, and He made a covenant with Abraham after reaching this new understanding. As the verse says,

> On that day, God made a covenant with Abram, saying: "To your descendants I have
> given this land, [. . . the lands of] the Kenites, the Kenizzites, the Kadmonites, the Hit-
> tites, the Perizzites, the Rephaim, the Amorites, the Canaanites, the Girgashites and
> the Jebusites."[48]

What is the difference between the giving of the land as a gift or as an inheritance?
Also, what is the significance of receiving the land of Israel as an inheritance?

Abraham particularly wanted to have the land of Israel for his offspring because,
as it is said, even before the Israelites took possession of the land, God's eyes were
focused on it from the beginning of the year until the end of the year. This was the
place where God desired to set a dwelling space for His Divine Presence.

The land of Israel can be seen as a unit of holy space, just as Shabbat is a unit of
holy time. Shabbat is the unit of time within the year that God chose, as it were, for
His day of rest, in that it is holier than the rest of the days. On this day, God reveals
His light the most. Similarly, the land of Israel is the unit of space within the world
that God selected as His own, and, if it can be said, it is there that He set up His house.

The Patriarchs wanted the space where the Divine Presence chose to dwell to be
the inheritance of their descendants so that they would always be under the wings of
the Divine Presence. As we have seen, the initial Divine response was, "All the land
that you see, I will give to you and to your offspring forever," as One giving permission to His friend, as well as to His children, to live in His house and enjoy the splendor of His Presence.

God's subsequent promise to give the land as an inheritance was of a different
quality. Since the Israelites were part of His very essence, if they inherited the land
they could be likened to a bride who comes to her husband's home after the wedding,
and in this house she eats with him and spends her time with him. This is what is
meant by an inheritance.

An inheritance differs from a present in that it is not an acquisition. When a son
inherits his father's property, people relate to him as if he were his father. All the
more in the case of a wife, who is bone from her husband's bones and flesh from his
flesh: wherever he lives she is there with him. And this is what God was telling Abraham: the Israelites would be worthy of receiving the land not only as a gift, but also
as an inheritance.

An inheritance is more significant than a gift in that if you receive something as
a gift, strictly speaking you have not fully acquired it. Although it is true that a person
only gives a present to one who has pleased him in some way, the value of the present
nevertheless supersedes that of the favor done to him. Such a present will not give rise
to a communication of hearts between giver and receiver, since the receiver feels that
he does not really deserve the gift, and, in a way, is embarrassed to face the giver.

Yet, when the Israelites received the land as an inheritance, and there—as it were—
they dwelt and ate with Him, their deep bond with the Holy One allowed them to
cleave to Him with perfect passionate attachment.

Abraham merited inheriting the land for his vibrant trust in God's personalized Providence. Initially, the Patriarch thought that Israel was under the influence of the constellations, and he had seen in the stars that he would not have a child. But God revealed to him that Israel is immune to planetary influence, and he believed this with all his heart.[49]

For this faith, Abraham merited descendants who would attain the high level of closeness in which they would surrender, body and soul, before the Holy One. Abraham nevertheless requested a sign, in the knowledge that a true inheritance necessarily had to be preceded by a gestation period and a birth, for otherwise it is a present rather than an inheritance. He therefore wanted God to make a covenant with him concerning the terms of Israel's initiation process.

The Divine answer came to him through the Pact of Halves:

> Know for sure that your descendants will be foreigners in a land that is not theirs for four hundred years. They will be enslaved and oppressed. But I will finally bring judgment against the nation who enslaves them, and they will then leave with great wealth.[50]

With these words, God was revealing to Abraham how the Israelites would reach the level of "essence of His essence" in order to be able to dwell in the land of Israel as heirs. They would have to go down to Egypt and suffer oppression. But throughout this gestation period, God would be with them in their sorrow, and, eventually, they would leave with great wealth.

The people of Israel essentially merited this bond because they rose above their despair when they found themselves sandwiched between the Red Sea and their pursuing enemies. They threw themselves into the sea, with total faith in His Providence. The anxiety that overcame them at seeing themselves cornered was greater than that which they had felt throughout their bondage, for the greatest of all "face-to-face" reunions was the one that occurred at the sea. As the Midrash puts it: "From mud and bricks I took you, and made you a bride."

The sages question whether Abraham was guilty in asking God, "How can I really know that it will be mine" since this question essentially brought about the decree of the Egyptian exile. As we have seen, the exile was necessary for Israel to become part of God's essence. Therefore, how can Abraham be blamed for questioning God?

Two Different Paths

Kabbalah explains that the bond based on becoming part of His essence can come about in two different ways. The first is to go back to nothing, to the very essence that created them, because only at that point can nature be changed. The second way is by rising up to the Source: in this dimension, the concentrated power of luminous Divine energy is of such intensity that the only possibility is total surrender to the Holy One.

The first way is illustrated by the Egyptian bondage: despite the hardship experienced, Israel managed to reach the point of total surrender, having shed any vestige of ego that had previously helped them to rationalize sin. As a consequence of this exile, the Israelites were now empty, ready to become One with their Creator both in body and in soul.

The second way is illustrated by the union of the Shabbat afternoon prayers. This rarefied soul-union builds up our soul power for the coming week, according to the teaching of the Ari that the world was created only for six days; the power of Shabbat enables it to be renewed on a weekly basis for the following six weekdays.

After reaching the total surrender of Shabbat afternoon there must be a separation for the next six days, for the world was created according to the above-mentioned principle of giving light and taking it away in order to maintain the flame of desire burning within the people of Israel. Beyond the level of closeness of the soul-union lies the level of total surrender which, in this dimension, must be followed by a separation in which the people of Israel pine for their former closeness.

God witnesses the struggle of the Community of Israel during the six weekdays to cleanse themselves of any transgression or bad trait that might block the total union of the coming Shabbat. As a result, when Shabbat comes, they are as dear to Him as on the first day.

Hence, immediately after Shabbat, we perform the Shabbat conclusion service, known as *Havdalah*, where we make a distinction between Shabbat and the coming weekdays. The *Havdalah* service is the aftermath of the surrender of Shabbat afternoon, which calls for a separation. During this time that the relationship is in a dormant state, the Community of Israel works on developing their spiritual structure through their Divine service of the week, to attain total union once again in the upcoming Shabbat *Musaph*/additional Amidah prayer. They surrender to Him again in the afternoon Amidah, where they become part of His essence, only to lose His closeness once again in the coming separation.

The Shabbat afternoon prayers are therefore a time of Divine favor where Creation is renewed, and God finds pleasure in Israel, His holy people. As we bring about a separation in the *Havdalah* service, we are in effect preparing for an even higher level of *oneg*/delight of the following Shabbat.

Every Shabbat is therefore reminiscent of the Egyptian exile. On Shabbat, however, the same end is attained by a different means, for on Shabbat the surrender is effected by rising in consciousness to our soul-root. When in contact with the radiant Infinite Light, Israel becomes like the moon who surrenders all she has to the sun. To that end, at the beginning of the Shabbat afternoon prayers we quote King David's line: "But I am [all] prayer."[51] David means, "In this prayer, my God, I am surrendering to You all that I have: my essence, my very existence, including my will and the desires that define me, until there is nothing left in me but You."

After this exalted moment the separation is renewed in the *Havdalah*, which led the sages to comment that if there is no *da'at*/intimate knowledge of God, there is no real *havdalah*/distinction between Shabbat and the weekdays. For the *da'at* brings with it the *bitul*/surrender, and only then is it appropriate to make the *havdalah* and separation.

In contrast, the *bitul*/surrender product of the Exodus from Egypt came about by going back to the time of gestation. Hence, Shabbat is known as the memento of the Exodus from Egypt in that both Shabbat and the exile had the common objective of surrendering to Him in order to become One with Him, but by two different paths. God desired that this objective be realized through the ecstatic surrender of the Shabbat experience rather than as a product of agonizing years of bondage.

By asking God to document the effects of surrender, "How can I really know that it will be mine?" Abraham switched from what was to be a spontaneous and willing surrender to a documented deal where the end result has to be rightfully earned. The exile then came to be in the Divine thoughts.

It is nevertheless undeniable, however, that the Israelites were far from the level of holiness of their forefather, and simply would not have attained such a level of surrender to the Divine on their own. Hence, were it not for the Egyptian exile it is likely that there would have never been a soul-union between the Holy One and the Community of Israel, His Companion of the soul.

Conclusions:
Finding Your Fire

IN THE PRECEDING CHAPTER we saw that what appeared to be spiritual falls of the Jewish people were really preparations for ascent toward a higher union. In this chapter we will see how to reach more quickly the end of the lonely stretches of time in which we feel that our inner spark is gone.

We have seen that on the anniversary of the destruction of the Temple we mourn the loss of our desire for intimate union with God, for the Temple is the only fuel that can reinstate this union.

Part of the mystery of Creation is that imbedded in each one of us is a spark that has the power to ignite our personal desire, lighting a fire that may blaze within us as it did while the cherubs were still in the Ark.

The Ari teaches that all the souls of Israel stem from the Torah. As we know, there are many different approaches to Torah study, be it legal, talmudic, esoteric, or the like. God used a particular way of interpreting the Torah to form each and every soul of Israel. Since the soul is compelled to leave the source from where she was formed in order to grow through birth into the physical world, she feels a profound lack that causes her unhappiness.

If from its early years, a child is taught to fill his lack with deep insights into all the approaches to Torah interpretation, each style in its due time as the child matures, the soul receives the pleasure she seeks and the tools she needs to identify the source of what she felt was lacking. The child then enters adulthood equipped with the appropriate Torah background: he can now make an educated decision to nourish his germinating desire for the form of Torah interpretation that attracts him the most.

A person who matures without having had a chance to immerse himself in the Torah finds it much more difficult to identify the nature of the lack he feels. Particularly in our days, in which the cherubs, source of our arousal toward the Divine, are no longer, the person estranged from the Torah confuses the lack he feels within with a desire for physical pleasures.

In a way, this can be compared to an orphan who translates his yearning for his parent's love into a constant need of physical rewards that help him feel secure in his present environment. This type of compensation is similar to the case of an adult who, lacking the passionate attachment of a distant spouse, fills the pervading emptiness with a material substitute that cannot fill the absence of an intimate bond.

It is important to understand that the longer a person takes to realize the source of his lack, the greater will be the difficulty in finding it. The reason is that, when unbridled, his desire will soon grow into a frenzied pursuit of new experiences that distract him from focusing on his spiritual quest.

Those who go beyond the physical in their search and immerse themselves in deep analysis of the Torah will benefit from God's personal help. They will become aware of the Divine Presence dwelling within them, and this awareness will lead their groping search toward the particular Torah source from which their soul was fashioned. Upon attaining this understanding, they will have reached the space of pure delight where nothing else matters. The lack they were born with will now be both fulfilled and intensified at its very source.

God longs for Israel not just to browse through the pages of His wisdom, but to struggle in the search for ever deeper Torah insights, to learn to know Him through the Torah. Our sages said, "The Torah, the Holy One, blessed is He, and Israel are One," for the soul-union between God and Israel is actualized through the Torah. Toiling in the Torah is the key God left with us to attain the intimate relationship where "they lift their eyes up to Mine while My eyes are on theirs."

Those fortunate enough to identify the form of Torah study that ignites their unique spark will gain more than the personal delight they can potentially derive from their study. They will unearth an inner fire powerful enough to fuel the constant effort that toiling in the Torah involves.

Furthermore, during the hours between midnight and dawn, the hidden light of Creation shines unrestrained and is available to all those searching for it. One who studies during these special hours will find that he grasps the material with a sharper quality of mind than at any other time. In addition, he becomes increasingly sensitized to the Divine Presence, whose closeness he is able to feel with awesome intensity during these hours.

As we once did on Sinai, we would all like to learn Torah by spontaneous perception through intimate contact with God. Yet, it is only by killing ourselves over it, by making an effort to give something we think we don't have—whether time, energy, or intellect—that we will show God the fire of our love for Him. It is in the demanding study of Torah that we will find the One Whom our soul loves.[1]

The path that leads us to unite with the Creator is represented as a ladder. The interruptions in our contact are as numerous as there are steps of ascent. When you realize that you can no longer feel the Divine energy that was vibrating within you, God may be telling you that your efforts to be close to Him are becoming slack and need to be increased. Your prayers are needed at this time, to entreat the Creator to give you back the inner fire that was giving you life, and to ask for His help in accepting how the most difficult moments in life are gifts of love that help you ascend.

If our ability to identify the Divine energy within us were permanent, the experience would soon turn into a routine that we would in time ignore. We must always remember that the Divine energy we now feel will not be there for long. Although the Divine energy has existed from the beginning of Creation, it will eventually be taken away; soon a Shabbat or a festival will come when you will realize that you no longer feel anything.

Knowing the fragility of the Divine energy within will energize you to devote yourself with utmost care to your Divine service, in fear of the slightest separation from God or of falling into obsessive patterns that could be the catalyst for your fire to cease burning. At the same time, your awareness will help you store Divine energy to light the times of darkness you know will inevitably come again, and thus ensure the continuation of your ascent. In fact, the famed Rabbi Yerucham Levovitz, spiritual leader of prewar Mir Yeshivah, claimed that the main objective of the "energy periods" was precisely the task to illuminate the darker times, filling them with meaning.[2]

Rabbi Nachman of Breslov offers a simple test to reveal whether you are making progress in your ascent. You may think you have conquered a negative pattern of behavior. Suddenly the old temptations return to haunt you, and threaten to undo a long and strenuous work, yet you find the strength to resist and rise to the occasion. You then know that you have climbed a step toward the Source of Light.

One of the leading kabbalists of today, the late Rabbi Yehuda Getz, constantly reminded his disciples that when there came a time in which their study no longer seemed meaningful, this was a sure sign that they were in the transition period to a higher level. The determination with which they persisted in their studies would speed this transition.

When you undertake your Divine service by ascending on your own ladder, God meets your fire from below with His own fire from above. Your self-arousal is crowned with access to the other dimension where the "high" of perceiving Divine energy stands in total differentiation from any human high, in that it is unmistakably blended with the fiery ecstasy of *oneg*/delight that permeates you.

You must remember that even when you fall, God's love still surrounds and supports you. The golden cherubs in the Holy Temple would only embrace when Israel and the Creator were in a bond of love. Yet on the day of the Temple's destruction, the very onset of the exile, when the Romans broke into the inner sanctuary, they found the cherubs locked in a loving embrace. Though we had fallen from the status of "beloved companion," God's love for us remained, like that of a father for a child.

Although the golden cherubs are no longer with us, the message of their loving embrace is more alive than ever. As we have seen, one who struggles up his personal ladder will find the One Whom his soul loves, not just on Shabbat and festivals, but in every prayer, every moment in which he will stop his activities and dwell on the intimate contact he has learned to cherish.

We have mentioned in the preface Rabbi Luria's comments about the personal signs that reward one who gives himself unrelentingly to his search for a direct contact with the Divine energy:

> There are some who finish praying and are unable to speak for a long time until the intensity of their personal signs begins to abate!

One may easily object that there is nothing extraordinary in Rabbi Luria's comment. There have been mystics in all generations since the creation of the world!

What is indeed extraordinary is that, after the initial effort in which you, the individual—not just as part of the nation—experience the joy of the personal bond, you will have opened a door that will not easily be closed. You may fall either into transgression or into self-indulgence, and if you do, you will not be spared the consequences: as the Israelites in the desert, you will find that the conscious awareness of living under Divine scrutiny is indeed a challenge.

The immense difference is that if you sink into the depth of depression at the thought of the barrier that you have just erected, you will soon feel your personal signs stirring you into action, gentle but persisting, pushing you to pick up the pieces and start again. Even though you may be reeling with physical or emotional pain, you will know that your present suffering is indeed a gift of love, and you will be able to say with a full heart in the morning prayers,

> We are fortunate—how good is our portion, how pleasant our lot, and how beautiful our heritage![3]

and on Shabbat,

> For I know that God is great, and [our Master] is greater than all gods.[4]

Like the love embrace of the cherubs that the Israelites were feeling as they were going into exile, you will realize that this proof of God's love—of which no one but you is aware—is a token of lovingkindness that at this point you hardly deserve. You will treasure it all the more, for it will represent a source of strength for you to draw upon, and persist on your ascent to the Source of light.*

---

* I dedicate this chapter to Dan Segre, who, upon reading an early version of the manuscript in which the preceding chapter was the final one, urged me to write a different conclusion. "Your final message to the reader cannot be that he will eventually lose his fire. You must write another chapter explaining how to regain it." It was at Dan's inspiration that I enlisted Rabbi Luria's help to write this conclusion. May *Hashem* grant Dan a speedy *refua shelema.*

Notes

PREFACE

1. It is the Jewish custom to include the initials *z"l*–which stand for the Hebrew expression *zichrono libracha*/may his memory be a blessing–after the name of departed sages. I have omitted this practice in order to lighten the English text.

2. Paraphrasing the Song of Songs 8:7. The people of Israel are referred to with the collective name "Israel."

3. Although an essay on the dangers of studying Kabbalah without the direct guidance of a master is beyond the scope of this book, I would like to share with the reader the example of a young man I will call Mark. Mark meditated on the holy Tetragrammaton and ended up in psychiatric treatment, having to interrupt his studies at Hebrew University for one year. The young man simply did not know that you have to be in a state of purity before coming in contact with the Divine forces, and that "beginning to keep Shabbat," as he told me bitterly he was doing, was not enough to come into contact with the holy Divine forces.

4. Rabbi Kaplan uses the example of the telephone in the transcripts of his classes on the *Sefirot*, the most basic modes of God's creative power. Most of these transcripts were published posthumously as *Inner Space: Introduction to Kabbalah, Meditation and Prophecy* (Jerusalem: Moznaim, 1990).

5. Transcripts on Jewish meditation.

6. Although some laws are discussed as needed, this is not a book of Jewish law and may not be used as one.

7. The often-used term "light" refers to the *Zohar's* "light that does not shine," which is a current of Divine energy and a light of understanding, rather than the more usual connotation of physical light.

8. The following discussion of prayer stems from Rabbi R. M. Luria, *Ori veYish'i: Tshuva uTefilah*, p. 146.

9. The terms *nefesh, ruach,* and *neshamah* are explained in chapter 3; *chayah* and *yechidah* are explained in chapter 29.

10. Transcripts of Rabbi Kaplan's classes on Jewish meditation are property of Rabbi Kaplan's estate.

INTRODUCTION: FIERY COALS

Adapted from Rabbi R. M. Luria, "Maamar Mar-eh Hasheneh," in *Geulat Mitsrayim*, pp. 138–44, and "Maamar Ner Shabbat veNer Chanukah, Samchem beBinyan Shalem," in *Or Yekarot*, pp. 219–23.

1. Deuteronomy 30:20, in *The Living Torah*, trans. Rabbi Aryeh Kaplan (New York: Moznaim, 1981). All further quotations from the Pentateuch will be from this edition. We may change the translation of some words in any given verse in order to fit the meaning that Rabbi Luria is expounding.

2. Proverbs 20:27, quoted from *Tanach: The Torah/Prophets/Writings*, The Stone Edition, ed. Rabbi Nosson Scherman (New York: Mesorah Publications, 1996). All further quotations from the Writings will be from this edition.

3. Song of Songs 3:1–2.

4. Jeremiah 31:19.

PART ONE
SHABBAT

CHAPTER 1. THE INFINITE LIGHT

Adapted from Rabbi R. M. Luria, *Bet Genazai*, vol. 1, preface.

1. The *Chabura Kadmaah*, mentioned in *Zohar* 3:219b. See *Kisey Melech* on *Tikuney Zohar* (Jerusalem, 5723) #7, *"BeAgada"* p. 7b; *Sichot HaRan* 278. The final edition of the *Zohar* was apparently written by Rabbi Abba. See Rabbi David Luria, *Kadmut Sefer HaZohar* 5:2, quoted from Rabbi A. Kaplan, *Meditation and Kabbalah* (New York: Schocken Books, 1985), p. 317, n. 28.

CHAPTER 2. SOUL-UNION OF SHABBAT

1. Rabbi R. M. Luria "Maamar Lech Lehodi'am," in *Bet Genazai*, vol. 1, pp. 39–42.

For a detailed and illustrated description of the creative tasks that are prohibited on Shabbat, see Rabbi Y. M. Stern, *The Book of Shabbos*, with color photographs of the *melachos*, translated by Rabbi D. Oratz (printed in Israel, 1995).

2. Rabbi R. M. Luria, "Maamar Ki Bo Shabat Micol Melachto," in *Bet Genazai*, vol. 2, pp. 395–98.

CHAPTER 3. THE ADDITIONAL SOUL

1. Adapted from Rabbi R. M. Luria, "Maamar neshamah yeterah beshabat," in *Bet Genazai*, vol. 1, pp. 85–89.

2. Exodus 12:21.

3. As taught by a disciple of the Gaon of Vilna, these wisdoms are subdivided as follows: (1) mathematics, astronomy, and geometry; (2) natural science (physics) and chemistry; (3) medicine, pharmacology, botany; (4) logic,

grammar, and syntax; (5) musicology and esoteric theory; (6) engineering and construction, architecture; (7) mind/body connection, psychology, parapsychology, and the brain-sciences.

4. Exodus 20:8–11.

5. Deuteronomy 5:12–15.

6. Exodus 31:13; Leviticus 19:3; 19:30; and 27:2; Isaiah 56:4; Ezekiel 20:12; 20:13; 20:16; 20:20; 20:21; 20:24; 22:8; 22:26; 23:38; 44:24, etc.

CHAPTER 4. REACHING THE SHABBAT DELIGHT

Adapted from Rabbi R. M. Luria, "Maamar Kavod ve Oneg beShabat," vol. 2, pp. 247–52, and "Maamar nachalat Ya'akov avicha," in *Bet Genazai*, pp. 564–67.

1. Isaiah 58:13–14. In *The Living Nach*, trans. Rabbi Yaakov Elman (New York: Moznaim, 1995). All further quotations from the Prophets will be from this edition. We may change the translation of some works in any given verse in order to fit the meaning that Rabbi Luria is expounding.

2. See chapter 8.

3. Genesis 28:20.

4. Genesis 25–28.

5. Genesis 28:15.

6. Genesis 29:18.

7. Psalms 37:4.

CHAPTER 5. THE LIGHT OF THE CROWN

1. Rabbi Chayim Vital, *Shaarey Kedushah* (Gates of Holiness), 4:3. I am grateful to Rabbi Abraham Sutton for reminding me of this beautiful explanation of the soul's attachment to the Creator.

2. Adapted from Rabbi R. M. Luria, *Bet Genazai*, vol. 1, pp. 249–50.

3. For those who don't know Hebrew, a good way to begin is to memorize the first blessing of the Amidah. When reciting this all-important first paragraph, dwell on the meaning of each word. Then, you may use a prayer book such as the *Metsudah Siddur* (New York: Metsudah Pubs., 1986), which provides a linear translation of every word in the prayer.

Those who pray following the Sephardic tradition may use *The Orot Sephardic Siddur,* ed. Rabbi Eliezer Toledano (Orot Inc., 314 5th Street, Lakewood, N.J. 08701), 1994. This is the first Sephardic prayer book with a linear translation.

4. I am grateful to Rabbi Moshe Schatz, for his clear explanation of the kabbalistic concept of *Ateret haYesod/*the Foundation Coronet.

5. Adapted from Rabbi R. M. Luria, *Bet Genazai,* vol. 1, pp. 197–200.

6. Exodus 30:13.

7. Adapted from Rabbi R. M. Luria, *Bet Genazai,* vol. 2, pp. 347–49, and 537–39.

8. Deuteronomy 4:35.

9. Exodus 33:6.

10. Adapted from Rabbi R. M. Luria, *Bet Genazai,* vol. 1, pp. 12–13; vol. 2, pp. 348–49 and 561–63.

Shabbat is first of all the day in which God rested from His creative activities, and secondly the day in which He sanctified His relationship with Israel to its former state in the Giving of the Torah. Consequently, everything is double on this day. In each of the three Shabbat meals, two breads are to be placed on the table, just like the double portion of Manna, and the two loaves of bread that were to be offered during Shavuot. Similarly, we offer a second Amidah prayer on Shabbat, known as *musaph.*

11. *The Complete Art Scroll Siddur, Nusach Sefard,* ed. Rabbi Nosson Scherman (New York: Mesora Pubs., 1985), p. 503.

12. Adapted from Rabbi R. M. Luria, *Bet Genazai,* vol. 1, pp. 197–200.

13. This will be the subject of chapter 7.

14. 1 Kings 19:12.

CHAPTER 6. SICKNESS OF THE SOUL

Adapted from Rabbi R. M. Luria, *Bet Genazai,* vol. 1, pp. 200–201; vol. 2, pp. 508–9 and 525–26.

1. Isaiah 44:1.

2. Proverbs 12:4.

3. Song of Songs 5:8.

4. Maimonides, *Mishneh Torah: The Laws of Repentance,* trans. R. E. Touger (New York: Moznaim, 1987), p. 221.

5. Our souls remain locked in their intimate bond until we say the parting paragraph added to the evening Amidah prayer.

6. Exodus 24:11.

7. Jeremiah 2:2.

8. Song of Songs 8:7; see the Introduction.

9. See Rabbi R. M. Luria, *Ori veYish'i,* vol. 2, *Teshuvah veTefilah,* p. 4b, quoting the *Shibole HaLeket.*

CHAPTER 7. HEARING THE ANGEL'S SONG

1. Exodus 3:2.

2. Psalms 19:10.

3. Song of Songs 8:7; see the Introduction.

4. See chapter 20.

5. "Keep Shabbat for it is holy"–Exodus 30:32, 37, 31:14, 35:2.

6. See chapter 2.

7. This is the secret meaning of the verse, "My glory I will not give to another"(Isaiah 42:8 and 48:11).

8. Avraham Greenbaum, *The Sweetest Hour (Tikkun Chatsot)* (New York: Breslov Research Institute [POB 587, Monsey, N.Y. 10952-0587] 1993), p. 52.

9. Rabbi Aryeh Kaplan, *The Handbook of Jewish Thought* (New York: Moznaim, 1979), chapter 9, p. 180.

10. See Rabbi R. M. Luria, *Bet Genazai,* vol. 1, pp. 219–21. Since the understanding of the Torah portion of the week is one of the objects, it is a good idea to read simultaneously a traditional translation based on Jewish sources but written in modern English, such as Rabbi Kaplan's *Living Torah* (New York: Moznaim, 1981).

11. *Bet Genazai,* vol. 1, pp. 208–15.

12. See chapter 5.

13. Isaiah 37:36.

14. The comparison of *oneg/*delight to the angel's song is culled from Rabbi Luria's work *Bet Genazai 'al haTorah vehaMo'adim,* vol. 3, section on Shabbat.

15. Rabbi Luria asks: "Since when do Israel's enemies deserve such sweet death?" He answers that the Assyrians were descendants of Ketura, the concubine Abraham married after Sarah's death.

16. Excerpt from a song written in the fifteenth century by an unknown author, in *Zemiroth: Sabbath Songs,* ed. Rabbi Nosson Scherman (New York: Mesorah, 1979), p. 295. The singer is asking for prophecy, hinting at the

verse "They saw a vision of the God of Israel, and under His feet was something like a sapphire brick, like the essence of a clear blue sky" (Exodus 24:10).

17. Amos 3:2.

CHAPTER 8. FROM SHABBAT TO THE FESTIVALS

The following comparison between Shabbat and festivals is adapted from Rabbi R. M. Luria, *Or Yekarot*, pp. 35–37.

1. Song of Songs 5:1.
2. Psalms 104:15.
3. *The Complete Art Scroll Siddur*, p. 223.
4. Psalms 105:43.
5. Psalms 2:11.
6. See chapter 5.
7. An illustration of this is found in the account of the revelation of the Divine Presence at the splitting of the Red Sea. The Israelites were so entranced with it that they sang spontaneously, and amidst the powerful energy that infused them, the women started to dance in praise of the Almighty.

PART TWO
FIRST TABLETS

CHAPTER 9. AFFLICTION

1. Adapted from Rabbi R. M. Luria, *Seder Lel Shemurim*, Preface.
2. See chapter 30.
3. Numbers 12:3.
4. See chapter 30.

CHAPTER 10
THE EXODUS: PASSIONATE COURTSHIP

Adapted from Rabbi R. M. Luria, *"Maamar Ahavat 'Olam Bet Israel,"* in *Torah veIsrael*, pp. 49–52.

1. Deuteronomy 16:3.
2. Genesis 15:13.
3. Song of Songs 6:5.
4. Exodus 32:11.
5. Proverbs 27:19.

CHAPTER 11. I, AND NOT AN ANGEL

Adapted from Rabbi R. M. Luria, "Maamar Ani velo Mal-ach," in *Lel Shemurim*, pp. 239–42.

1. Jeremiah 2:2.
2. Exodus 32:4.
3. Exodus 32:11.
4. Exodus 32:14.
5. Exodus 3:12.
6. Exodus 20:2.

CHAPTER 12. THE SONG AT THE SEA

Adapted from Rabbi R. M. Luria, "Maamar Ahavat 'Olam Bet Israel," in *Torah veIsrael*, pp. 49–52.

1. Rabbi Levy Itzchak of Berdichev, *Kedushat Levi*.
2. *Akeidat Itschak*.
3. Psalms 92.
4. Psalms 92:2, 6.

CHAPTER 13
TEFILLIN: REMEMBER THE EXODUS

Adapted from Rabbi R. M. Luria, "Maamar Tefillin Zecher Litsiat Mitsrayim," in *Seder Lel Shemurim*, pp. 317–20.

1. See chapter 5.
2. The image of the Song of Songs, "love is as strong as death," is thus explained in Rabbi de Vidas, *Beginning of Wisdom*, "Gate of Love," chapter 3.
3. Exodus 24:10.
4. Proverbs 27:19.
5. Jeremiah 2:2.
6. Exodus 19:4.
7. Exodus 13:3, 9.
8. Exodus 13:11, 16.
9. Deuteronomy 6:4, 8.
10. Deuteronomy 11:13–18.
11. *Sefer haIkarim*.

CHAPTER 14
THE *TSITSIT* AND THE SPLITTING OF THE SEA

Adapted from Rabbi R. M. Luria, "Maamar Chutey Tsitsit veKeryat Yam Suf," in *Shirat haYam*, pp. 266–68.

1. Numbers 15:38.
2. Numbers 15:37–39.
3. Within a person, the brain (intellect) usually receives more light than the heart (emotions), which in turn receives more than the

liver (instincts). It is much easier for a person to understand and accept truth intellectually by studying than to absorb it into his emotions or his instincts by changing his behavior.

4. Exodus 13:3, 9.
5. Numbers 15:39–40.
6. Rabbi Menachem M. Kasher, *Israel Passover Haggadah* (New York: Shengold Publishers, 1983), p. 27.
7. Even though the splitting of the sea occurred on the seventh day after the Exodus, we count from the day before the Exodus, the fourteenth of Nisan, in which the Israelites were to fulfill the commandment of the Paschal Lamb. See chapter 3.
8. Exodus 11:4.
9. Exodus 10:23.
10. Exodus 15:2.
11. Deuteronomy 4:34.
12. "Tzitzith: A Thread of Light," in *The Aryeh Kaplan Anthology*, vol. 2 (New York: Mesora Publications, 1991), pp. 205–6.
13. Tractate *Menachot* 44a.
14. Today, the art of producing the *techelet* dye has been lost and the blue thread is no longer attached.
15. Exodus 20:8.
16. Deuteronomy 5:12.
17. *Kiddush* literally means sanctification, and refers to the prayer pronounced over a cup of wine at the onset of the Shabbat meal.
18. Hosea 2:21–22.

CHAPTER 15. "SEVEN PERFECT SABBATHS"

Adapted from Rabbi R. M. Luria, *Torah veIsrael*, "Maamar Sheva' Shabbatot Shelemot," pp. 6–11.

1. See Eliahu Kitov, *The Book of Our Heritage* (New York: Feldheim Publishers, 1978), vol. 2, pp. 356–75.
2. See chapters 1–8.
3. Exodus 31:14.
4. Rabbi Eliyahu Dessler, *Strive for Truth*, vol. 3, trans. Aryeh Carmell (New York: Feldheim, 1989), pp. 68–69.
5. Deuteronomy 16:9.
6. Aryeh Kaplan, *Inner Space*, pp. 68–69.
7. Moshe Chayim Luzzato, *The Path of the Just* (New York: Feldheim, 1985), p. 329.

CHAPTER 16
"WE WILL DO AND WE WILL HEAR"

Adapted from Rabbi R. M. Luria, *Torah veIsrael*, Introduction, and "Maamar hasagat haTorah veKabalat haTorah," pp. 142–49.

1. See Rabbi Aryeh Kaplan, "Waters of Eden: The Mystery of the Mikvah," in *The Aryeh Kaplan Anthology*, vol. 2, and Tehillah Abramov, *The Secret of Jewish Femininity* (New York: Targum Press, 1988).
2. Psalms 82:6–7.
3. See chapter 12.
4. Psalms 40:9.
5. Exodus 24:3.
6. Exodus 24:6.
7. *Avodat Israel.*
8. Exodus 21:11.
9. Exodus 24:7–8.
10. R. J. Zwi Werblowsky, *Joseph Karo: Lawyer and Mystic* (Philadelphia: The Jewish Publication Society, 1980).
11. Song of Songs 1:2. Unpublished interpretative translation of Abraham Sutton.
12. Tractate *Shabbat* 89a.

CHAPTER 17. CHILDREN OF THE LIVING GOD

Adapted from Rabbi R. M. Luria, "Amalut baTorah ledavka Bo," in *Amalut baTorah*, pp. 75–77; and from "Amalut baTorah veDiglo 'alay Ahava," ibid., pp. 110–12. The volume *Amalut baTorah* (Toiling in the Torah) is the last one written by Rabbi Luria to date.

1. Exodus 24:12.
2. Rashi
3. Rabbi Saadia Gaon. The Ten Commandments contain 620 letters, each letter corresponding to one of the 613 commandments found in the Torah. The seven remaining letters correspond to seven commandments added by rabbinic jurisdiction.
4. Tractate *Makkot* 42:21.
5. Rabbi Aryeh Kaplan's oral teachings.
6. Rabbi Chayim Vital, star disciple of the Ari, emphasizes in his *Shaare Kedushah* (Gates of Holiness) that the fact that many of the commandments relate to the Temple service and are therefore not applicable does not prevent one who is worthy from attaining the highest level of Divine inspiration in our time. For a

critical discussion of the commandments, see *Sefer haChinuch* (The Book of [Mitzvah] Education), ed. Charles Wengrov (New York: Feldheim, 1984).

7. Exodus 19:6.

8. Song of Songs 3:11.

9. As taught by the sixteenth-century kabbalist Rabbi Moses Cordovero (1522–1570), dean of the Sefad school.

10. See chapter 7.

11. I can still hear the computer bell ringing repeatedly as I translated this line: "Not every person can attain the full level of *devekut* of 'my soul is sick for your love." Puzzled, I looked at the original Hebrew once again, and realized that I had inadvertently mistranslated one word. The text reads: "Not every person *merits* attaining the full level of *devekut* of 'my soul is sick for your love,' however."

This incident reminded me of the time when I finished chapter 5 and attempted to print it: five times I gave the command to print, but nothing happened. I paid attention to the first page of the chapter and realized that I had added one sentence that was not in the original text: "This high level of communion in prayer is only within the reach of an elite group of people." I removed the sentence and the chapter was printed.

12. Psalms 8:5.

13. Song of Songs 2:4.

14. Song of Songs 8:6–7.

15. See chapter 1.

16. The following section is adapted from Rabbi R. M. Luria, *Torah veIsrael*, pp. 149–54.

17. Exodus 33:4.

18. Deuteronomy 4:4.

PART THREE
SECOND TABLETS

CHAPTER 18
SERVANT, CHILD OR SOUL-COMPANION?

1. The following section is adapted from Rabbi Luria's *Ori veYish'i: Yamim Noraim*, pp. 56–57.

2. The discussion about *Yedid Nefesh* is adapted from Rabbi R. M. Luria's *Or HaMikdash*, pp. 14–19.

3. *In Honor of Shabbos*, ed. Abraham Sutton (Jerusalem: Targum/Feldheim, 1996), pp. 77.

4. Psalms 122:8.

5. Exodus 34:29.

6. Deuteronomy 7:6–8.

7. The relationship viewed from above to below is adapted from Rabbi R. M. Luria, *Ori veYish'i: Yamim Noraim*, pp. 1–15.

8. Deuteronomy 7:7–8.

9. Hosea 3:1.

10. "I brought [the Israelites] out of Egypt, and they are My servants."–Leviticus 25:55.

11. Psalms 122:8.

12. Deuteronomy 11:22.

13. Deuteronomy 10:14–15.

14. Song of Songs 8:6–7.

15. Proverbs 27:19.

16. The discussion of the reward is adapted from Rabbi R. M. Luria, *Ori veYish'i: Yamim Noraim*, pp. 6–8.

17. Deuteronomy 6:5–9.

18. Deuteronomy 11:13–21.

19. *The Path of the Just*, ed. Shraga Silverstein (New York: Feldheim, 1980), 1:1.

20. The section on Ephraim is adapted from Rabbi R. M. Luria, *Ori veYish'i*, pp. 240–52.

21. Jeremiah 31:17–18.

22. Genesis 18:27.

23. Jeremiah 31:19.

24. Deuteronomy 3:23–6:17.

25. Deuteronomy 4:4.

26. Deuteronomy 7:12–11:25.

27. Deuteronomy 7:12.

CHAPTER 19. ELUL: "HE PLACED HIS LEFT HAND UNDER MY HEAD"

The following section is adapted from Rabbi R. M. Luria, *Ori veYish'i: Yamim Noraim*, pp. 212–17; *Ori veYish'i: Zeman Simchatenu*, pp. 214–17, and *Yamim Noraim*, pp. 220–22.

1. Exodus 24:7. *Naaseh veNishma'* is generally rendered as "we will do and we will obey"; "we will do and we will hear" is the literal translation. See chapter 16 for an interpretation.

2. Amos 3:2.

3. Song of Songs 7:11.

4. Song of Songs 6:3.

5. Ashkenazic Jews sound the Shofar in Elul. Among the Sephardim, North-African Jews also

sound it throughout Elul, but other Sephardic Jews only sound it from Rosh Hashanah through Yom Kippur.

6. Psalms 89:16.
7. Jeremiah 13:11.
8. Psalms 33:3.
9. Psalms 98:6.
10. Psalms 100:1.
11. Song of Songs 8:6–7.
12. Psalms 94:1.
13. Proverbs 20:4.
14. Psalms 89:3.
15. Song of Songs 2:6.
16. Song of Songs 2:6.

CHAPTER 20
DRAWING DOWN THE HIDDEN LIGHT

Adapted from Rabbi R. M. Luria *Ori veYish'i: Yamim Noraim*, pp. 36–41.

1. Numbers 29:1.
2. *Hallel*: Psalms of praise recited on the New Moon and festivals.
3. Psalms 81:4.
4. Psalms 2:9.
5. Psalms 27:1.
6. Jeremiah 2:2.
7. Jeremiah 31:19.
8. Amos 3:6.
9. *Mishneh Torah: The Laws of Repentance*, 3:3, trans. R. E. Touger.
10. *Shaarey Orah*, chap. 9.
11. Rabbi Aryeh Kaplan, *The Light Beyond* (New York: Moznaim, 1981), p. 187.
12. *Avot* 2:4.
13. R. Akiva Tatz, *Living Inspired* (New York: Targum/Feldheim, 1993), p. 106.
14. Song of Songs 2:5.
15. Song of Songs 8:5.

CHAPTER 21
KING ABOVE, KING BELOW

Adapted from Rabbi R. M. Luria, *"Maamar 'hanoten beyam derech,'"* in *Teshuvah uTefilah*, pp. 22–30 and from *"Maamar Yom Kippur Yom Chatunato,"* in *Teshuvah uTefilah*, pp. 281–83.

1. Deuteronomy 17:14–15.
2. I Samuel 8:2, 20.
3. In his Tractate *Hilchot Melachim*.

4. I Samuel 8:7.
5. See chapter 3.
6. I Samuel 16:1–3.
7. "And the Lord said, 'You shall take a heifer with you, and you shall say, "I have come to slaughter [a sacrifice] to the Lord"'" (I Samuel 16:2).
8. Psalms 25:16.
9. Psalms 102:1.
10. *The Complete Art Scroll Siddur*, p. 115.
11. I Chronicles 29:23.
12. II Chronicles 9:23.
13. Proverbs 23:26.
14. Exodus 15:18.
15. Rabbi Yosef Dov Soloveitchick, "Surrendering to the Almighty," in *Light* 17 Kislev, pp. 11–17, p. 15.

CHAPTER 22
RETURN TO ME OUT OF LOVE

Adapted from Rabbi R. M. Luria, "Maamar Teshuvah bechol hashana ubeYom haKippur" and "Shuvu Elai vaAni ashuva alechem," in *Ori VeYish'i: Yamim Noraim*, pp. 265–76.

1. Deuteronomy 30:2.
2. Deuteronomy 30:1–2.
3. *Yesod veShoresh ha'Avodah* (Foundation and Root of the Divine Service), final epistle.
4. Leviticus 16:30.
5. Jeremiah 13:11.
6. *Gates of Repentance* (New York: Feldheim 1966).
7. In fact, the source of sadness lies in this erred belief that God is distant.
8. An increasing number of Torah scholars are currently working on the relationship between Torah and science. See Rabbi Moshe Schatz, *Sparks of the Hidden Light: Seeing the Unified Nature of Reality through Kabbalah* (Jerusalem: The Ateret Institute, 1998) [Fax 972-2-653-5438]; and Rabbi David Toledano, *The Cosmos–Enigma and Resolution*, first published in Hebrew in *"Machshavot I.B.M."* (Israel, 1993, no. 65) An English translation is available upon request.)
9. The rights of the firstborn, which Esau sold Jacob, entailed his personal involvement in the Divine service, and included the God-given ability to use the stimulation of the senses as a

means of attaining a state of communion with God. See chapter 4.

10. Rabbi Chayim Yosef David Azulay, 1724–1806.

11. *Mishneh Torah: The Laws of Repentance,* trans. R. E. Touger, 3:4, p. 60.

12. Ibid., 2:2, p. 22.

13. Ezekiel 36:25.

14. Jeremiah 17:13. The usual interpretive translation of this verse is "God is Israel's hope (*mikveh*)." We are quoting the verse with the literal understanding of the word *mikveh.*

15. Tractate *Yoma* 8:9.

16. Malachi 3:7.

17. Numbers 14:20.

CHAPTER 23. ETERNAL JOY

1. Adapted from Rabbi R. M. Luria, *Ori ve-Yish'i: Zeman Simchateinu,* pp. 148–49.

2. Song of Songs 2:6.

3. As pointed out by the *Torah Temimah* in the commentary to the verse "I am my Beloved's and His desire is for me" (Song of Songs 7:11).

4. Deuteronomy 16:14–15.

5. Leviticus 23:40–41.

6. *Hilchot Lulav* 8:12–13. The special water libation was performed only during the seven days of Sukkot. All other libations in the Temple were of wine poured on the altar, but during the seven days of Sukkot water was poured simultaneously with the wine libation appended to the daily offering. This water pouring was performed only in the morning after the offering of the daily morning meal offering. See *The Art Scroll Mishnah Series: Moed* (New York: Mesorah Publications, 1980).

7. Isaiah 12:3.

8. *The Art Scroll Mishnah Series: Moed,* vol. 3, *Succah* 5:1, p. 121.

9. Adapted from Rabbi R. M. Luria, *Ori ve-Yish'i: Zeman Simchateinu,* pp. 156–60.

10. Deuteronomy 28:47.

11. Psalms 100:2.

12. Psalms 2:11.

13. Isaiah 62:5.

14. Adapted from Rabbi R. M. Luria, *Ori veYish'i: Zeman Simchateinu,* pp. 128–30.

15. The thirteen attributes of God's com-

passion are derived from Exodus 34:6: "God (1), merciful (2) and gracious (3), slow (4) to anger (5), and abundant in love (6) and truth (7). Keeping mercy (8) to the thousandth generation (9), forgiving sin (10), rebellion (11) and error (12), and cleansing (13)."

16. Deuteronomy 4:35.

17. On the discussion of the widespread fraud behind the protection against evil of the so-called kabbalistic amulets and the like, see Rabbi Yaakov Hillel, *Faith and Folly: The Occult in Torah Perspective,* adapted by E. van Handel from the Hebrew work *Tamim Tiheyeh* (Jerusalem: Yeshivath Hebrath Ahavath Shalom, distributed by Feldheim Publishers, 1990).

18. Psalms 89:3.

19. The *etrog* and the *aravah,* then, represent two extreme types of Jews. They are bound together with the *lulav,* for just as the date of the palm tree has a sweet taste but no fragrance, so Israel is made up of those who are filled with Torah but lack good deeds, and with the *hadas,* for just as the myrtle has a pleasant fragrance but no taste, so Israel is made up of those who perform good deeds but have no Torah knowledge.

See *Pathways to the Torah: The Arachim Seminar Source Book,* and *Yeshivat Aish HaTorah,* ed. A. Sutton (Jerusalem, 1988), p. B34, quoting the Midrash *Vayikra Rabbah* 30:12.

20. See Rabbi Moshe Cordovero, *The Palm Tree of Deborah,* chap. 1.

21. Exodus 34:30.

CHAPTER 24. REJOICING WITH GOD

Adapted from Rabbi R. M. Luria, "Maamar Shemini Atzeret Chag Bifne Atsmo," in *Zeman Simchatenu,* pp. 232–35, and "Maamar Iniane Shemini Atseret," ibid., pp. 223–25.

1. Except for Rosh Hashanah.

2. See chapter 17.

3. Deuteronomy 4:4.

4. Deuteronomy 4:24.

5. Isaiah 10:17.

6. Song of Songs 2:5.

7. Song of Songs 7:11.

8. Song of Songs 8:1.

9. Song of Songs 8:3.

10. Jeremiah 13:11.
11. See Proverbs 8:22.
12. Genesis 1:1-2.
13. Psalms 27:4.
14. Isaiah 60:19.

PART FOUR
DEALING WITH CONCEALMENT

CHAPTER 25. DAYS OF
AFFLICTION: DARKNESS BEFORE DAWN

Adapted from Rabbi R. M. Luria "Parashat Massey veYemey ben haMetsarim," in *Or haMikdash* pp. 237-41. I am grateful to L. Bokobsa for the valuable suggestions that helped me include this chapter in the book.

1. Numbers 33:1-2.
2. Rabbi Yehudah Loevy ben Betzalel (1513–1609) in his *Netzach Israel*.
3. Numbers 33:14, 16, 38.
4. Psalms 63:1-3.
5. When the Israelites left Egypt and received the Torah, they were meant to enter the Holy Land immediately. But they became frightened of the powerful nations dwelling in the land, and they wept. The day of weeping in the desert was Tisha B'Av, and God declared it a day of weeping throughout the generations. It was the day on which the two Temples were destroyed. It would be the day of expulsion of the flowering Jewish community of Spain; King Ferdinand of Aragon set the final date for the expulsion on the second of July 1492, which then coincided with the ninth of Av. The ninth of Av is also the day on which World War I broke out, a war that led to the Holocaust of World War II.
6. Paraphrasing Numbers 33:2.
7. See chapter 23.
8. Psalm 73:1.
9. Allusion to the morning blessings: "Do not bring us . . . into the power of challenge, nor into the power of scorn," in *The Complete Art Scroll Siddur*, p. 23.
10. Numbers 12:3.
11. Psalms 34:15.
12. Zechariah 14:7.
13. Psalms 112:4.

CHAPTER 26
TISHA B'AV: CALL FROM THE DIVINE

Adapted from Rabbi R. M. Luria, "Maamar Giluy HaShechinah beMishkan, Bait Rishon uSheni," in *Or Mikdash*, pp. 40-42.

1. Genesis 28:10.
2. The following interpretation of Jacob's dream is adapted from Rabbi R. M. Luria, *Or Yekarot*, pp. 151-55.
3. The word "already" attempts to convey the Hebrew wording of the verse, *ki ba hashemesh*, which literally means "because the sun had come," implying that the sun, as the expression goes, dropped from the clouds, or in other words, set suddenly. Hence, the Midrash suggests that instead of *ki ba hashemesh* (the sun had set) we should read *kibah hashemesh* (He extinguished the sun).
4. Exodus 25:8.
5. See section "Jacob's Ladder" in chapter 4.
6. See chapter 28.
7. *Mishneh Torah: The Laws of Repentance*, trans R. E. Touger, 7:4, p. 160.
8. Exodus 32:1.
9. Exodus 32:4.
10. Exodus 28:30.
11. *Tsidkat haTsadik*, number 222.
12. Proverbs 1:24.
13. Song of Songs 3:4.
14. Proverbs 27:19.
15. *Kol haMekadesh Shevi'i;* see the English version of this song in the compilation of Shabbat songs, *In Honor of Shabbos*, ed. Abraham Sutton (Jerusalem: Targum/Feldheim, 1996), pp. 27-29.

CHAPTER 27. "MY EYES, MY EYES,
ARE FLOWING WITH TEARS!"

Adapted from Rabbi R. M. Luria, "Maamar Tammuz Av Tre 'Enayim," in *Or HaMikdash*, pp. 189-92.

1. Lamentations 1:16.
2. Numbers 14:14.
3. Deuteronomy 16:16.
4. Exodus 32:20.
5. See chapter 2.
6. Song of Songs 6:5.
7. Isaiah 52:8.
8. See *Amalut baTorah*, p. 63.

9. See chapter 13.

10. Numbers 23:21.

11. Second of the five laments recited in the midnight weekly prayer, expressing our mourning for the Temple. It was written by Rabbi Chayim haKohen, who was the disciple of Rabbi Chayim Vital. Translation my own. It is included in A. Greenbaum's *The Sweetest Hour: Tikkun Chatsot.*

CHAPTER 28
THE SYMBOLISM OF GARMENTS

Adapted from Rabbi R. M. Luria, "Maamar uMordechay Yatsa milifne haMelech biLebush Malchut," in *Orah veSimchah: 'Inyane Purim,* pp. 199–203.

1. Esther 1:4.

2. The Torah refers to these as "for honor and for splendor"; Exodus 28:2.

3. Esther 1:10, 11.

4. Esther 4:1.

5. Esther 4:1–2.

6. Esther 4:4.

7. Esther 5:1.

8. Esther 4:1–2.

9. Proverbs 27:19.

10. Song of Songs 2:14.

11. Psalms 63:4.

12. Genesis 3:1.

13. Isaiah 33:17.

14. Exodus 33:6.

15. Proverbs 10:12.

16. Isaiah 61:10.

17. Deuteronomy 8:4.

18. See chapter 30.

19. Esther 4:13–14.

20. "Nevertheless, they re-accepted it in the days of Ahasuerus, for it is written, 'The Jews observed and willingly accepted'" (Esther 9:27) [Tractate *Shabbat,* 88a].

21. Esther 8:16.

CHAPTER 29. *ATERET HAYESOD/*
THE FOUNDATION CORONET

Adapted from Rabbi R. M. Luria, *Or Yekarot,* pp. 47–65 and 78–80.

1. Ecclesiastes 7:14.

2. For an overview of the exiles, see Rabbi Hersh Goldwurm, *The Book of Daniel: Transla-*

tion and Commentary (New York: Mesorah Publications, 1979), pp. 104–5.

3. As quoted from ibid., p. 105: *Hilchot Melachim,* ch. 11, appendix to *Mishneh Torah,* ed. Pardes, compiled by Rabbi K. Kahane from the relatively uncensored Rome edition, 1480, and others.

4. Jeremiah 4:23.

5. Esther 6:14.

6. Isaiah 11:2. A question surfaces here about the Egyptian exile. Why is it not alluded to in the second verse of Genesis? We may answer that Egypt represents the root of all evil in Creation, and if the four exiles were graphically illustrated as a tree with four main branches, Egypt would be the roots which, although responsible for giving life to the tree, are underground and thus not seen. In addition, the Egyptian exile is not represented in the account of Creation by a verse in physical letters.

7. Tractate *Midot* 2:3.

8. See chapter 4, and A. Kaplan, *Inner Space,* pp. 15–20.

9. As taught by Aristotle, the Greeks saw God as the "unmoved and First Mover." God was considered to be the eternal source of the life and movement of the universe, but actually unaware of the existence of the world which he "moved." The gods of mythology were part of educational laws to inculcate certain moral principles to the nation.

See Renford Bambrough, *The Philosophy of Aristotle* (New York: New American Library, 1963), p. 128, and Alfred Edward Taylor, *Platonism and Its Influence* (New York: Cooper Square Publishers, 1963), p. 121.

10. Jeremiah 13:11.

11. The third step involves drawing blood from the wound. See *Bris Milah,* ed. Rabbis N. Scherman/M. Zlotowitz (New York: 1985), p. 99.

The Islamic powers, descendants of Ishmael, were also given the commandment of the circumcision, but they merely have to remove the foreskin, without having to flip back the membrane over the glans. Forming a crown in the most intimate part of the body is only relevant for Israel, who are bound to God at the Foundation Coronet.

12. Genesis 18:1; see Tractates *Shevuot* 35b and *Shabbat* 127a.

13. Teddy Kollek, "Attractive Religion," *Jerusalem Post*, Friday, January 13, 1995, p. 11.

14. Amos 3:2.

15. Job 19:26.

16. Concentrating their efforts in denying Israel's inner connection to the Foundation Coronet, the Greeks issued decrees against the revelation of this principle as it was manifested in Shabbat, the circumcision, and the observance of the festivals, in particular Sukkot where the Crown of the kingdom of Heaven was crystallized in a "face-to-face" bond.

17. See chapter 8.

18. Ezekiel 39:7.

19. See Introduction; *Or Yekarot*, p. 57; Tractate *Shabbat* 22b.

20. See chapter 28.

21. See chapter 26.

22. Zechariah 2:14; translation my own.

CHAPTER 30
SHOVAVIM/"REBELLIOUS CHILDREN"

Adapted from Rabbi R. M. Luria's chapters on the *Shovavim*, *Or Yekarot*, pp. 259–74.

1. *Even haEzer* 21–25.

2. *Shaar haGilgulim*.

3. Genesis 11:1–9.

4. Genesis 18:20–38.

5. Genesis 38:6, 10.

6. *Zohar* (London: Soncino Press, 1978), vol. 2, p. 312, and vol. 3, p. 7.

7. *Zohar*, vol. 3, p. 7.

8. *Shaar Maamare Rashbi* 19a.

9. Exodus 34:29.

10. Rabbi Chayim Volozhyn, *Nefesh haChayim* (The Soul of Life) 1:15.

11. Genesis 49:6.

12. Song of Songs 2:1.

13. It is important to note that the Ari (*Shaar HaCavanot*) refers to the section of the morning prayers concerning the preparation of the incense spices burned by the High Priest every morning in the Temple (*pitum haketoret*). He teaches that the man who reads this carefully is thereby protected against involuntary emission of sperm.

14. *Jewish Meditation*, pp. 122–23.

15. Psalms 107:10.

16. Psalms 89:9.

17. Exodus 1:12.

18. Mishnah: Tractate *Yoma* 8:9.

EPILOGUE: I LOST MY FIRE!

Adapted from Rabbi R. M. Luria, "Maamar vehine Mitsrayim nosea acharehem, vayir-u meod," in *Shirat haYam*, pp. 56–59, and "Maamar anochi HaShem asher hotseticha meeretz Mitsrayim," in *Geulat Mitsrayim*, pp. 265–80.

1. See Rabbi Aryeh Kaplan, *Inner Space*, pp. 120ff.

2. We find a similar development in the first couple, Adam and Eve. The Ari draws our attention to the creation of Eve, noting that the Bible adjoins to the creation of Adam the cryptic statement "male and female He created them" (Genesis 1:27), while farther on, we find "[God] took one of [Adam's] ribs . . . and built it into a woman" (Genesis 2:21–22). Initially, the Ari explains, Eve was created independently from Adam, rather than "a bone from his bones," and as a result, there was no emotional tie binding her to him.

Hence, in the second account of Eve's creation, Adam exclaims, "*Now this* is bone from my bones and flesh from my flesh" (Genesis 2:23), thus stating his recognition of his earthly soul mate. Thereafter, the newly created Eve would be what Kabbalah calls "a being emanated—separated from its source of creation—that always seeks the reattachment to her original source."

God's second creation of Eve would set the model for every human couple, that would initially be created as one being, and then separated into soul mates. As a result, after coming into the world as humans, they would instinctively look for each other, not finding satisfaction in any other being until the moment of reunion came, and, like Adam, they would feel within "Now *this* is the bone from my bones and flesh from my flesh." In contrast, points out the commentator Raavad regarding animals, the female species was created independently from the male species, as indeed we can judge from the aloofness noticed in the mating patterns of most animals.

3. Isaiah 55:1.

4. Genesis 46:4.

5. Exodus 12:41.

6. Isaiah 63:9.

7. End of Torah portion *Ekev* (Deuteronomy 11:13–21).

8. Jeremiah 2:1.

9. Exodus 8:15.

10. Exodus 14:31.

11. Exodus 14:19.

12. Exodus 15:2.

13. Exodus 19:11.

14. Exodus 14:31.

15. See chapter 12.

16. "The third day arrived. There was thunder and lightning in the morning, with a heavy cloud on the mountain, and an extremely loud blast of a ram's horn. The people in the camp trembled. Moses led the people out of the camp toward the Divine Presence. They stood transfixed at the foot of the mountain." (Exodus 19:16–17)

17. Deuteronomy 5:26.

18. See chapter 6.

19. Exodus 14:3.

20. Exodus 14:15.

21. Psalms 145:9.

22. Exodus 14:25.

23. Zechariah 2:12.

24. Jeremiah 23:7-8.

25. Exodus 24:10.

26. Psalms 135:4; from *The Metsudah Tehillim* (New York: Metsudah Publications, 1983).

27. Psalms 94:14.

28. Exodus 32:32.

29. See Exodus 30:12.

30. Exodus 16:2.

31. Exodus 17:3.

32. Exodus 17:4.

33. Song of Songs 5:6.

34. Exodus 17:7.

35. Exodus 33:5-6.

36. Exodus 32:11.

37. Exodus 32:14.

38. Exodus 32:32.

39. Exodus 32:34.

40. Exodus 20:3.

41. Exodus 20:13.

42. Genesis 15:8.

43. Genesis 15:10.

44. Genesis 15:17.

45. Genesis 15:12.

46. Genesis 13:15.

47. Genesis 15:70.

48. Genesis 15:18-20.

49. Rashi on Genesis 15:5.

50. Genesis 15:13-14.

51. Psalms 109:4.

CONCLUSION: FINDING YOUR FIRE

I am particularly grateful to Rabbi Luria for his invaluable guidance for this final chapter, enriching it with his personal guidance and experience.

1. Adapted from Rabbi R. M. Luria, *Amalut baTorah*, Introduction.

2. *Daat Torah: Maamarim* on Genesis.

3. *The Complete Art Scroll Siddur*, p. 31.

4. Psalms 135:5.

Works of
Rabbi Rafael Moshe Luria

BOOKS ON TALMUDIC INTERPRETATION

Sefer Avnei Shoham: colel chidushim ubiurim be'inyanei Masechet Berachot.
Sefer Avnei Shoham: colel chidushim ubiurim be'inyanei Masechet Shevi'it.
Sefer Avnei Shoham: colel chidushim ubiurim be'inyanei Masechet Nidah.
Sefer Avnei Shoham: colel chidushim ubiurim be'inyanei Masechet Mikvaot.
Sefer Avnei Shoham: colel chidushim ubiurim be'inyanei Masechet Chalah.
Sefer Avnei Shoham: colel chidushim ubiurim be'inyanei Masechet Shevi'it.
Sefer Avnei Shoham: colel chidushim ubiurim be'inyanei Masechet Chulin; part one.
Sefer Avnei Shoham: colel chidushim ubiurim be'inyanei Masechet Chulin; part two.
Sefer Avnei Shoham: colel chidushim ubiurim be'inyanei Masechet Avodah Zarah.
Sefer Avnei Shoham: colel chidushim ubiurim be'inyanei Masechet Ribit.
Sefer Avnei Shoham: colel chidushim ubiurim be'inyanei Masechet Ketubot.
Sefer Avnei Shoham: colel chidushim ubiurim be'inyanei Masechet Yebamot.
Sefer Avnei Shoham: colel chidushim ubiurim be'inyanei Masechet Gittin.
Sefer Avnei Shoham: colel chidushim ubiurim be'inyanei Masechet Kidushin.
Sefer Avnei Shoham: colel chidushim ubiurim be'inyanei Masechet Baba Kamma.
Sefer Avnei Shoham: colel chidushim ubiurim be'inyanei Masechet Baba Metsi'a.
Sefer Avnei Shoham: colel chidushim ubiurim be'inyanei Masechet Baba Batra.
Sefer Avnei Shoham: colel chidushim ubiurim be'inyanei Masechet Nedarim.
Sefer Avnei Shoham: colel chidushim ubiurim be'inyanei Masechet Shabbat.
Sefer Avnei Shoham: colel chidushim ubiurim be'inyanei Masechet Pesachim.
Sefer Avnei Shoham: colel chidushim ubiurim be'inyanei Masechet Mo'adim.

BOOKS ON KABBALAH AND JEWISH THOUGHT

Sefer 'Amalut BaTorah (Toiling in the Torah): colel maamarim ubiurim bedivrei chazal vehaAri z"l bema'alat vechashivut 'amalut be'omekah shel Torah. 1995.

Bet Genazai: 'Al HaTorah (House of Treasures: On the Torah); from *Bereshit* to *Shemot*.

Bet Genazai: 'Al HaTorah; from *Bemidbar* to *Devarim*.

Bet Genazai: 'AlhaMo'adim (House of Treasures: On the Festivals). 1979.

Sefer Bet Genazai (House of Treasures On Shabbat): *colel maamarim ubiurim 'al derech haavodah meyusadim 'al yedei haAri z"l Luria be'inyanei Shabbat.* 2 vols, 1993.

Sefer Geulat Mitsrayim (On the Exodus from Egypt): *colel maamarim ubiurim 'al derech ha'avodah meyusadim 'al yedei haAri z"l Luria be'inyan gezerat berit ben habetarim veyetsiat mitsrayim.* 1989.

Sefer Or Hamikdash (Light of the Temple): *colel maamarim ubiurim 'al derech haavodah meyusadim 'al yedei haAri z"l Luria be'inyanei haMikdash binyano, chorbano ubinyano veyemei ben hametsarim.* 1993.

Sefer Or Yekarot (Precious Light: On Chanukah): *colel maamarim ubiurim 'al derech haavodah meyusaydim 'al yedei haAri z"l Luria be'inyanei Chanukah.* 1992.

Sefer Orah veSimchah (Light and Joy: On Purim): *colel maamarim ubiurim 'al derech haavodah meyusadim 'al yedei haAri z"l Luria be'inyanei Purim upirush Megillat Esther.* 1993.

Sefer Ori veYish'i (Light and Salvation: On the Days of Awe). *Yamim Noraim: colel maamarim ubiurim 'al derech haavodah meyusadim 'al yedei haAri z"l Luria be'inyanei Yamim Noraim, Rosh haShanah veYom haKipurim vecavanat hateki'ot.* 1993 (2nd edition).

Sefer Ori veYish'i (Light and Salvation: Repentance and Prayer). *Teshuvah uTefilah: colel maamarim ubiurim 'al derech haavodah meyusadim 'al yedei haAri z"l Luria be'inyanei Teshuvah uTefilah.* 1991.

Sefer Ori veYish'I (Light and Salvation: Time of Our Joy): *Zeman Simchatenu. Chelek Shelishi: colel maamarim ubiurim 'al derech haavodah meyusadim 'al yedei haAri z"l Luria be'inyanei chag haSukkot veShemini Chag Hatseret.* 1992.

Sefer Seder Lel Shemurim (Passover Eve: Night of Vigilance): *colel maamarim ubiurim 'al derech haavodah meyusadim 'al yedei haAri z"l Luria be'inyanei seder leyl Pesach vehagadah shel Pesach.* 1990.

Sefer Shirat haYam (Song at the Sea): *colel maamarim ubiurim 'al derech haavodah meyusadim 'al yedei haAri z"l Luria be'inyanei keri'at yam suf veshirat hayam.* 1991.

Sefer Torah veIsrael (Torah and Israel: On Shavuot): *colel maamarim ubiurim 'al derech haavodah meyusadim 'al yedei haAri z"l Luria be'inyanei Matan Torah veKneset Israel.* 1991.

Simchah shel Ma'alah (Joy on High: On Marriage).

Simchah shel Mitsvah (Joy of Observing a *Mitsvah:* On the Use of *Tefillin*).

Rabbi Luria's books are distributed by the author himself in Jerusalem, but they can be purchased in Jewish bookstores in Brooklyn, New York. The author is sometimes listed as Rabbi Moshe Luria, and other times as Rabbi Rafael Moshe Luria, because the name Rafael was added to his own in the course of a grave illness, in accord with Jewish tradition. Rabbi Luria is currently working on a kabbalistic interpretation of the Pentateuch.

Index of Names and Subjects

Index of Passages